Cinematic Psychotherapy

T0383764

This book investigates the therapeutic potential and efficacy of audiovisual languages, deepening the integration of film studies into neuropsychiatry and strategic psychotherapy.

Within a theoretical framework including documentary studies, self-representational and amateur theories, and strategic psychotherapy, the book describes the key notions and methodologies for using audiovisual language in clinical therapy practice and autism spectrum disorder (ASD) interventions. The book, a review and update of the Italian *Cinema terapeutico: Linguaggi audiovisivi e percorsi clinici*, showcases the healing potential of creative participatory processes and self-representations that occur thanks to the relocation and amateurization of the contemporary cinematic experience. The authors propose an experimental therapeutic protocol, Video-Pharmakon, which aims to serve as a new integrated method for taking care of children and adolescents with ASD and their families. The protocol is illustrated in its methodologies and phases and supported through case studies.

Scholars and practitioners of art therapy and narrative-based medical approaches, professionals working with clients with ASD, and any other student or professional interested in ASD, psychotherapy, and film studies will find this a valuable resource for current practice and future research interventions.

Anna Chiara Sabatino, PhD, Adjunct Professor of Audiovisual Storytelling and Fellow Researcher in Visual Culture at the University of Salerno, PhD in Communication Sciences and Graduated Director at Italian National Film School. She is a documentary filmmaker, an Italian Miur Certificated Film Education Trainer and Expert. She also teaches Directing Techniques at VHEI, Valletta Higher Education Institute of Malta. Her ongoing research is focused on cinematic agency, amateur audiovisual narratives, and methodological applications for therapeutic images.

Valeria Saladino, PhD, clinical psychologist, criminologist, PhD in Developmental Psychology and post doc in Clinical Psychology at the University of Cassino and Southern Lazio. She is interested in new addictions, sexual offending, and the use of new technologies in the field of treatment, and has published articles and books on the topic. She works in the University Mercatorum of Rome as a professor and collaborates with the University of Salerno and "Magna Graecia" University of Catanzaro. She also works in Italian correctional facilities for adults as a psychologist.

Cinematic Psychotherapy

Audiovisual Languages, Therapeutic Strategies, and Autism Narratives

Anna Chiara Sabatino and
Valeria Saladino

Routledge
Taylor & Francis Group

LONDON AND NEW YORK

Designed cover image: © Getty Images

First published 2024
by Routledge
4 Park Square, Milton Park, Abingdon, Oxon OX14 4RN

and by Routledge
605 Third Avenue, New York, NY 10158

Routledge is an imprint of the Taylor & Francis Group, an informa business

© 2024 Anna Chiara Sabatino and Valeria Saladino for the English updated and revised edition

The right of Anna Chiara Sabatino and Valeria Saladino to be identified as authors of this work has been asserted in accordance with sections 77 and 78 of the Copyright, Designs and Patents Act 1988.

First English edition published 2024

Originally published as Cinema terapeutico. Linguaggi audiovisivi e percorsi clinici by Anna Chiara Sabatino, Valeria Saladino, Valeria Verrastro. © 2021 by Carocci editore, Rome.

British Library Cataloguing-in-Publication Data
A catalogue record for this book is available from the British Library

Library of Congress Cataloging-in-Publication Data
Names: Sabatino, Anna Chiara, 1991- author. | Saladino, Valeria, 1990- author.
Title: Cinematic psychotherapy : audiovisual languages, therapeutic strategies, and autism narratives / Anna Chiara Sabatino and Valeria Saladino.
Other titles: Cinema terapeutico. English
Description: First English edition. | Abingdon, Oxon ; New York, NY : Routledge, 2024. | Originally published as Cinema terapeutico : linguaggi audiovisivi e percorsi clinici by Anna Chiara Sabatino, Valeria Saladino, Valeria Verrastro. | Includes bibliographical references and index. |
Identifiers: LCCN 2023031277 (print) | LCCN 2023031278 (ebook) |
ISBN 9781032374994 (hardback) | ISBN 9781032374949 (paperback) |
ISBN 9781003340508 (ebook)
Subjects: MESH: Autism Spectrum Disorder–therapy | Motion Pictures | Psychotherapy--methods | Child | Adolescent | Case Reports
Classification: LCC RC553.A88 (print) | LCC RC553.A88 (ebook) |
NLM WS 350.8.P4 | DDC 616.85/882--dc23/eng/20230929
LC record available at https://lccn.loc.gov/2023031277
LC ebook record available at https://lccn.loc.gov/2023031278

ISBN: 978-1-032-37499-4 (hbk)
ISBN: 978-1-032-37494-9 (pbk)
ISBN: 978-1-003-34050-8 (ebk)

DOI: 10.4324/9781003340508

Typeset in Times New Roman
by Taylor & Francis Books

Contents

Figures

Introduction

Anna Chiara Sabatino and Valeria Saladino

Storytelling is a fundamental aspect of human experiences as it represents life itself. Illness and therapy are no exception. In fact, self-narrative acts as an essential component of psychotherapy and involves a form of self-healing from psychic distress and disease. Starting from these premises, our work investigates the therapeutic potential and efficacy of audiovisual forms and language, deepening their integration with clinical practice. Whether treating mental, psychological, or biological disorders, any therapeutic approach is characterized by self-narrative characteristics, since it cannot be separated from the patient's experience, which generates pathological and pharmacological *fabula*.

Such a principle is the necessary cornerstone of our research, illustrating and recounting it in all its theoretical, methodological, and applicative domains. The book, which is the development of its Italian version, *Cinema Terapeutico*, is structured as follows. In Chapter 1 we propose a definitional and operative interweaving between narrative and therapeutic dispositive, outlining differences and commonalities in their logic, functioning, and constitutive elements. In Chapter 2 we concisely circumscribe the theoretical framework of audiovisual self-narratives, specifically within participatory and performative documentary forms and amateur expressions and manifestations, with detail on the bodily involvement and peculiar gestures that such productive practices imply and involve. In the context of Narrative Medicine, the theoretical background of audiovisual therapeutic potential is declined according to the concept of agency, with the aim of framing the roles and dynamics of the "Therapeutic Set". In this perspective, Chapter 3 proposes a historical, selective, and targeted reconnaissance of audiovisual therapeutic approaches, which we define as Cinematherapy, Filmtherapy, Documentary Videotherapy, and Therapeutic Filmmaking. These therapeutic strategies must be distinguished based on their function, their medium specificity and the patient's role in their making. In fact, he/she goes from being a spectator to becoming an actor, the main character of her/his narrative therapy, to a "*spectauthor*", who can experience her/his movie viewing and the process of making it, as both spectator and author. Chapter 4 illustrates the principles of

DOI: 10.4324/9781003340508-1

strategic psychotherapy and the construction of the relationship between psychotherapist and patient, with the goal of examining the theoretical-practical correlations with audiovisual language starting from the concept of mental representation in psychotherapy. Chapter 5 proposes a literature review of art-based therapies that grounds their functioning on the presence of a group process, with the active involvement of the therapeutic team: such specificity is one of the key points of our methodological proposal, which will be fully illustrated in Chapter 6, dedicated to the description and analysis of the *Video-Pharmakon* research-intervention protocol for patients with autism spectrum disorder and their families.

The Video-Pharmakon pilot protocol and project has been developed at the Videotherapy and Therapeutic Filmmaking Outpatient Clinic for Neurodevelopmental Disorders of the Child Neuropsychiatry Department of the "San Giovanni di Dio e Ruggi D'Aragona" hospital in Salerno, inaugurated in 2019. The Video-Pharmakon protocol is accurately illustrated in all its methodological and application development stages, procedures, and objectives, as well as epistemological, diagnostic, and clinical perspectives, and purposely exemplified by four case studies to which the protocol has been applied, showing the first results and evaluations. The present work aims to propose a new integrated and interdisciplinary methodology that has been designed and tested through five years of clinical and applied research.

We hope our methodological and clinical proposal can be an incentive to explore this important issue through further research and interventions. A complex commitment and dedication are needed to realize experimental and applicative research such as this.

We thank Professors Giangennaro Coppola, Filippo Fimiani, and Filippo Petruccelli for their dedication and valuable guidance, without whom we could not have taken the first steps in this human and professional adventure. We are very grateful to the Institute for the Study of Psychotherapies, School of Specialization in Brief Psychotherapies with a Strategic Approach, for assisting with the start of this research project, and to the Society for Research in Videotherapy and Therapeutic Filmmaking (Refit), of which we are members and founders, for supporting our ongoing research. The application of the experimental protocol could not have been achieved without the valuable collaboration of Grazia Maria Giovanna Pastorino, Chiara Napoli, Marianna Venosa, Jacopo Brucculeri, and Rosa Oliviero. Our gratitude goes especially to the families who trusted and relied on us and without whom we would not have achieved the results we discuss and articulate here.

Although this volume is the result of an ongoing exchange of ideas and was conceived together by the authors, Chapters 1, 2, and 3 were written by Anna Chiara Sabatino, Chapters 4 and 5 by Valeria Saladino, and Chapter 6 by Anna Chiara Sabatino and Valeria Saladino.

Chapter 1

Self-Representational Grounds for Therapeutic Dispositive

Anna Chiara Sabatino

Cinema and Therapy: A Double *Dispositif*

Cinematic experience is characterized by a spectatorial fruition that mainly consists of aesthetic involvement and sensorial determinations (Andriopoulos, 2002). Regarding the peculiar relationship between the movie and its viewer, Christian Metz doubles the subject of filmic enunciation, locating it, on the one hand, in the point of view that sets the *mise-en-scène*; on the other hand, in the spectator's gaze toward the screen (Metz, 1977). Such a magnetic encounter between the audience and the movie (Gordon, 2001) activates mechanisms of suggestion that recall hypnosis functioning (Bellour, 1988) in a movie theatre, thanks to the convergence of all the cinematic spectacle elements: from the movie screen and the dark room, to the projection taking place facing the seated bodies of the spectators.

As pre-hypnotic situation (Barthes, 1980), filmic discourse involves both a gaze and a scene, the event represented and the recipient of the representation. The functioning of cinematic apparatus was theorized by Jean Louis Baudry who elaborated the Apparatus Theory in *Cinéma: effets idéologiques produits par l'appareil de base* (1970) and *Le dispositif: approches métapsychologiques de l'impression de réalité* (1975). According Baudry's elaboration, a cinematic situation is made possible by the material conditions of the movie projection, rather than of the fruition itself: the cinematic apparatus, understood as a signifying, non-neutral medium, is described as the holder of an ideology derived from a monocular perspective, from which the displayed objects are organized and the viewing subject is pigeonholed (Baudry, 1970). If the basic apparatus coincides with the technical equipment necessary for the movie and projection making, the dispositive implies metapsychological effects exerted on the spectator, who experiences her/his projected desire through the simulating cinematic machine, in a way that is very similar to a dreaming situation.

The notion of dispositive as apparatus, inscribed in a theory of representation that involves a viewer bound to believe the impression of reality produced by the screen, evolves almost naturally into a psychoanalytically

DOI: 10.4324/9781003340508-2

inspired reading: just as the childhood phase of the mirror which leads the child to assemble a first image of the "Self" (Baudry & Williams, 1974; Lacan, 1966), the camera fosters favorable conditions for the representation of a subject who unitarily shows her/himself before the eyes of the spectator, despite being narratively parcelled out into frames. Triggering the self-imagining instead of (and thanks to) the apparatus, which is opportunely concealed or removed, cinema can act as substitute psychic apparatus following a set dominant ideology (Baudry, 1970). The ideological effects thus lead the viewer to identify with the eye of the camera and to experience the illusion of coinciding with a transcendental, disembodied, omnipotent subject, free to inhabit the scenic space without limits.

In this perspective, Baudry advances a comparison with the dispositive as imagined by Plato in the Seventh Book of the *Republic*, a dark cave (the movie theater); prisoners immobilized in their places (the spectators in their chairs, endowed with very little mobility); a large fire behind the prisoners illuminating the wall at the back of the cavern (the projector with its beam of light); a series of silhouettes passing in front of the fire while remaining behind the prisoners (the film itself); shadows cast on the background wall, created by the silhouettes passing in front of the fire (the screen image) (cf. Kaplan, 1990). Just as the slaves in the cave, the spectators witness a play of shadows and light: only a process of projection can identify shadows with real things and beings, and attribute to them this reality which, when reflected upon, they so conspicuously lack (Morin, 1956). In this sense, cinema allows for one and only one form of experience in which the subject has no room for maneuver: the cinematic spectator is a pure passive subject, since he has no room for action; everything happens far away, out of his reach (Morin, 1956).

The dispositive thus described is configured as a simulating machine not because it reproduces reality, but because it resembles the psychic apparatus of the spectator (Bellour, 1988). Within the psychoanalytic framework and, in agreement with Baudry, Christian Metz describes the primary cinematic identification, thanks to the pure gaze of the film – first, of the camera lens, and then the projector of the movie theater (Baudry, 1975) – and a more conscious form of secondary identification, with the characters of the fictional story, which is linked both to the represented and shown characters and to some structural aspects of the cinematic dispositive itself.

The image on the screen, at once resembling and different, recognizable and phantasmal, places the viewer in a singular condition of "suspension of disbelief", which triggers a dual mechanism that allows, at the same time, adherence to and divergence from the truth of the images flowing on the screen. The cinematic viewer is emotionally affected as s/he chooses to believe in the fiction of what s/he sees, but at the same time s/he is also aware of being at the movie theatre. Even more than the theatrical spectator, the cinematic one is a double subject, split, involved in a mental and bodily mechanism that pushes her/him to grasp the meaning of the story, inviting her/him to be active and aware, and, simultaneously, asks her/him to surrender to its fascination, passively abandoning to the seduction of the moving images.

Cinema erases, according to Metz, the traces of the subject of visual enunciation in order to leave a space that the viewer illusorily occupies as the subject of enunciation (Metz, 1977). Baudry's and Metz's psychoanalytic approach highlights the metapsychological dimension of cinema as a mode of activating the spectator's desire, while, in the same years, Michel Foucault was elaborating his own subjectivation analyses though referring to very different contexts and situations (Foucault, 1975). Introducing an idea of a non-filmic disciplinary dispositive, while recalling its institutionality as well as its situationality, Foucault clarifies that the dispositive is configured as a grid which regulates and determinates power relationships. While in the Anglo-Saxon debate the concept of the cinematic apparatus has been defined as the point of intersection between the text, the meaning, and the spectatorial interpretation (Flitterman-Lewis et al., 1992), in the French landscape, beginning with Foucault, the cinematic dispositive becomes the interweaving of the constitutive of the cinematic experience itself.

In this perspective, the notion of dispositive has been defined as anything that is able to determine, intercept, shape, and control the gestures, conducts, opinions, and discourses of living beings (Agamben, 2006, p. 21). Between the two major classes of living beings or substances and dispositives, there is a third subject, which is configured as the result of bodies and dispositives' interaction (Agamben, 2006, p. 22). Agamben's definition, further expanding the implications of the Foucaultian dispositive, focuses on the dynamic of mutual exchange between the device and the user, emphasizing the complexity of subjectification processes and spaces of action (cf. Deleuze, 1989). In Agamben's theoretical declination, the dispositive becomes capable of orienting the involved and committed subjects not only in submissive terms of subjection, but of subjectification.

Within a so-described open configuration, a double dispositive is methodologically definable and applicable, to which both the spectator embedded in the cinematic dispositive and the patient in the therapeutic setting voluntarily access, crossing a material and experiential, symbolic and epistemic threshold. Unlike the prisoner of the Platonic cave evoked by Baudry, immersed in daydreaming and illusion, the patient-spectator can be contextualized within a double dispositive in which psychotherapy and cinema aim to activate a different processing of experiences, affects, and emotions, bringing to consciousness deep aspects of the Self (Mitry, 1997). If the dispositive acts by creating a dynamic balance analogous to a multilinear skein composed of lines of a different nature (Deleuze, 1983), and thus activates an *autopoiesis* for involved subjects, this is even more true within a bifid machine such as *Therapeutic Cinema*, in which the components interact by mutual interference as lines of subjectivation (Deleuze, 1983).

Cinema and psychotherapy can indeed expand their effects in mutual contaminations, arising from the encounter between therapeutic interview and audiovisual images, both relational and narrative, able to create new spaces of self-representation and sense-making. In delineating the profile of a spectator who is also a patient, however, the viewer could still be framed as a mere part of a dispositive with doubled and enhanced power, binding even more strictly wills, beliefs, and actions of the spectator as patient. To dispel this risk, it is necessary to recall how the polarity between activity and passivity of the spectatorial subject can be measured during the cinematic illusion. Although strictly framed in pre-determined conducts, the viewer's affective involvement, characterized by a high proprioceptive and attentional level, as well as in the co-construction and interpretation of meaning, both of the film and of the therapeutic story, is an indispensable condition, along with the immersive enjoyment of the audiovisual narrative. Complementary to the alert inactivity of the "hypnotized" spectator (Bellour, 1988), the active passivity of the patient-spectator manifests itself when the cinematic experience calls her/him to participate: it is the participatory act, the adherence that begins with the ritual of access to the movie theater (Feldmann, 1956), along with the patient's consent to therapy.

It is, therefore, vital the relational pact between the engaged subject and the functioning of the dispositive itself: without such dynamic interplay of relationships articulating mutually connected discourses and practices (Tortajada & Albera, 2015), *le dispositif n'existe pas*. The impression of reality that the movie leaves on the patient-spectator is literally imprinted on her/him (Gallese & Guerra, 2012), while intervening in the reality outside the screen and the movie theater, outside the technical and technological dispositive: the movie and the cinematic experience involve the viewer in a specific praxis of human being's confrontation with her/himself, consequently setting in motion the transformation of human practices (Bertram, 2019). Within the described double dispositive, the engaged subject can be summoned, and practically involved, into the construction of self-fictional identity capable of triggering beneficial and effective narratives.

Audiovisual Self-Representation and Amateur Practices

Even fictional identities, which play a crucial role in accessing the dual dispositive so far described, should be based and constituted on self-narratives. Nevertheless, self-narratives can consist in multiple forms of representation, theoretically and methodologically distinguished by means of *mise-en-scène* and production.

If the "autobiography" label can be attributed to any text in which the authorial intentionality of recounting one's own life is evident (Lejeune, 1980), the self-narrative instance should determine, at least in principle, the annulment of the distance separating the narrating self from the protagonist self and, consequently, the overlapping-convergence of points of view, in an ever-present game of cross-references between life and tale (Genette, 1972). In this direction, Lejeune argues that the constraints of autobiographical writing concern first and foremost the implicit agreement between reader and author, such as to stand as a guarantee of the reliability of the narrative, necessarily an account of events actually experienced, thus inscribing literary autobiography within an autobiographical pact that provides for the coincidence between author, narrator, and narrated character (Bottalico & Chialant, 2005).

The interaction between the origins of the literary autobiography and the audiovisual language has long been debated (Lejeune & Nysenholc, 1987). According to Elizabeth Bruss, the audiovisual medium proves to be unsuitable for the autobiographical medium because it constitutively carries an impossible identity fusion between author-narrator and main character, between the narrated self in the diegetic space and the living self in the extradiegetic space. Self-centered literary productions are indeed characterized, according to Bruss, by at least three elements necessary for the effectiveness of such a narrative: the value of truth, arising from the possibility of comparison with real documentary sources that allow the reliability of the narrative to be verified; the value of the act, determined by the stylistic connotations of that particular narrative; and the value of identity, which draws together in a single individual the author, the narrator, and the protagonist of the autobiographical act. According to Bruss, the film language would not allow the affirmation of any of these values. Indeed, cinematic repertoire would be divided internally between movies that record reality (documentaries) and those that reconstruct it (fiction films). In attempting to recount a true fact, the value of true would be linguistically challenged by the manipulation, in one sense or another, operated by these two registers. With respect to the value of act, then, the audiovisual language, even in its most literal and direct expression of subjectivity, the subjective shot, proves to be inadequate, being only a weak substitute for the position of the narrating subject, which is hidden behind the camera's placements and movements (Bruss, 1980).

Cinema, therefore, would not be able to restore the fusion, typical of the literary text, between the author-narrator and the main character, because of the clear separation between the spectator and the movie characters: hence the crisis of the value of identity. If the reader accepts that the narrative is filtered by the subjectivity of the narrator, the cinematic spectator confronts the double representation of both the filmed characters on the screen and the narrative instance which directs the camera point of view along the movie. The visual presentification that cinema is able to construct would, therefore, become the cause of the narrative ineffectiveness of the autobiographical film genre. According to Elizabeth Bruss the autobiographical configuration of the self appears incompatible with the cinematic medium since it would violate the principles that for literary autobiography had long been fundamental (Bruss, 1980); for Philippe Lejeune, instead, *l'écriture du "Je"* can be configured *au cinéma* as well (Lejeune, 1980), within an autobiographical space that includes, among the various media forms, the audiovisual production with autobiographical content.

In an elastic and versatile space, Bellour inscribes the self-portrait form as a further possibility of dealing with subjective experience. On the one hand, in fact, autobiography, conveyed by cinematic language becomes fragmentary, limited, dissociated, uncertain; on the other hand, it tends instead to overlap with an experience that, being autobiographical, is also its opposite – the self-portrait (Bellour, 1990). If temporal delimitation is identified as an essential characteristic of autobiographical narrative, the self-representational dispositive, in contrast, is connoted by a discontinuous bricolage constituted through anachronistic montage (cf. Beaujour, 1980).

Audiovisual self-portraits, in this sense, are characterized by their versatile configurations, according to an amateur rhetoric historically ascribable to New American Cinema, that stylistically establishes an artisanal film practice through autobiographical and diaristic filmmaking (Gernalzick, 2006; Monterrubio Ibáñez, 2016). By rejecting the structures of professional cinema by testing the boundary between avant-garde and amateurism, authors like Maya Deren, Stan Brakhage, and Jonas Mekas are the forerunners of stylistic features of contemporary amateur authors through grassroots (Casetti, 2015) and non-professional storytelling practices. Beginning with a substantial modification of spectatorial and user status, the amateur, eventually cinephile (Baumbach, 2012), no longer just prosumer (Jenkins, 1992, 2006; Toffler, 1980) practices poaching (De Certeau, 1980) and therefore defines her/his own textual participation (Fiske, 1992). The control the spectator/user acquires over her/his own fruition experience constitutes the first step toward a continuous and ongoing participation, which is performative, as well increasingly oriented toward medium awareness and alphabetization. The operations of retrieval, cataloging, alteration, morphing, and photoshopping (Rascaroli, 2014) through technological portability and accessibility allow the users to manage their own level of participation and textual commitment.

In this perspective, amateur self-representational forms can be configured as everyday audiovisual transfigurations by ordinary people (Chalfen, 1987, 1988). As it becomes easier to import, manipulate, and export materials, the user-bricoleur – to borrow a Lévi-Strauss definition (1966) – personally reviews and recombines the vast amount of accessible sources, using whatever tools and know-how are available. The practice of *remixing it yourself* (Campanelli, 2012), proliferates in what Manovich calls the "software age" (2008), which has led to significant innovation in devices and dispositives' expressive possibilities. Mobile media (Ferraris, 2005; Prédal, 2008) provide a useful element of reflection for the re-definition of the figure of a user capable of contributing to the exploration and implementation of self-made narratives (Odin, 2014; Schleser, 2014). Thanks to the smartphone configuration, the frontal camera is literally embedded, "part of a hand-camera assemblage whose possibilities and limitations are mutually determined by technical photographic parameters (available light, field of view, angle, etc.) and the physical potential and constraints of the human body" (Frosh, 2015, p. 1612).

With the advancement of web and social media representations, mobile film-making (Baker et al., 2009; Schleser, 2011) and *film de poche* (Odin, 1995) made with the mobile phone, illustrate the applicative potential of audiovisual self-narrative, following home movies' production modes and rhetorics. As shown in the main studies on this topic (Aasman, 2012; Jenkins, 2015; Zimmermann, 1995), home movies create "a different amateur space [...] characterized by a specific mode of communication" (Cati, 2011, p. 320), mainly affective, but no less culturally connoted. The amateur, argued Stan Brakhage (1971), devotes himself first and foremost to the act of loving, filming things and people that are dear to him in order to immortalize them, to save them from death (Bazin, 1984). Ancestors of production modes and rhetorics employed by mobile film-making are home movies, filmed within the home environment and among the earliest amateur audiovisual forms (Odin, 1995). Such amateur and home mode is well defined by Judi Hetrick who makes a punctual distinction between home movie and home mode, systematizing textual and expressive manifestations of vernacular video (Aufderheide, 1995; Moran, 2002): vernacular video can be considered as a new and more circumscribed category to describe those non-fictional videos made by non-professional cameramen in an attempt to narrate as faithfully as possible the life around them. Such a vernacular label can encompass a broader genre of audiovisual products identified first by defining the role of their creator, then by the equipment used, and finally by the content of the footage. The addition of the adjective "community" to "vernacular video" marks home movies' shift toward the public, social, and civic dimensions, with the goal of depicting life away from the home and private environment (Hetrick, 2006, pp. 78–79).

In its historical progression, the vernacular video transcends domestic boundaries and reaches the public and social dimension, as is the case with *Life in a Day* (2011), in which YouTube users are invited to film a day in their lives and upload their video on YouTube on a set day. Considered by the director himself as "a collective auto-ethnographic experiment" (Dodes, 2011), in this participatory and user-generated movie (Gubbins, 2012; Petraitis, 2019) the audiovisual materials are reconfigured into new, often fractured and fragmented forms, mostly by amateurs (Birchall, 2008). Audiovisual expressions such *Life in a Day*, largely self-representational, renew the possibilities of self-inscription inside the cinematic dispositive, significantly impacting the traditional definition of amateurism and the theoretical reformulation of the nexus between amateur and author, consequently developing, expanding, and intensifying the long tradition of self-portrait (Mirzoeff, 2016).

These reflections conceptually can be applied to the selfie, which can be considered one of the evolving manifestations and contemporary expressions of the self-portrait genre. Rather than a "royal" portrait, the selfie is configured as a contextual portrait and connected image, whose authenticity is attested by its personal realization, which preferably must be visible in the picture (Gunthert, 2013a). Defined by Alisa Tifentale as "a symptom of media-driven and influenced social narcissism [and] a way to control the image others have of us", "a masturbation of the self" (2014, pp. 5–7), the selfie was defined as self-obsession driven (Krauss, 1976), but only apparently such a generative element can be considered as the driving force of such digital self-representations. While Narcissus was only interested in his own reflection, the selfie on the contrary presents itself as an interaction proposal in a conversational context (Gunthert, 2013a). The heir to live snapshot photography, sharing the legacy of an *instant* aesthetic but also the characteristic of exhibiting its visual codes, thus creating an identifiable and reproducible culture (Gunthert, 2013b), the selfie contributes to the democratization of self-representation (Freund, 2011), while distinguishing itself by its conversational nature. The practice of the selfie belongs more than ever to the amateur, both user and producer, we have discussed so far: thanks to the mobility of the equipment and its almost unconditional availability, the amateur user finds her/himself constantly performing inevitable practices of everyday life self-narrativization. The constant mediatization of experience to which the prosumer is summoned is configured as a fundamental narrative propeller, as well as an essential component of an identity construction that can only be self-representative (Cati & Grassilli, 2019; Sabatino, 2019), shaped by the digital technologies of the Self (Rascaroli, 2014).

Documentary and Performative Filmmaking

Forms of amateur audiovisual self-representation traverse the history of the documentary genre and develop and evolve within it. This relationship between documentation and self-representation is to be understood not only from a representative or stylistic perspective, but also with respect to the positioning of the author, filmmaker, or director. Regarded as the art of staging (Ejzenštejn, 1989), since the early twentieth century directing has been attributed to the so-called US *director* and the French *metteur en scène* (Mackendrick & Cronin, 2005) – both responsible for coordinating stagings and departments. Toward the end of the 1950s, the *politique des auteurs* (Bazin, 1984) is characterized by the affirmation of the authorial centrality of the director, since "beautiful or ugly, a film always resembles the one who signs its realization" (Gandini, 1998, p. 176). As a result of the spread of lightweight cameras that offer a wider audience the opportunity to experiment with a new language, especially since the new tools can be used by only one person, a new documentary strand and a new role of the filmmaker stylistically emerges. This artistic profile takes charge of every creative and realization phase personally, bringing the production to an entirely artisanal dimension and differentiating from the historical filmmaker role (Naficy, 2001; Rouch, 1978).

Based on this authorial model, on the one hand, Direct Cinema, a rib of American Documentary starting with documentarists such as Richard

Leacock and Frederick Wiseman, veers toward a documentary mode that is as objective as possible and, stylistically, tries to conceal the presence of the author in favor of an apparently unmediated and direct representation. On the other hand, an exemplary work such as *Chronique d'un été* (1963) shows Jean Rouch and Edgar Morin not bothering to be present with voices and bodies in interviewing the documentary participants, expounding their own point of view by commenting on the work in progress and posing questions and reflections through first-person interventions. It is the French ethnologist Jean Rouch himself who argued that film images do not arise exclusively from the gaze and work of the filmmaker, but rather from the dialogue between the *filmeur* and the *filmé* (Monterrubio Ibáñez, 2021).

Implementing the collaborative video inaugurated by Flaherty, since the mid-1940s Jean Rouch has been basing his anthropological and authorial research on the participatory practices of shared anthropology, which aims to establish narrative cooperation between observer and observed (Pink, 2008). This mode, first *collaborative*, then *shared*, has been described in its evolution by many scholars who have proposed a classification (see Bruzzi, 2006; Nichols, 1991), starting from Bill Nichols who replaced the term *interactive* with *participatory* (2001). Such terminological shift stemmed from the need to give greater prominence to the co-presence of the filmmaker and the *filmé* by conceiving them as participants to the same extent in the constructive activity of the documentary, rather than emphasizing their mutual and natural influence during the production stages of the documentary. Within this methodological frame, the interviewer shifts from external observation to a more participatory attitude that allows her/him to blend in with the observed subjects and to access the status of social actor her/himself.

Participatory documentary highlights the praxis of the truthful encounter between the filmmaker and the represented subject in its evenemential characterization in front of the camera, in its constituting as an encounter, contact, and confrontation that would not exist if not in function of the camera and the narrative that is accomplished with it. The reflections on the status of documentary images have often set out to define the documentary idea investigating their role in the construction of the real itself (Aguayo, 2019; Bertozzi, 2018).

In this perspective, performative documentary does not focus attention on an object of study external to the representation, but "sets out to demonstrate how embodied knowledge provides entry into an understanding of the more general processes at work in society" (Nichols, 2010, p. 201). The concept of performativity, which has traversed and permeated numerous disciplinary fields, from linguistics to sociology (Austin, 1955; Goffman, 1959; Searle, 1969), until it reached a more accomplished formulation in performance studies in the 1990s (Auslander, 2003; Schechner, 1988), is based on a productive and relational circularity within the mechanism of production/reception, which performatively activates a hermeneutic system in which emission and reception are simultaneous and complementary (Sabatino, 2020).

During a documentary filming the act of documentation adopts performative modality not so much in its production process, but while building up the relationships with the *filmé* (Moraldi, 2015). The statute of performativity seems to consist, therefore, in the act of collaborative and participatory documenting in a de-gerarching escalation between the representing and the represented instance, in which the latter does not give itself only as a passive interlocutor, a "subject" to be documented, but rather as a culturally active interlocutor and agent, participating in the communication process with its own cultural bearing and point of view redefining itself, in a way, as co-author. The act of documentary filming consists in creating a *shared social field*, in which the performative act gives rise to a relational dynamic, a negotiation between the filmmaker and reality itself, and thus, in depth, a performance (Bruzzi, 2006). The documentary is configured as an "ideal tool for capturing the truth of a performance that unfolds in front of the camera being explicitly guided by it (Perniola, 2014).

Compared to the more self-conscious and expressive forms of non-fiction cinema (Bruzzi, 2006), the performance of the filmmaker, who instead of hiding, makes explicit and articulates her or his presence in the narrative, representatively interrupts the privileged relationship between filmed subjects and the viewer, exposing the authorial performance, in a way that is both critical and affective. The performance we are referring to is primarily inscribed in the everyday and in the roles that social actors play in the narrative field. In *The Presentation of Self in Everyday Life*, Erving Goffman (1959) already reflected on the modes of everyday self-presentation in different social contexts, arguing that the presentation of self depends on different roles assumed according to singular occurrences, without the ontological and descriptive dependence of theatrical performance (Auslander, 2003; Carlson, 1996). In line with Goffman, Michael Renov has investigated the ways in which the filmmaker's expression of subjectivity interacts with the narrated reality, especially in the first-person essay, in which the speaking subject actively uses the cinematic apparatus as a means of self-expression (Rascaroli, 2009; Renov, 2004, 2009). Such a first-person narrative implies a visual dimension that more effectively presents the self and the power of subjective expression in relation to a culture dominated by images and mediated experiences. However, it would remain an ambivalent tool, both for representing subjectivity and for constituting it precisely through the narrative act. According to Renov, in fact, subjectivity is a multilayered construction of the imagined, interpreted, and assigned self (2004), which is based not only on the self but also on the relationship with otherness, becoming both personal and intersubjective. In this sense, the documentary dispositive is always employed not only to relate to the world, but also to construct a Self (image and representation) that presents itself to the other.

Such a recursive relationship is echoed by Alisa Lebow (2012), for whom the Self is transformed into a subject by means and effect of its own relationship with the Other, producing and defining itself through the sur-rounding context with which it interacts. The conception of an authorial Self and a represented Other as mutually involved in a process of defining and redefining subjectivity offers a further compelling argument for conceptualiz-ing the filmmaker's presence as a productive subject rather than as a witnes-sing gaze. When the filmmaker is present within the documentary frame, actively engaged in the "collision" (Beattie, 2004) between reality and its representation, her/his subjectivity constitutes a specific and unique factor contributing to the material filmmaking process.

We can, therefore, distinguish two possible declinations of the filmmaker's role within the autobiographical and self-portrait audiovisual texts: on the one hand, the filmmaker as the subject-author of the narrative; on the other hand, the filmmaker as the subject-object of the narrative. If in the first nar-rative scenario the filmmaker is considered as a key figure who performs her or his authorial subjectivity with self-representational forms, content, goals, in the second one her or his authorial role is narratively determined by her or his own presence in the storytelling or by being its content focus through auto-biographical narratives (Griffiths, 2013). The presence of the filmmaker in audiovisual texts can be articulated in these terms: in one way, author and representing subject, in the act of representing; in another way, subject and represented object, diegetically present as main character protagonist in the articulation of the plot.

In leading us back toward amateur self-narrative, which is particularly important in the therapeutic uses of cinema and audiovisual languages we are going to discuss, Stan Brakhage's amateur's manifesto (1971) comes to mind:

> "Amateur" is a word which, in the Latin, meant "lover" […]. An amateur is one who really lives his life – not one who simply "performs his duty" – and as such he experiences his work while he's working – rather than going to school to learn his work so he can spend the rest of his life just doing it –; and the amateur, thus, is forever learning and growing thru his work into all his living in a "clumsiness" of continual discovery that is beautiful to see, if you have lived it and can see it […]. The amateur photographs the persons, places, and objects of his love and the events of his happiness and personal importance in a gesture that he can act directly and solely according to the needs of memory. […] It is for this reason that I believe any art of the cinema must inevitably arise from the amateur, "home-movie!" making medium. And I believe that the so-called "commercial", or ritual, cinema must inevitably take its cues from the film of amateurs rather than, as is too often the case these days, the other way around.
>
> (Brakhage, 1971)

From this text clearly emerges how the filmmaker-amateur is capable of creating her/his own film because of new technical resources, but above all because the love for everyday existence inspires her/his own narratives, that easily and often involves her/himself, becoming self-narratives.

But if this is partly valid for the everyday user, who narrates for the sake of the narrative itself, different is the discourse that could be articulated for the serious amateur (Buckingam et al., 2009, p. 59), who is primarily passionate about the techniques and languages through which narrative is creatively packaged, rather than out of "clumsy" love for the narrated content, as is the case for the everyday user.

To the theoretical mosaic assembled so far, we also find it useful to add the reflections of Cecilia Sayad (2013) who, beginning with Butler's (1993) notion of performativity, examines how repeated acts and performative gestures can be employed by certain authors to highlight their distinct artistic identities. Focusing on fictional and documentary movies in which the presence of the filmmaker manifests as diegetically significant, Sayad explores the relationship between the author, the object of the narrative, and the narrative field, arguing that the performance of the director or filmmaker in the role of authorship emphasizes specific gestures that define her or his authorial identity, eventually making it recognizable.

In this direction, the bodies and gestures inscribed in the amateur audiovisual field are not insignificant but, indeed, have a fundamental importance, as we shall see, even in therapeutic approaches that make use of moving images.

Narrative Bodies and Gestures

According to the phenomenological and neurophenomenological conception (Gallagher, 2006; Shapiro, 2019; Varela et al., 1991), looking at specific performative actions in the spectator brings about particular neurobiological phenomena, since not only the filmmaker but also the spectator is, first and foremost, lived body. Based on this assumption, it is possible to understand performance and performative practices as modes of persistence and transmission, which are fundamentally accomplished in and through the body (Elsaesser & Hagener, 2015, pp. 124–145).

The mirroring of the actions, emotions, and affective states of another human being, activated through the mechanism of "embodied simulation" (Gallese, 2005; Gallese & Guerra, 2019), allows a viewer not only to immediately identify with the other – in the flesh, intra – and extra-specific, in image, still or moving – but to experience firsthand her or his experience, acted and felt, directly in her or his own body. The bodily nature of the cinematic spectator has been noted, as Susan Sobchack (2004) well describes, within film experience theory (Barker, 2009; Crary, 1990; Marks, 2000; Shaviro, 1994): on the one hand, on the screen as a semiotic effect of cinematic representation and as a semantic property of cinematic objects, and, on the other hand, "off the screen in the spectator's phantasmatic psychic formations, cognitive processes, and basic physiological reflexes that do not pose major questions of meaning" (Sobchack, 2004, p. 60).

According to the phenomenological approach, the objective body, *Körper*, is always subjectively experienced as "one's" body, and *Leib*, instinctively and actively engaged in producing meaning and significance in and about the world. As lived body, the subject exercises a vision that is always embodied, since movie viewing has no meaning apart from the body which experiences it (Sobchack, 2004). By experiencing a film, the viewer's body is, therefore, involved in its totality in a process of reversibility of perception – as Merleau-Ponty (1945) noted, in a dialectic of non-separateness between what is shown on the screen and what comes into contact with it off the screen: all bodies of filmic experience – those on the screen and those off it – are potentially subversive bodies, endowed with the capacity to function both figuratively and literally, since they are pervasively and diffusely situated in the movie experience.

If the spectator in a traditional cognitivist conception (Bordwell, 1989; Carroll, 1990) is "mind", and in a phenomenological reading (Grodal, 2017) is "body", the "spectator-organism" proposed by Adriano D'Aloia and Ruggero Eugeni (2017) seems in some ways to be the synthetic and most recent figure of an interdisciplinary reflection that accepts the challenges of contemporary experimental sciences in a way that is neither reductionist nor prejudicial. Placing themselves in different disciplinary domains, Neurocinematics and Psychocinematics are, in fact, characterized by a distinct vocation that is both experimental and applicative, animated by the dual desire to discover something new about both the human brain and cinema, while Neurofilmology takes on, in broader and more interdisciplinary terms, the hermeneutic and heuristic bearing of neuroscientific investigations – neurobiology, neurolinguistics, and neurocognitivism – specifically within the field of cinematic spectator experience. What is called the *Mind-Movie Problem*, concerning the ways in which a two-dimensional moving image manages to harpoon our consciousness with considerable force, is firmly connected with the *Mind-Body Problem*, which questions conscious and cognitive experience and the ways in which it relates to the physical materiality of the body and brain (McGinn, 1989).

The modes of cinematic presence and the capability of inhabiting the space-time filmic fiction need, in short, to be investigated in the light of a multimodal spectatorial conception, particularly useful for a clinical approach that wants to take on, first and foremost, the embodiment of the patient's pathologies and dysfunctions. It does not seem possible to speak of the effects of vision only on a psyche and an unconscious, both paradoxically disembodied and, therefore, understood in reductionist terms mirroring those imposed by the cognitive sciences; it is preferable to discuss the influences on a *Cinesthetic Subject* in its entirety: a living subject who

> both touches and is touched by the screen – able to commute seeing to touching and back again *without a thought* and, through sensual and cross-modal activity, able to experience the movie as both here and there rather than clearly locating the site of cinematic experience as onscreen or offscreen.
>
> (Sobchack, 2004, p. 71)

As an operational and descriptive notion, embodied simulation is the experimental evidence that, between real-world perception and screen-mediated perception, there is a dimensional rather than a categorical difference. There is, however, one aspect that uniquely characterizes the relationship with fictional reality and which Gallese and Guerra, not without references to classical and modern theories of theatrical fruition, call "liberated simulation" (Gallese & Guerra, 2019). The viewer of a fictional narrative, free from direct and problematic involvements with everyday reality, observes the narrated reality from a safe distance: such a fruitional mode is appropriately declined in terms of "liberated" simulation, eventually free from the intrusiveness of the real world and our grip on it. The viewer finds her/himself, on the one hand, motionless, nailed to her/his seat, and, on the other, virtually mobile, a prisoner of both the liberated cinematic vision (Bellour, 1990) and the lived and suffered images of his singular perceptual and existential experience. In spectatorial reception, there is no separateness between body and mind, but there is

> a continuity between the physiological and affective responses of my own body and the appearances and disappearances, the mutations and perdurances, of the bodies and images on screen. The important distinction is not the hierarchical, binary one between bodies and images, or between the real and its representations. It is rather a question of discerning multiple and continually varying interactions among what can be defined indifferently as bodies and as images.
>
> (Shaviro, 1994, pp. 255–256)

If, in sketching the fruitional profile of the viewer, reflections on the body and its involvement are necessary, with respect to the role of the filmmaker as an autonomous producer of audiovisual narratives, such reflections are inescapable. Particularly interesting is Gallese and Guerra's observation on the relationship between the body of the film and that of its creator. The interaction between the film as a lived body and its viewer can go so far as to consider the movie as the crossroad of three different bodies: the body of the spectator, the body of the film, and the body of the filmmaker, as MacDougall wrote regarding images we make, which are

> in a sense mirrors of our bodies, replicating the whole of the body's activity, with its physical movements, its shifting attention, and its conflicting impulses toward order and disorder. [...] Corporeal images are not just the images of our bodies; they are also images of the body behind the camera and its relations with the world.
>
> (MacDougall, 2006, p. 3)

Filmmakers would be supposed to create, layer by layer, a living object sharing perceptual and cognitive structures with its viewer. (Gallese & Guerra, 2012, p. 189)

Therefore, the three bodies mentioned in amateur self-representative practices really seem to coincide: the new spectators are performatively involved, both users and producers, potentially amateur filmmakers acting in an audiovisual field and creating their own self-portrait and autobiographical narratives primarily through a bodily act. In this sense, in her article "Amateur versus professional", Maya Deren identifies the great advantage the amateur enjoys over the professional: freedom, both artistic and physical – "the most important part of your equipment is yourself: your mobile body, your imaginative mind, and your freedom to use both" (Deren, 1965, p. 45). Indeed, it may well be said that rather than self-portraits, as we will elaborate later, these are self-portrait gestures, "ways of doing, rather than objects to be shown" (Villa, 2012, p. 312).

Gesture, as Agamben (2000) argues, is indeed inscribable in the dimension of action, but it holds together in itself the three components of acting (*agere*), doing (*facere*), and bearing the burden of it on oneself (*gerere*). While sometimes these three domains do not coincide, audiovisual self-representational gesture highlights their ambivalence, as the self-representational subject appropriates fragments of the world that it recognizes as its own because it anchors them to an intimate dimension and therefore appropriates them; on the other hand, however, it does not metabolize and assimilate them, precisely because they are external and foreign, and therefore it spits them out, giving "birth to the Self as an Other" (Villa, 2011, p. 27).

This double movement of protention and retraction evokes a gestural dimension that Marcel Mauss called the technique of the body (1936), whereby the mediality from the organ consists in its nature as a medium that already contains the tool by which it is to be empowered. If Leroi-Gourhan (1993) highlights the essential role of the technique as a gestural extension and Flusser (1991), in his phenomenology of gesture, lingers on and analyzes the capacity of the tool to extend bodily faculties, Jousse (1991) argues that cinema is, for all intents and purposes, not a gaze, but a body endowed with its own acted thought that constitutes, finally, the extension of a human gesture. If the spectator initiates the vision through the touchscreen, the amateur filmmaker brings the narrative to life through the gesture of filming oneself through her/his own body (Belting, 2005). The spectator-performer takes responsibility for her or his own gesture, bringing into play, with feeling and perception, her or his own sensitive flesh (Fontanille, 2004).

Here, then, the amateur gesture acquires exquisitely performative characteristics, transforming itself through and within the media reality in which it is contextualized and deployed, no longer only through the gaze, but through the physical and pragmatic involvement of its user. The camera becomes a kind of extension and self-poietic remodeling of the amateur operator's body, contained as it is within a portable device such as the camera built into the cell phone, generating an image in which "a structuring presence capable of transferring a phenomenon that characterizes the cine-amateur practice"

(Cati, 2011, p. 39) is clearly visible at every stage. Amateur authorship thus seems to be configured in the very presence and agency of the subjects involved in the first person, in their physical and material inscription within the self-portrait dispositive, especially through the gesture of turning the screen toward one's face and starting the recording (Rascaroli et al., 2014; Sayad, 2013). They are, in this sense, true audiovisual gestures, conveying a representational activity aimed at refiguring the material reality through a mode of existence and an emergent movement that allows one to engage in an intentional act of embodied consciousness, belonging to an always situated, phenomenological body (De Rosa, 2019; cf. Grespi, 2019).

Audiovisual gesture (Chare & Watkins, 2017) can, in this sense, be distinguished into at least two categories: on the one hand, filmed gesture, shown and represented within the movie itself, and on the other hand, filmic gesture, which coincides with the act of filming: "actually, the two aspects – the filmic gesture, in all its aesthetic and linguistic complexity, and the filmed gestures, in their more or less pure mediality – while conceptually distinguishable, are linked in practice by an inextricable thread: the act of filming creates or transforms the framed gestures, the chain of moving images affects their appearance" (Grespi, 2017, p. 101; cf. Blümlinger & Lavin, 2018).

Inscribed in this theoretical framework, amateur self-representational gesturality seems to embody, literally, the actualization of the filmic gesture in the moment of contextual creation of the self-portrait and autobiographical work. Such filmic gesture becomes, however, a crystallization of the filmed gestural content by the author himself, as writes Jean-Luc Nancy (2000) about the gaze of the portrait, whose subject can only really show itself through a stroke. In the case of audiovisual gestures, the stroke corresponds to the built-in gesture of lingering or moving, of choosing the frame, of looking into the camera or placing oneself behind the screen, of starting and stopping the shot. The mobile-filmmaker and the amateur-user, employing rhetorics that achieve, through sensory extension, a plastic construction of the self, act in a gestural environment in which the point of view is prothesized and developed, acquiring subjective characters. This type of gesturality, exquisitely amateur, gives body to a narrative that is configured both as a narrated object and as a narrative of the gestural act.

The gestural dimension we described unfolds, in our opinion, interesting definitional and methodological perspectives for the application of audiovisual languages in the context of psychotherapeutic clinical pathways. Forms of amateur audiovisual self-representation, necessarily embodied, act in fact within a particular reflexive device, sometimes participatory, but first of all autonomic-narrative, an element that, as we shall see below, constitutes itself as particularly useful for the exploration of its agentive potential.

References

Aasman, S. I. (2012). Smile, wave or blow a kiss… Home movies and tele-technologies from the hearth. In S. Kmec & V. Thill (Eds.), *Tourists & nomads: Amateur images of migration* (pp. 161–169). Jonas Verlag.

Agamben, G. (2000). Notes on gesture. In *Means without end: Notes on politics* (Vol. 20, pp. 48–59). University of Minnesota Press.

Agamben, G. (2006). *Che cos'è un dispositivo.* Nottetempo.

Aguayo, A. J. (2019). *Documentary resistance: Social change and participatory media.* Oxford University Press.

Andriopoulos, S. (2002). Spellbound in darkness: Hypnosis as an allegory of early cinema. *The Germanic Review: Literature, Culture, Theory,* 77(2), 102–116. doi:10.1080/00168890209597860.

Aufderheide, P. (1995). Vernacular video: For the growing genre of camcorder journalism, nothing is too personal. *Columbia Journalism Review,* 33(5), 46.

Auslander, R. (2003). *Performance: Critical concepts in literary and cultural studies.* Routledge.

Austin, J. L. (1955). *How to do things with words.* Harvard University Press.

Baker, C., Schleser, M., & Molga, K. (2009). Aesthetics of mobile media art. *Journal of Media Practice,* 10(2–3), 101–122. doi:10.1386/jmpr.10.2-3.101_1.

Barker, J. M. (2009). *The tactile eye: Touch and the cinematic experience.* University of California Press.

Barthes, R. (1980). Upon leaving the movie theater. (A. Bertrand & S. White, Trans.). In T. Hak Kyung Cha (Ed.), *Apparatus: Selected writings* (pp. 3–4). Tanam Press.

Baudry, J. L. (1970). Cinéma: Effets idéologiques produits par l'appareil de base. *Cinéthique,* 78, 1.

Baudry, J. L. (1975). Le dispositif: Approches métapsychologiques de l'impression de réalité. *Communications,* 23, 56–72.

Baudry, J. L., & Williams, A. (1974). Ideological effects of the basic cinematographic apparatus. *Film Quarterly,* 28(2), 39–47. doi:10.2307/1211632.

Baumbach, N. (2012). All that heaven allows: What is, or was, cinephilia? *Film Comment,* 48(2), 47–53.

Bazin, A. (1984). *La Politique des auteurs: entretiens avec Jean Renoir [et al.]* (Vol. 3). Cahiers du cinéma.

Beattie, K. (2004). The camera I: Autobiographical documentary. In K. Beattie (Ed.), *Documentary Screens: Non-Fiction Film and Television* (pp. 105–124). Palgrave Macmillan.

Beaujour, M. (1980). *Miroirs d'encre.* Seuil.

Bellour, R. (1988). La machine à hypnose. *CinémAction,* 47, 67–72.

Bellour, R. (1990). *L'Entre-images, Photo, cinema, video* (Vol. 1). La Difference.

Belting, H. (2005). Image, medium, body: A new approach to iconology. *Critical Inquiry,* 31(2), 302–319. doi:10.1086/430962.

Bertozzi, M. (2018). *Documentario come arte. Riuso, performance, autobiografia nell'esperienza del cinema contemporaneo.* Marsilio.

Bertram, G. W. (2019). *Art as human practice: An aesthetics.* (N. Ross, Trans.). Bloomsbury Publishing.

Birchall, D. (2008). Online documentary. In T. Austin & W. de Jong (Eds.), *Rethinking documentary: New perspectives, new practices* (pp. 278–284). Open University Press.

Blümlinger, C., & Lavin, M. (2018). *Gestes filmé, gestes filmiques*. Mimésis.

Bordwell, D. (1989). A case for cognitivism. *Iris*, 9, 11–40.

Bottalico, M., & Chialant, M. T. (2005). *L'impulso autobiografico. Inghilterra, Stati Uniti, Canada… e altri ancora*. Liguori.

Brakhage, S. (1971). In defense of the "amateur" filmmaker. *Filmmakers Newsletter*, 4 (9–10), 20.

Bruss, E. E. (1980). Eye for I: Making an unmaking autobiography in film. In J. Olney (Ed.), *Autobiography: Essays theoretical and critical* (pp. 296–320). Princeton University Press.

Bruzzi, S. (2006). *New documentary*. Routledge.

Buckingam, D., Pini, M., & Willett, R. (2009). "Take back the tube!": The discursive construction of amateur film-and video-making. In D. Buckingham & R. Willett (Eds.), *Video cultures: Media technology and everyday creativity* (pp. 51–70). Palgrave McMillan.

Butler, J. (1993). *Bodies that matter: On the discursive limits of "sex"*. Routledge.

Campanelli, V. (2012). Remix it yourself: A do it yourself ethic. *Comunicação e Sociedade*, 22, 8–15. doi:10.17231/comsoc.22(2012).1271.

Carlson, M. (1996). *Performance: A critical introduction*. Routledge.

Carroll, N. (1990). *The philosophy of horror: Or paradoxes of the heart*. Routledge.

Casetti, F. (2015). *The Lumière galaxy: Seven key words for the cinema to come*. Columbia University Press.

Cati, A. (2011). Figure del sé nel film di famiglia. *Fata Morgana*, 15, 35–44.

Cati, A., & Grassilli, M. (2019). The migrant as an eye/i: Transculturality, self-representation, audiovisual practices. *Cinergie: Il Cinema e le altre Arti*, 8(16), 1–11. doi:10.6092/issn.2280-9481/10228.

Chalfen, R. (1987). *Snapshot versions of life*. Bowling Green State University Popular Press.

Chalfen, R. (1988). Home video versions of life-anything new? *Society for Visual Anthropology Newsletter*, 4(1), 1–5.

Chare, N., & Watkins, L. (2017). *Gesture and film: Signalling new critical perspectives*. Routledge.

Crary, J. (1990). *Techniques of the observer*. MIT Press.

D'Aloia, A., & Eugeni, R. (2017). *Teorie del cinema: Il dibattito contemporaneo*. Raffaello Cortina.

De Certeau, M. (1980). *L'invention du quotidien*. Gallimard.

Deleuze, G. (1983). *Cinéma 1. L'image-mouvement*. Éditions de Minuit.

Deleuze, G. (1989). Qu'est-ce qu'un dispositif? Michel Foucault philosophe. In *Rencontre internationale, Paris, 9–11 janvier 1988* (pp. 185–195). Seuil.

Deren, M. (1965). Amateur versus professional. *Film Culture*, 39(1), 45–46.

De Rosa, M. (2019). On gesture, or of the blissful promise. *Necsus: European Journal of Media Studies*, 8(2), 113–128. doi:10.25969/mediarep/13141.

Dodes, R. (2011, 22 July). "Life in a Day" director aims to elevate YouTube videos into art, interview to Kevin Macdonald. *The Wall Street Journal*. www.wsj.com/articles/BL-SEB-66274.

Ejzenštejn, S. M. (1989). *La regia. L'arte della messa in scena*. Marsilio.

Elsaesser, T., & Hagener, M. (2015). *Film theory: An introduction through the senses*. Routledge.

Feldmann, E. (1956). Considération sur la situation du spectateur au cinéma. *Revue Internationale de Filmologie*, 7(26), 83–97.

Ferraris, M. (2005). *Dove sei? Ontologia del telefonino*. Bompiani.

Fiske, J. (1992). The cultural economy of fandom. In L. A. Lewis (Ed.), *The adoring audience: Fan culture and popular media* (pp. 30–49). Routledge.

Flitterman-Lewis, S., Stam, R., & Burgoyne, R. (1992). *New vocabularies in film semiotics*. Routledge.

Flusser, V. (1991). *Gesten: Versuch einer Phänomenologie*. Bollmann Verlag.

Fontanille, J. (2004). *Soma et séma. Figures du corps*. Maisonneuve et Larose.

Foucault, M. (1975). *Surveiller et punir: Naissance de la prison*. Gallimard.

Freund, G. (2011). *La photographie en France au XIXe siècle*. Bourgois.

Frosh, P. (2015). The gestural image: The selfie, photography theory, and kinesthetic sociability. *International Journal of Communication*, 9, 22.

Gallagher, S. (2006). *How the body shapes the mind*. Clarendon Press.

Gallese, V. (2005). Embodied simulation: From neurons to phenomenal experience. *Phenomenology and the Cognitive Sciences*, 4(1), 23–48. doi:10.1007/s11097-005-4737-z.

Gallese, V., & Guerra, M. (2012). Embodying movies: Embodied simulation and film studies. *Cinema: Journal of Philosophy and the Moving Image*, 3, 183–210.

Gallese, V., & Guerra, M. (2019). *The empathic screen: Cinema and neuroscience*. Oxford University Press.

Gandini, L. (1998). *La regia cinematografica. Storia e profili critici*. Carocci.

Genette, G. (1972). *Figures III*. Seuil.

Gernalzick, N. (2006). To act or to perform: Distinguishing filmic autobiography. *Biography*, 1–13. www.jstor.org/stable/23541011.

Goffman, E. (1959). *The presentation of self in everyday life*. Doubleday.

Gordon, R. B. (2001). From Charcot to Charlot: Unconscious imitation and spectatorship in French cabaret and early cinema. *Critical Inquiry*, 27(3), 515–549.

Grespi, B. (2017). *Il cinema come gesto. Incorporare le immagini, pensare il medium*. Aracne.

Grespi, B. (2019). *Figure del corpo. Gesto e immagine in movimento*. Meltemi.

Griffiths, T. (2013). Representing history and the filmmaker in the frame. *Doc On-Line: Revista Digital De Cinema Documentário*, 15, 39–67.

Grodal, T. (2017). How film genres are a product of biology, evolution and culture – an embodied approach. *Palgrave Communications*, 3(1), 1–8.

Gubbins, M. (2012). Digital revolution: Active audiences and fragmented consumption. In D. Iordanova & S. Cunningham (Eds.), *Digital disruption: Cinema moves on-line* (pp. 67–100). St Andrews.

Gunthert, A. (2013a). *Le selfie, emblème de la photographie connectée*. http://histoir evisuelle.fr/cv/icones/2846.

Gunthert, A. (2013b). *Viralité du selfie, déplacements du portrait*. http://histoirevisuelle. fr/cv/icones/2895.

Hetrick, J. (2006). Amateur video must not be overlooked. *Moving Image*, 6(1), 66–81.

Jenkins, C. (2015). *Home movies: The American family in contemporary Hollywood cinema*. Bloomsbury Publishing.

Jenkins, H. (1992). *Textual poachers: Television fans and participatory culture*. Routledge.

Jenkins, H. (2006). *Fans, bloggers, gamers: Exploring participatory culture*. New York University Press.

Jousse, M. (1991). *Anthropologie du geste*. Gallimard.

Kaplan, E. A. (1990). *Psychoanalysis and cinema*. Routledge.

Krauss, R. (1976). *Video: The aesthetics of narcissism*. The MIT Press.

Lacan, J. (1966). *Ecrits*. Seuill.

Lebow, A. (2012). *The cinema of me: The self and subjectivity in first person documentary*. Columbia University Press.

Lejeune, P. (1980). *Je est un autre. L'autobiographie de la littérature aux médias*. Seuil.

Lejeune, P., & Nysenholc, A. (1987). Cinéma et autobiographie: problèmes de vocabulaire. *L'écriture du JE au cinéma*, 7–14.

Leroi-Gourhan, A. (1993). *Gesture and speech*. MIT Press.

Lévi-Strauss, C. (1966). *The savage mind: The nature of human society series*. University of Chicago Press.

Macdougall, D. (1998). *Transcultural cinema*. Princeton University Press.

Mackendrick, A., & Cronin, P. (2005). On film-making: An introduction to the craft of the director. *Cinéaste*, 30(3), 46–54. www.jstor.org/stable/41689874.

Manovich, L. (2008). *Software takes command*. http://softwarestudies.com/soft book/manovich_softbook_11_20_2008.pdf.

Marks, L. U. (2000). *The skin of the film: Intercultural cinema, embodiment, and the senses*. Duke University Press.

Mauss, M. (1936). Les techniques du corps. *Journal de Psychologie*, 32, 3–4.

McGinn, C. (1989). Can we solve the mind-body problem? *Mind New Series*, 98(391), 349–366. doi:10.1093/mind/xcviii.391.349.

Merleau-Ponty, M. (1945). *Phenomenology of perception*. Gallimard.

Metz, C. (1977). *Le signifiant imaginaire: psychanalyse et cinema* (Vol. 1134). Union générale d'éditions.

Mirzoeff, N. (2016). *How to see the world: An introduction to images, from self-portraits to selfies, maps to movies and more*. Basic Books.

Mitry, J. (1997). *The aesthetics and psychology of the cinema*. Indiana University Press.

Monterrubio Ibáñez, L. (2016). Identity self-portraits of a filmic gaze: From absence to (multi) presence. *Comparative Cinema*, 8, 63–73.

Monterrubio Ibáñez, L. (2021). The filmmaker's presence in French contemporary autofiction: From filmeur/filmeuse to acteur/actrice. *New Review of Film and Television Studies*, 19(4), 533–559.

Moraldi, S. (2015). *Questioni di campo. La relazione osservatore/osservato nella forma documentaria*. Bulzoni.

Moran, J. M. (2002). *There's no place like home video*. University of Minnesota Press.

Morin, E. (1956). *Le cinéma ou l'homme imaginaire: Essai d'anthropologie*. Les éditions de Minuit.

Naficy, H. (2001). *An accented cinema: Exilic and diasporic filmmaking*. Princeton University Press.

Nancy, J. L. (2000). *Le regard du portrait*. Éditions Galilée.

Nichols, B. (1991). *Representing reality*. Indiana University Press.

Nichols, B. (2010). *Introduction to documentary*. Indiana University Press.

Odin, R. (1995). *Le film de famille: Usage privè, usage public*. Meridiens Klincksieck.

Odin, R. (2014). Quand le téléphone portable rencontre le cinema. In L. Allard, L. Creton, & R. Odin (Eds.), *Téléphone mobile et création* (pp. 37–54). Armand Colin.

Perniola, I. (2014). *L'era postdocumentaria*. Mimesis.

Petraitis, M. (2019). Be part of history – documentary film and mass participation in the age of YouTube. *Research in Film and History*, 2, 1–26.

Pink, S. (2008). Visual anthropology. In T. Bennett & J. Frow (Eds.), *The Sage handbook of cultural analysis* (pp. 632–653). Sage Publications.

Prédal, R. (2008). *Le cinéma à l'heure des petites cameras*. Klinksieck.

Rascaroli, L. (2009). *The personal camera: Subjective cinema and the essay film*. Wall-flower Press.

Rascaroli, L. (2014). Working at home: Tarnation, amateur authorship, and self-inscription in the digital age. In L. Rascaroli, G. Young, & B. Monahan (Eds.), *Amateur filmmaking: The home movie, the archive, the web* (pp. 229–242). Blooms-bury Publishing.

Rascaroli, L., Young, G., & Monahan, B. (2014). *Amateur filmmaking: The home movie, the archive, the web*. Bloomsbury Publishing.

Renov, M. (2004). *The subject of documentary*. University of Minnesota Press.

Renov, M. (2009). First person films: Some thesis of self-inscription. In T. Austin & W. de Jong (Eds.), *Rethinking documentary: New perspectives, new practices* (pp. 29–39). Open University Press.

Rouch, J. (1978). On the vicissitudes of the self: The possessed dancer, the magician, the sorcerer, the filmmaker, and the ethnographer. *Studies in the Anthropology of Visual Communication*, 5(1), 2–8. doi:10.1525/var.1978.5.1.2.

Sabatino, A. C. (2019). Lo schermo performativo e il suo sguardo sugli autoritratti audiovisivi. The performative screen and its look on audiovisual self-portraits. *Journal of Communication*, 15, 69–88. doi:10.1285/i22840753n15p69.

Sabatino, A. C. (2020). Performance. In *International lexicon of aesthetics* (Vol. 3). Mimesis.

Sayad, C. (2013). *Performing authorship: Self-inscription and corporeality in the cinema*. Tauris.

Schechner, R. (1988). *Performance theory*. Routledge.

Schleser, M. (2011). *Mobile-mentary: Mobile documentaries in the mediascape*. Lap Lambert Academic.

Schleser, M. (2014). Connecting through mobile autobiographies: Self-reflexive mobile filmmaking, self-representation, and selfies. In M. Berry, & M. Schleser (Eds.), *Mobile media making in an age of smartphones* (pp. 148–158). Palgrave Pivot.

Searle, J. R. (1969). *Speech acts: An essay in the philosophy of language*. Cambridge University Press.

Shapiro, L. (2019). *Embodied cognition*. Routledge.

Shaviro, S. (1994). *The cinematic body*. University of Minnesota Press.

Sobchack, V. (1991). *The address of the eye: A phenomenology of film experience*. Princeton University Press.

Sobchack, V. (2004). *Carnal thoughts: Embodiment and moving image culture*. University of California Press.

Tifentale, A. (2014). The selfie: Making sense of the "masturbation of self-image" and the "virtual mini-me". *Selfiecity.net*, 1–24. https://selfiecity.net/#theory

Toffler, A. (1980), The rise of the prosumer. In Id., *The third wave* (pp. 265–288). Morrow.

Tortajada, M., & Albera, F. (2015). *Cine-dispositives: Essays in epistemology across media*. Amsterdam University Press.

Varela, F. J., Thompson, E., & Rosch, E. (1991). *The embodied mind: Cognitive science and human experience*. The MIT Press.

Villa, F. (2011). Time-lapse self-portrait. L'autoritratto e la cosa metamorfica. *Fata Morgana*, 5(15), 25–34.

Villa, F. (2012). *Vite impersonali. Autoritrattistica e medialità*. Pellegrini.

Zimmermann, P. R. (1995). *Reel families: A social history of amateur film*. Indiana University Press.

Chapter 2

The Therapeutic Set
Methodological Integrations

Anna Chiara Sabatino

Embodiment and Living Images

We have extensively described how the negotiations between everyday user and the documentary dispositive, performative, and possibly participatory imply the involvement of creative, agential, and gestural domains. The embodiment of everyday audiovisual acts still remains an essential element to be explored, particularly in its relation to technologies and the images they produce and mediate.

If the spectator's viewing experience is bodily, almost like the filmmaker who confronts, body to body, the world to be filmed, along with Belting (2005) we can deduce a fundamental part of our reflection on the therapeutic potential of the creative process. In the essay *Image, Medium, Body*, the German art historian argues that images do not exist in themselves, but happen: they take place through transmission and perception. Such a reflection moves from the distinction between picture and image (Mitchell, 1994, 2005), where *picture* refers, strictly speaking, to the materiality of the image, the physical support and its location in material space, while *image* is used to describe the virtual presence of the represented subject. Indeed, any visible image reaches the viewer through an inevitable mediation, which might be the body itself, both percipient and agent. The body as a living medium in the activities of image perception, projection, and production is thus the first piece by which users interact with a medium in order to be able to explore images as if they were alive. It is precisely from the idea of a *living image* that William Mitchell (2005) wonders what images want, defining them as living entities capable of circulating, communicating, and directly addressing a request or an appeal to the recipient. Mitchell moves, therefore, his reflection from the weakness rather than the power of the image: the objects of his investigation are not only works of art, but especially common iconic objects, in which he detects the true desire of images "to change places with the beholder, to transfix or paralyze the beholder, turning her or him into an image for the gaze of the picture [...]. The power they want is manifested as *lack*, not as a possession" (Mitchell, 2005, p. 36). Elaborating a subaltern

DOI: 10.4324/9781003340508-3

image model, Mitchell argues that the images' desire is inversely proportional to their power, therefore compensating through desire their real powerlessness.

Such a strategic shift, meaning the construction of images not as sovereign and disembodied spirits, but as subaltern subjects functioning as both intermediaries and scapegoats in the social field of the visible, does not mark the desire of the image as the desire of the artist, of the viewer, or even the figures within the image. What images want does not coincide with the message they communicate or the effect they produce, because "what pictures want in the last instance, then, is simply to be asked what they want" (Mitchell, 2005, p. 48).

The hermeneutic and relational vis-à-vis desire theorized by Mitchell is juxtaposed with the ability of images to return the gaze to the viewer. David Freedberg reflects on the psychosomatic reactions and responses to very different iconic objects, choosing to develop an interdisciplinary approach on image theories which diverges from the intellectual constructions of the critic and scholars, and lingers, instead, on people's actions and reactions (Freedberg, 1989). Far from elaborating a specific theory of reaction and history of fruition, Freedberg sets out to explore, by accessing different iconic genres, from pornography to popular sacred iconography, from idolatrous veneration to iconoclastic actions, the power of images in relation to their encounter with their users.

The gaze of images can sting, as Roland Barthes (1980) claims when he sets the concept of *studium* as the starting point and defines it as the trigger which activates the relationship between the Spectator, and the photographer who made it, the Operator. Barthes argues that *studium* reception implies to connect and understand the photographer's intentions in order to question them, since the concept of culture itself (from which *studium* derives) is an implicit contract between creators and consumers. But the image, according to the French theorist, has the power to strike and provoke particular suggestions, such as individual behaviors may do, when the *punctum* comes to break the *studium*. While the *studium* empties images of their engaging potential, showing and illustrating the represented content, the *punctum* does not intercept their meaning, but the iconic element that, starting from the scene, pierces the viewer like an arrow (Barthes, 1980). The presence of a detail, a dazzling pole of spectatorial attention, stings the viewer through an unleashed image force of expansion, playing on the delicate balance of the interplay between material and immaterial. Images, according to Bredekamp (2010), enjoy, in fact, an alien corporeity, since they cannot be fully traced back to that human dimension to which they owe their realization: once produced, they become autonomous and instill emotions and feelings.

The term "material" seems to be no longer sufficient to describe how pictures as physical supports convey mental images, notes Hans Belting (2005, p. 77). Indeed, the less the viewers are aware of the visual medium, the more they focus on the image, as if images come from themselves (cf. Casetti, 2015; McLuhan, 1964). Images can be experienced or produced through a living medium, the body, which allows us to acquire them through perceptual processes, store them through mnemonic processes, reactivate, create, and transform them through creative and productive processes. On the basis of a reversibility between subject and object founded on a *passion of the material* (Sobchack, 2004), media can be subjectivized through the interaction with technical and technological objects and the involvement of a subject who is always embodied and enworlded. In other words, material objects, in contact with the engaging subject, somehow come alive. Such animation activity of the subject recalls an iconic lifegiving attitude that has tended, since ancient times, to consider iconic objects as substitutes for bodies themselves. Peculiar material images are, in fact, attributed the power to give body to the absence of the represented figures by their presence, particularly in certain cultic and ritual practices of the deceased and deities, activating a dialectic whereby both image and medium take life from the analogy with the body. We might speak, using Baudrillard's expression, of a symbolic exchange between dead body and living image, representing the presence of an absence as funda-mental and paradoxical image ontological status. Taking on the burden of the images' presentification, the pictures conveyed by audiovisual techniques and media refer both to the represented subject and to their material character-istics, triggering a process of "re-presentation" of the original.

In returning to our specific research interests, the produced objects, as well as the technologies and techniques, can only be embodied by a subject engaged in an intentional, material and technological production of objects that acquire an individual identity in time and space. In the context of the delicate relationship between the materiality and immateriality, we intend to delve into the potential reversibility of audiovisual representations and con-textualize them within the methodological frame of iconic agency, particu-larly regarding the therapeutic potential of moving images.

Iconic Agency in Audiovisual-Based Approach

Images, then, desire, want, touch, but they can also acquire a *figuractive* nature (Pinotti & Somaini, 2016), as they contribute to constructing our reality not as its emanations, but as a necessary condition of it. In this sense, the notion of *Bildakt* elaborated by Horst Bredekamp (2010) summarizes the iconic capacity to trigger reactions and actions on the part of the user. The iconic act is not an intentional disposition of the subject, but that particular capacity of images themselves to perform or undergo actions, generating chains of cause and effect. The schematic iconic act, peculiar to mimetic works of art – such as statues, tableaux vivants, automata – consists of the exchange between life and artifact; the substitutive iconic act, on the other hand, insists on the possibility of the artifact replacing the body, in particular posing the weighty question of authen-ticity and iconoclasm in contexts of war or control of power; the intrinsic iconic act, finally, calls into question the shaping of form in relation to our gaze (Bre-dekamp, 2010).

Within a specifically art-historical field, the *Theorie des Bildakts* argues that images do not undergo, but rather produce perceptual experiences and behaviors performing the iconic act itself, by summoning exercise and application of human symbolic faculties and capacities. The *imagines agentes*, understood as material representations and *pictures* capable of intervening on the existing reality, do not acquire power only by virtue of their belonging to the artistic sphere as works of art: according to some scholars, they are configured as forms of operativity that potentially concern all iconic phenomena involving the construction of scopic relations between producers and users. Agency, in this sense, as defined by anthropologist Alfred Gell in his classic *Art and Agency* (1998), is not exclusively about works of art: anthropological theory of art cannot afford to have as its primary theoretical term a category or taxon of objects which are *exclusively* art objects because the whole tendency of this theory, as I have been suggesting, is to explore a domain in which "objects" merge with "people" by virtue of the existence of social relations between persons and things, and persons and persons *via* things (Gell, 1998, p. 12).

Starting from the assumption that the aesthetic properties and sensible effects of artifacts cannot be abstracted from the anthropological processes and social settings in which such objects exist, function, and act on and with people, Gell's agency theories are based on the premise that any thing, person, or living being can, in theory, constitute themselves as art objects. Agency field of inquiry is delineated primarily with respect to "material" indexes – "the visible, the physical, the thing", as Gell points out – and their power to catalyze that particular cognitive process called, in the footsteps of Peirce's semiotics, abduction of agency.

The relation with the "index", which, following Charles Pierce, is understood as a "natural sign" from which the observer is able to draw a causal inference and trace the intentions or capacities of the agent-creator, Gell describes the abductive process as the initial moment of a broader inductive process in which a hypothesis serves as a possible explanation of an empirical fact. Borrowing such logic from semiotics, the anthropologist reflects on the roles that artifacts assume in processes of social interaction and their constitution as "indexes", connected as much to the material producers as to the recipients of products. The term agency is thus used by Alfred Gell with a double meaning: on the one hand, as the human faculty to act on things, and, on the other hand, as the power of artifacts to act on human beings: the concept of agency provides a cultural framework for thinking about causality, regarding creative experiences, products and events being intentionally conceived by a person-agent or thing-agent. Whenever an event is considered to happen because of an "intention" belonging to the person or thing initiating the causal sequence, it is an instance of agency. Action cannot be conceived, claims Gell, in other than social terms within an explicit relational structure.

Artifacts, therefore, are also bearers of agency of their creators and for their users: this agency lives through theirs, enriching itself autonomously in the system of social relationships, exercising its capacity to infer constructively about reality, as well as acquiring the dual role of action of the individual on things and influence of things on the individual. The social "agent" is defined by Gell both as a subject capable of intentionally and manifestly causing the occurrence of events, and as an object, an artifact whose causality must be taken physically, socially, and ritually into account.

We must, therefore, make a distinction, which will be very useful for a redefinition of the therapeutic setting: on the one hand, we have intentional beings that, because of their inherent capacity to produce actions, are defined as primary; on the other hand, objects, artifacts, which, since referable to primary agents, can be labeled as secondary – "artefacts, dolls, cars, works of art, etc. through which primary agents distribute their agency in the causal milieu, and thus render their agency effective" (Gell, 1998, p. 20). Determining themselves as derivatives of primary agentivity, secondary agents are created by the actions and productions of their creators, imparting and enacting, voluntarily and deliberately, but are agency themselves. In fact, the agentive relationship, Gell clarifies, functions by virtue of the art nexus (Gell, 1998, pp. 12–27), the peculiar relationship between agent, i.e., the creator, and user (patient) such that the recipient coincides with the user-patient and the agent acts on her or him through the index that conveys her or his agency. Social agency is exclusively relational and provides a patient for each agent and, reciprocally, an agent for each patient. Such a complex network of relationships gives rise to a wide variety of combinations in both active and passive ways, as is then illustrated in the dissertation of *Art and Agency*, which proposes the application of the relational schema between the elements of the art nexus and the roles played by them. Giuseppe Pucci aptly summarizes the agentive functioning:

> members of a community as observers or users (patients or recipients) infer by abduction from the art objects (indexes) a certain quality or intentionality (agency) of the creators (agents). Producers and recipients, art object and referent (prototype) enter into a complex of social relationships – called by Gell art nexus – that gives rise to a wide variety of combinations, each component being able to operate bi-directionally, both actively and passively.
>
> (Pucci, 2008, pp. 35–36)

If, according to Alfred Gell, art objects are extensions of the agency of those who create or use them, they actively or passively participate in relationships between human beings. The French sociologist Henri Lefebvre, in *The Critique of Everyday Life*, also ascribes to images a social use, asserting that the image is an act that implies the intention or will for an effect: either to contribute to the realization of the possible or the depiction of the impossible, to prepare a project of choice, or to seduce and reach out to the other human being. The image as a social act is the image of an act (Lefebvre, 1961). In a perspective that investigates their effectivity, performativity and efficacy (Leone, 2014),

> images become visual objects or social actors, even before they are representations of something, punctual elements, dispersed and piled up, that ask for and perhaps impose not contemplation and distancing, but, precisely by virtue of their autonomy and degree of abstraction, a performance and an action.
>
> (Malavasi, 2017, p. 11)

In defining a history of the body that speaks of its demarcation, marks and signs that subdivide it, diminish it, and deny it in its difference and radical ambivalence in order to organize it into a structural material of exchange/sign (Simonigh, 2011), the absence of bodies is replaced by iconic presence, and images come to life and act on the bodies of viewers. As is well known, in *Ontologie de l'image photographique*, André Bazin described the "mummy complex" as the origin of man's psychological need to defeat death through images. While such a complex harks back to the ancient practice of embalming among the Egyptians, it finds full fulfillment, according to Bazin, only with the advent of photography and, later, cinema – "dynamic mummification", as Eisenstein would write in the same years (cf. Kleiman & Somaini, 2016; Subini, 2010), since both media are finally able to satisfy the need to "save being by means of appearance" (Bazin, 1945, p. 3) thanks to their constitutive characteristics. When cinema was still only a distant dream, other thinkers prophesied the technological miracle of restoring life as such:

> the future will see the replacement of motionless photographs, frozen in their frames, with animated portrait that can be brought to life at the turn of a handle. Physiognomic expressions will be preserved as voices are by the phonograph. It will even be possible to combine the latter with the Phonoscope to complete the illusion... we will do more than analyse, we will bring back to life.
>
> (Demenÿ quoted in Burch, 1990, p. 26)

In these typically modern myths, the life-restoring and life-instilling act of an "animated portrait" is made possible by a technical gesture not devoid of ritual and magical valences: the images do not provide information but live and act at the same time on their producer and recipients, through the same media, tools, and supports. With Gell, we can argue, in fact, that the agency of images is not recognizable in advance but only *ex post*, from their acting on the setting in which they are inscribed and from the effects they cause on the peculiar configuration of the causal environment of which they are at the same time the product and the engine (Gell, 1998). For the art nexus to be established, the agentivity of images must somehow be recognized not as subjugating acceptance of an already given cause, but as verifying the actualization of the image's potentiality to act and as ratifying its power in action. This is what happens in consecrations and rituals, which transform objects into images and media (Belting, 2005). If ritual is an individual or collective act always faithful to certain rules that constitute its rituality, its (real or presumed) efficacy is not resolved in the empirical concatenation of cause and effect (Cazeneuve, 1971). The *causal milieu* matters and we will elaborate on this later, since it is within a material and singular environment that things and people – image, medium, and body – interact and act.

Ritual acting, in this sense, is not to be understood as the symbolic re-enactment of a social covenant handed down or codified in written form, but as a gestural action performance through specific body techniques, that intervene not only with the purpose of presentifying symbolization, but also as an agent that triggers a movement, constantly and cyclically renewing and confirming the symbolic orders, but also, at the same time, mutating them (Harth, 2003, p. 250). Through an embodied intervention that is an extension of the producer's consciousness and mind (extended mind) on and in artifacts, understood as intentionally produced objects acting as indexes of agency, such artifacts acquire a social capacity (social agency) "in ways theoretically equivalent to those present in flesh-and-blood persons" (Freedberg, 2008, p. 9).

Such a life-giving drift of the iconic, for some, might be rejected, since images, not necessarily to be understood as subjects, perhaps want nothing at all, except that we leave them alone, without forcing them to be living organisms (Rancière, 2009, p. 131). But here we believe that it is neither possible to evade the production processes of pictures, processes on which their relationship with the reality, and vice versa, is based, nor to ignore the fact that images can be, for all intents and purposes, ways of worldmaking (Goodman, 1978), rather than merely passive objects or representational tools.

Agential Participatory Self-Narratives

Alfred Gell never ceases to highlight how, on the one hand, his conception of agency is inescapably relational and contextual, and on the other hand how "anthropological relationships are real and biographically consequential ones, which articulate to the agent's biographical 'life project'" (Gell, 1998, p. 11). It seems, for these reasons, that agency theory may be applied and contextualized in documentary practices, particularly performative ones. According to Bill Nichols, documentary aims to change the way the world is seen and approached through the exercise of imaginative, rhetorical, and persuasive skills (Nichols, 2001). If the only truth that documentary produces is participation to the reality (Bertozzi, 2018), it is undeniable that cinema was born as a documentary and, as such, gained its first powers (Comolli, 2004). In this sense, Renov (2004) argues that the performative approaches that characterize that strand of subjective, first-person, and confessional contemporary documentary aim to shape life through audiovisual narratives and texts.

We have already highlighted the way in which the performative documentary modality, rather than having as its primary purpose documentation itself, is constituted as a process to be traced and represented, a contact and a ritual dynamic that refers to no other referent than itself and its own performative bearing (Moraldi, 2015, p. 82). But still little we have lingered on the matter of audiovisual fieldwork: now, once we have acquired methodological awareness of the moving images agency, we are better able to understand how "social and ritual dynamics intersect with scenic dynamics related to the presence of the machine" (Moraldi, 2015, p. 87).

Following the notion of enactivity proposed by Francesco Marano (2007) and borrowed from Varela (1992), Simone Moraldi (2015) theorizes a ritualized set in which the documentary encounter and relationship are activated and self-regulated. Similar to the double dispositive, narrative and therapeutic, previously described and to which we shall return, in the audiovisual documentary field there is a double rituality, contextual to the internal dynamics and their evenemential component, and diegetic, linked to the recording in progress. Where enaction involves the overcoming of the dualism between subject and object (cf. Grodal, 1997; Marks, 2000), the presence and action of a recording apparatus lend a "ritual charge" to what happens: the *milieu* in which a ritual action takes place is itself charged with a further, second-level rituality by virtue of the presence of the device; the dynamics characterizing the social field in which the ritual takes place meet and intersect with the ritual dynamics that take place at the moment the button is pressed and the video device starts recording.

In the context of the non-fiction practices dispositive, the ritualizing charge is thus superimposed on an existing ritual charge, easily resulting in phenomena of performative surplus (Gauthier, 1995) by subjects called to self-representational practices triggered by the dispositive presence (Moraldi, 2015). Such ritualizing charge also applies in self-representation and its "parallax effect" (Ginsburg, 1995), which determines the narrative repositioning of those subjects who generally are observed by the observers. The so described de-gerarchization process, historically referring in postcolonial studies to indigenous self-narratives (cf. Turner, 2002; Worth & Adair, 1972), would similarly concern the drift of the self-portrait form toward the contemporary selfie, which in some ways profanes its tradition. As Gunthert (2013a) appropriately points out, the selfie pragmatically acts on the portrait democratization front (Freund, 2011), and allows a better understanding of popular culture manifestations. Through a linguistic, usage, and production shift, the selfie redefines the self-portrayal genre, diverging from the tradition of the careful set up of pictorial portrait, and configures itself as the outcome of a performative, often improvisational act.

During the twentieth century the development of this amateur genre for the exclusive use of the producer and her/his affective context encouraged the proliferation of live shots. Nevertheless, such desire for authenticity and immediacy does not easily colonize self-representation territory. The selfie realizes the paradoxical birth of the *portrait d'occasion*, as Gunthert defines it (2013b), showing a self-image snapshot. With respect to the sacralization and rituality that governs the setting, the genre, and the iconic agency, amateur self-representation acts, conversely, in profanatory ways, where profanation is meant as *counter-dispositive*, are able to restore to common and free use what was previously accessible only to particular social conditions and technical skills (Agamben, 2006, pp. 21–22), precisely as happens with the selfie. By preferring the expression *self-produced* over adjectives such as amateur, private, or vernacular, Gunthert chooses to materially refer to the practice, to the profanatory and productive act to which contemporary self-representational processes are, as already extensively discussed, inextricably intertwined.

In agreement with Dubois (1983) we can argue that the photographic image is unthinkable outside the very act that makes it be, whether this passes for the receptor, the producer, or the referent of the image, since it is inseparable from its referential situation. Now, the amateur image, particularly in the case of the selfie, is necessarily "gestural" (Frosh, 2015), as it is clearly illustrated from the presence of the photographing arm within the frame. The performativity of the image-act, in the selfie as a specific object of analysis, thus comes to be, almost literally, a *limb-image* (Giusti, 2019, pp. 30–31), understood as a crutch to the construction of our digital and performative identities. Although acknowledging its categorization as an emanation of the referent (Barthes, 1980) rather than as a representation of reality (Sontag, 1977), the indexicality of the selfie is peculiarly characterized by its correspondence to the performed action rather than by being the trace of reality imprinted on the photographic medium (Frosh, 2015). Far from the conception of a representation that benefits from the transference of reality due to the mechanical process initiated by the analogical medium (cf. Bazin, 1945), the indexical functioning which was already fundamental in Gell's agency theory can be conceived no longer as tributary to the reality to which it refers, but, rather, as a deictic regime hosting the process and the producer.

The connective performance to which Frosh refers is embodied in the production of a trace of reality that, rather than referring ontologically to an external referent, concerns its own maker, who is involved in a deissic circle, being both object and subject of the image. Acting in and about the present time, the practice of the selfie "not only composes technicity and embodiment in the moment of image production; it also constitutes a deictic movement of the body that draws attention to the immediate context of image viewing and to the activity of a viewer" (Frosh, 2015, p. 1615).

The gestural image thus takes shape as an image thanks to a deissic relationship, which materially binds it to its producing subject and its produced object as both subject and author of the narrative act. The product of such a gestural act is an artifact, handmade and autographic, whose identity depends on the technical and existential conditions of the history of its production, bearing an identity trace of the one who made it: the amateur video is finally configured as an index and material expression of the will and the creative act of its agent (cf. Gell, 1998).

This is how the profanatory and self-representative act dropped into everyday life has to be understood as the outcome of the interplay between bodily movements and contextual interactions mediated by technologies and medial languages innervating the everyday life: such self-experience can be configured as a transformative process, implying an embodied, embedded and gestural evenementionality within a performative agency context and process (Fischer-Lichte, 2008). In an amateur-oriented dispositive, the "material" index of the audiovisual self-portrait is also capable of activating, by virtue of the agency acquired through gestural processuality, a threshold between the subject and its self-representation which may determine material and factual interchange between the two dimensions (reality and representation). In fact, if the conversational and interpolative nature of the selfie has the power to undo the out-of-frame and share the viewer's "here and now" (Deleuze, 1983), in its audiovisual declination it becomes capable of looking back at its own author.

To describe and define the cinematic screen, film studies have employed, among others, three major metaphors: the screen as a window to reality, as a picture representing a world, and as a mirror that returns to us a reflection of things and ourselves. This last metaphor, in particular, illustrates the importance of the complex relationship between the subject, its self-representation, and the surface on which it is represented and shown. In a self-representational form such as the selfie, for example, the viewer's gaze rests, through the mediation of the screen, on an audiovisual text that, at the same time, addresses its interlocutor.

Amateur audiovisual self-representation can only play out in the relationship between the constituent elements of producer, product, and viewer, but it cannot ignore the fact that nowadays the viewer can be the material maker of the representation but also be represented by its own self-representation. Screens have the power to give body and depth to a network of vicissitudes and experiences, generating a tension capable of structurally transforming the space, a poetic and poietic reversibility (Baudrillard, 1997) determining a transfusion of reality into the screen and vice versa.

In the framework of theoretical and methodological proposal we have so far described, the traditional oppositional binary between spectatorial position and observed representation object is set aside in favor of an active, performative, and participatory dynamic that finally makes the user a "spectator" of a narrative that, literally, watches and re-watches her/him back. The potentially therapeutic agency of amateur audiovisual self-narratives is determined, therefore, by the activation of a threshold suspension (Pinotti, 2017), with the consequent permeability between the on-screen narrative and the off-screen reality. Such powerful permeability and reversibility may be configured through the deployment of complex narrative processualities and by means of flexible and interchangeable roles that regulate both the fieldwork and the representation functioning.

Narrative Medicine and Audiovisual Therapeutic Agency

The "narrative" approach, which belongs to psychotherapy as well as to the cinematic universe, has emerged within a more general narrative orientation in epistemology and the human sciences, and has been further fostered by the development of the humanities in clinical and evolutionary psychology (Hillman, 1979). In fact, many psychotherapists locate the core of the therapeutic process in self-narrative, since stories help human beings to construct and reconstruct their worlds by a simple narrative (White & Epston, 1990) and imaginative exercise on their lives' narrative. Viewed from this perspective, not only does the pathological condition acquire its own clinical and experiential story and, eventually, can be considered as a particular narrative form, but also, together with diagnosis and treatment, it constitutes an articulated and broader narrative structure and a true, complex story of care.

While differing in specific methodologies, therapeutic interventions can be defined as forms of storytelling, varying in genre and style, characterizing the vast landscape of the psychotherapeutic movement, which has used since its emergence and still uses "narrative means" (Parry & Doan, 1994; Payne, 2006; White & Epston, 1990). For a long time, in psychotherapy the essential factors of change have been linked to cognitive processing and increased levels of awareness, as we will explore further on. However, over the past two decades a profound epistemological renewal has swept through psychotherapeutic theories and practices, leading to new conceptions characterized by greater attention to the relational and intersubjective aspects, as well as to the empathic, emotional, and affective components, together with nonverbal elements, physiognomic and body language (Leijssen, 2006; Moschini, 2018).

The empathic relationship and narrative talk that characterize the therapeutic relationship expand further with the advent of Narrative Medicine (Charon, 2001, 2017; Greenhalgh & Hurwitz, 1999). The evasion of narrativity from the psychological fieldwork toward Evidence-Based Medicine starts questioning a highly reductionist and medicalizing framework of medicine and its application and practice in various clinical care settings.

Following the publication of *The Illness Narratives* (Kleinman, 1988), generally considered the birth act of Narrative Medicine, the versatility and potential of a narrative clinical approach have been highlighted, mainly since "clinical method is an interpretive act which draws on narrative skills to integrate the overlapping stories told by patients, clinicians, and test results"

(Greenhalgh, 1999, p. 323). If an evidence-based medical setting tends to refer to the disease rather than to the sick person, in the spirit of medical humanities the doctor sets the medical relationship as patient-centered instead of doctor/disease centered, encouraging the emergence of a real storytelling, about the illness and about the self.

With this purpose of systematizing medical narrative approaches and methodologies, the Consensus Conference organized by the Istituto Superiore di Sanità in 2014 establishes the guidelines for Narrative Medicine clinical practice: in this context, Narrative Medicine is defined as a methodology of clinical-care intervention based on a specific communicative and narrative competence, which aims to acquire, understand, and integrate the different points of view of those involved in the care process (ISS, 2015, p. 13). Aiming to dispel terminological and definitional ambiguities, Narrative Medicine is therefore a story-telling-based approach that, on the one hand, is described as a method of intervention to improve patients' quality of life, including their clinical and psychological parameters, and, on the other hand, as a research tool that contributes to the collection of biographical, as well as clinical, data of patients. In this regard, the Istituto Superiore di Sanità identifies four theoretical and clinical approaches (ISS, 2015, pp. 13–15): as regards our following reflections, the integration of the Narrative Therapy in the psychological, psychotherapeutic, psychiatric, and neuropsychiatric fields is most relevant.

In the humanistic-narratological approach, founded by American scholar Rita Charon (2008), Narrative Medicine becomes a humanistic tool that allows for pragmatic interpretation and interaction with patients' suffering and personal story, especially in clinical practice through the application of narrative skills. The phenomenological-hermeneutic approach, on the other hand, which has its roots in Husserlian phenomenology, Gadamer's hermeneutics, as well as Ricoeur and Taylor's reflections, highlights the importance of narrative as a hermeneutic and dialogical trigger based on the encounter of a constructive multiplicity of viewpoints arising from the roles involved in the process of care (Wahn, 1965; Minkowski, 1970). Finally, the socio-anthropological approach takes the assumption that medicine must necessarily consider the cultural system that influences the pathological experience of the sick person (ISS, 2015).

If Narrative Medicine aims at the shared construction of a personalized care pathway, the lack of an unambiguous and shared definition of Narrative Therapy (cf. Charon, 1993; Hunter, 1991; Shapiro, 1993), as well as of the approaches that identify narrative tools as methodologies of intervention, persists. Medical narratives are based on the interaction between a narrative experience of illness and the social and cultural instances of which the subject is the bearer, therefore providing an entirely new scenario of complexity for health practitioners and caregivers. As a result of the depersonalization of physicians' intervention and action, the narrative reappears on the scene when medicine "seems to lose its effectiveness in the relationship with the patient and in the management of those states of suffering that are not yet pathology but are now no longer health" (Virzi & Signorelli, 2007). During the diagnostic interview, Evidence-Based Medicine tends not to read in the patient's body her/his biography but only pathology (Galimberti, 2000), acquiring from the patient's narrative the elements that guide the formulation of a diagnosis oriented by an exclusively clinical gaze.

It seems to us, however, that all therapeutic histories are co-(re)constructed from the patient's narrative derivatives, even if the clinical model established by medical practice stipulates that the physician directs the time and manner of consultation with questions aimed at investigating symptoms, constructing diagnostic hypotheses, and prescribing treatments. The importance and irreplaceable function of the relationship highlighted by neuroscience is shared by a medical practice capable of "recognizing, appropriating, interpreting and being moved by the stories of illness" (Garrino, 2015, p. 36). The story the patient tells outlines the meaning s/he attributes to the illness, while setting a therapeutic relationship able to investigate the multiple interweavings between the physical symptoms and verbal and nonverbal manifestations, associating different and distant, even contradictory, events and elements to build a storyline that gives meaning to her/his illness (Misale, 2017, p. 75).

Enrolled in a holistic dynamic, both psychic and bodily, the patient's role can evolve within a narrative-oriented clinical approach, which determines the shift from the patient as passive recipient of therapy to an active and co-creative participant into a Narrative Therapy. However, it is essential that the physician also works on the idiographic, purposeful, and singular creation of a balanced mix between Narrative-Based Medicine and Evidence-Based Medicine, aimed at the biological and psychological well-being of the patient. Within medical humanities health staff training can, now more than ever, shape and mold the contemporary physician profile into its narrative-oriented upgrade. As Edward Shorter (1985) states, while the modern physician was able to establish an instrumental relationship where hospital interests prevail, the post-modern physician experiences an even more drastic reduction in her/his relational skills, although capable of even more effective and accurate diagnosis and treatment. During psychotherapeutic treatment, therapeutic change is experienced in *now moments*, unexpected and unaccustomed events that disrupt and destabilize the setting status quo, insinuating into its relational here-and-now a kairological time and a dense present which may be appropriately grasped by therapist and patient (cf. Stern et al., 1998). From the point of view of less reductionistically oriented neuroscientific studies, the healing power of the therapeutic relationship responds to a neurobiological situation no less unreflective and immediate, without which even that mutual mirroring between doctor and patient would not occur.

Beginning with an alliance between neuroscience and psychotherapy (Onnis, 2015), an investigation on Narrative Medicine applications that use audiovisual language and media could be desirable. If the concept of the sensory motor system, closely related to that of embodied simulation, can legitimately refer to the therapeutic relationship, it is no less plausible that the affective baggage arising from the personal histories and contexts emerges during the psychotherapeutic journey requiring, both from the therapist and the patient, an emotional, cognitive, and pragmatic processing that allows their virtuous use in terms of beneficial transformative opportunities for sub-jectivization and healing. It can, therefore, be hypothesized that also the enhancement of the empathic aspects of the therapeutic relationship, within unreflective, pre-linguistic and precategorical dynamics activated by mirror neurons, is an essential channel of transformative events, enabling mirroring phenomena that have to take into account the narrativity enacted within the audiovisual therapeutic dispositive. The body assumes, in this sense, a key role in the process of re-constituting the Self and enacting narrative behaviors that, we shall see, make use of images as very powerful facilitators.

Let us briefly return to Narrative Medicine. As stated in the Consensus Conference, different approaches are outlined. First, the humanistic narrato-logical approach, centered on the importance of listening respectfully to stories of illness and considering them to all intents and purposes a funda-mental element of the process of care; second, the phenomenological-herme-neutic approach, which emphasizes how structures of meaning result from the interaction and fusion of different narratives; third, the socio-anthropological approach, which highlights the multiplicity of levels, clinical, personal, and social (sickness), within which health communication takes place (ISS, 2015, p. 15). In identifying the tools that are and can be used, it is therefore a priority objective not only "to frame the narrative approach in the context of empowerment and the transition from paternalistic medicine to the relation-ship model in which the patient is a partner and not just the object of care" (ISS, 2015, p. 19), but also to cultivate its true innovative potential, which "lies precisely in demonstrating that Evidence-Based Medicine can gain fur-ther effectiveness through the integration of the patient's point of view, gath-ered through her/his own illness narrative" (Fioretti, 2017, p. 62).

Here, however, we do not attempt to examine those medical narrative approaches that foster the humanization of clinical practice but, rather, focus on the application of Narrative Medicine as Therapeutic Set of tools and techniques.

Through the co-construction of "therapeutic plots" (Mattingly, 1994), which constitute a space for continuous renegotiation of meanings between caregivers and patients, the model that we are going to propose is based on the narrativization and, indeed, the re-narrativization of patients' life stories by means of their own creative and personal contribution. In the wake of the de-gerarchization of the narrative point of view we previously discussed, through medical narratives patients are placed at the center of their own therapeutic treatment, not only as spectators and main characters, but as authors and directors as well. Moreover, it does not seem to us a coincidence that, in Gell's agency theory, the user who comes into contact with the index of agency, the recipient, is also referred to as a *patient* – a patient, however, who "in any given transaction in which agency is manifested, there is [...] *another potential agent*, capable of acting as an agent or being a locus of agency" (Gell, 1998, p. 22). The roles of agent and patient are thus reversible and, indeed, the patient has to also be considered capable of acting, eventually, as an agent. In fact, "patients" in agent/patient interactions are not entirely passive; they may resist" (Gell, 1998, p. 23).

By acting with their own hands on their self-narratives, patients gradually slip into a position that is no longer passive but active and performative, transforming themselves from patients to agents, into a documentary field that is constituted as a transitional context, concrete and materially moldable, and, above all, narratively therapeutic.

References

Agamben, G. (2006). *Che cos'è un dispositivo*. Nottetempo.

Barthes, R. (1980). *La chambre claire: Note sur la photographie*. Cahiers du cinema Gallimard.

Baudrillard, J. (1997). *Art and artefact*. Sage.

Bazin, A. (1945). Ontologie de l'image photographique. *Qu'est-ce que le cinéma*, 1, 11–19.

Belting, H. (2005). Image, medium, body: A new approach to iconology. *Critical Inquiry*, 31(2), 302–319. doi:10.1086/430962.

Bertozzi, M. (2018). *Documentario come arte. Riuso, performance, autobiografia nell'esperienza del cinema contemporaneo*. Marsilio.

Bredekamp, H. (2010). *Theorie des bildakts*. Suhrkamp.

Burch, N. (1990). *Life to those shadows*. University of California Press.

Casetti, F. (2015). *The Lumière galaxy: Seven key words for the cinema to come*. Columbia University Press.

Cazeneuve, J. (1971). *Sociologie du rite: Tabou, magie, sacré*. Collection SUP/Le sociologue.

Charon, R. (1993). The narrative road to empathy. In H. M. Spiro *et al.* (Eds.), *Empathy and the practice of medicine: Beyond pills and the scalpel*. Yale University Press.

Charon, R. (2001). Narrative Medicine: A model for empathy, reflection, profession, and trust. *JAMA*, 286(15), 1897–1902. doi:10.1001/jama.286.15.1897.

Charon, R. (2008). *Narrative Medicine: Honoring the stories of illness*. Oxford University Press.

Charon, R. (2017). *The principles and practice of Narrative Medicine*. Oxford University Press.

Comolli, J. L. (2004). *Voir et pouvoir: l'innocence perdue, cinéma, télévision, fiction, documentaire*. Editions Verdier.

Deleuze, G. (1983). *Cinéma 1. L'image-mouvement*. Éditions de Minuit.

Dubois, P. (1983). *L'acte photographique*. Labor.

Fioretti, C. (2017). La ricerca in Medicina Narrativa. Una revisione degli studi sull'esperienza di malattia dei pazienti. In V. Covelli (Ed.), *Medicina Narrativa e Ricerca*.

Riflessioni teorico-metodologiche multidisciplinari per la raccolta e l'analisi delle narrazioni dei pazienti (pp. 57–68). Libellula Edizioni.

Fischer-Lichte, E. (2008). *The transformative power of performance: A new aesthetics.* Routledge.

Freedberg, D. (1989). *The power of images: Studies in the history and theory of response.* University of Chicago Press.

Freedberg, D. (2008). Antropologia e storia dell'arte: la fine delle discipline? *Ricerche di storia dell'arte*, 31(1), 5. doi:10.7374/72553.

Freund, G. (2011). *La photographie en France au XIXe siècle.* Bourgois.

Frosh, P. (2015). Selfies. The gestural image: The selfie, photography theory, and kinesthetic sociability. *International Journal of Communication*, 9, 22. doi:1932-8036/2015FEA0002.

Galimberti, U. (2000). *Il corpo.* Feltrinelli.

Garrino, L. (2015). *Strumenti per una medicina del nostro tempo. Medicina narrativa, Metodologia Pedagogia dei Genitori e International Classification of Functioning (ICF).* Firenze University Press.

Gauthier, G. (1995). *Le documentaire un autre cinéma.* Nathan Université.

Gell, A. (1998). *Art and agency: An anthropological theory.* Clarendon Press.

Ginsburg, F. (1995). The parallax effect: The impact of aboriginal media on ethnographic film. *Visual Anthropology Review*, 11(2), 64–76. doi:10.1525/var.1995.11.2.64.

Giusti, S. (2019). Immagine-atto/immagine-arto: La fotografia come protesi tra performance e comportamento nell'era della condivisione con le fotocamere in rete. *Mediascapes Journal*, 12, 23–40.

Goodman, N. (1978). *Ways of worldmaking.* Hackett.

Greenhalgh, T. (1999). Narrative based medicine in an evidence based world. *BMJ*, 318(7179), 323–325. doi:10.1136/bmj.318.7179.323.

Greenhalgh, T., & Hurwitz, B. (1999). Why study narrative? *BMJ*, 318(7175), 48–50. doi:10.1136/bmj.318.7175.48.

Grodal, T. (1997). *Moving pictures: A new theory of film genres, feelings, and cognition.* Clarendon Press.

Gunthert, A. (2013a). *Le selfie, emblème de la photographie connectée.* http://histoir evisuelle.fr/cv/icones/2846.

Gunthert, A. (2013b). *Viralité du selfie, déplacements du portrait.* http://histoirevisuelle. fr/cv/icones/2895.

Harth, D. (2003). Corpo e memoria. Il significato dell'agire rituale per la costruzione e l'interpretazione degli ordini simbolici. *Iride*, 16(2), 243–256.

Hillman, J. (1979). *The dream and the underworld.* Harper Colophon.

Hunter, K. M. (1991). *Doctors' stories: The narrative structure of medical knowledge.* Princeton University Press.

Istituto superiore di sanità (ISS). (2015). *Conferenza di Consenso. Linee di indirizzo per l'applicazione della medicina narrativa in ambito clinico-assistenziale, per malattie rare e cronico-degenerative. Il sole 24 ore sanità.* www.medicinanarrativa.network/wp-content/uploads/2021/03/Quaderno_n._7_02_CONSENSUS-CONF-FINALE_compressed.pdf

Kleiman, N., & Somaini, A. (2016). *Sergei M. Eisenstein: Notes for a general history of cinema.* Amsterdam University Press.

Kleinman, A. (1988). *The illness narratives: Suffering, healing, and the human condition.* Basic Books.

Lefebvre, H. (1961). *De la vie quotidienne*. L'Arche.

Leijssen, M. (2006). Validation of the body in psychotherapy. *Journal of Humanistic Psychology*, 46(2), 126–146. doi:10.1177/0022167805283782.

Leone, M. (2014). Immagini efficaci/Efficacious Images. *LEXIA*, 17, 1–788.

Malavasi, L. (2017). Fare cosa, con quali immagini? *Cinergie: Il Cinema e le altre Arti*, 6(11), 10–12.

Marano, F. (2007). *Camera etnografica: Storie e teorie di antropologia visuale*. Franco Angeli.

Marks, L. U. (2000). *The skin of the film: Intercultural cinema, embodiment, and the senses*. Duke University Press.

Mattingly, C. (1994). The concept of therapeutic "emplotment". *Social Science & Medicine*, 38(6), 811–822. doi:10.1016/0277-9536(94)90153-90158.

McLuhan, M. (1964). *Understanding media: The extensions of man*. McGraw-Hill.

Minkowski, E. (1970). *Lived time: Phenomenological and psychopathological studies*. Northwestern University Press.

Misale, F. (2017). Medicina narrativa e uso formativo nel cinema. In B. Morsello, C. Cilona, & F. Misale (Eds.), *Medicina narrative: Temi, esperienze e riflessioni* (pp. 73–82). Roma Tre Press.

Mitchell, W. J. T. (1994). *Picture theory: Essays on visual and verbal representation*. University of Chicago Press.

Mitchell, W. J. T. (2005). *What do pictures want? The lives and loves of images*. University of Chicago Press.

Moraldi, S. (2015). *Questioni di campo. La relazione osservatore/osservato nella forma documentaria*. Bulzoni.

Moschini, L. B. (2018). *Art, play, and narrative therapy: Using metaphor to enrich your clinical practice*. Routledge.

Nichols, B. (2001). Il cinema amatoriale. In G. P. Brunetta (Ed.), *Storia del cinema mondiale: Teorie, strumenti, memorie* (Vol. 5, pp. 319–352). Einaudi.

Onnis, L. (2015). *Una nuova alleanza tra psicoterapia e neuroscienze. Dall'intersoggettività ai neuroni specchio. Dialogo tra Daniel Stern e Vittorio Gallese*. Franco Angeli.

Parry, A., & Doan, R. E. (1994). *Story re-visions: Narrative therapy in the postmodern world*. Guilford Press.

Payne, M. (2006). *Narrative therapy*. Sage.

Pinotti, A. (2017). Self-negating images: Towards an-iconology. *Proceedings MDPI*, 1(9), 856. doi:10.3390/proceedings1090856.

Pinotti, A., & Somaini, A. (2016). *Cultura visuale. Immagini, sguardi, media, dispositivi*. Einaudi.

Pucci, G. (2008). Agency, oggetto, immagine. L'antropologia dell'arte di Alfred Gell e l'antichità Classica. *Ricerche di storia dell'arte*, 31(1), 35–40. doi:10.7374/72556.

Rancière, J. (2009). Do pictures really want to live? *Culture, Theory & Critique*, 50(2–3), 123–132. doi:10.1080/14735780903240083.

Renov, M. (2004). *The subject of documentary*. University of Minnesota Press.

Shapiro, J. (1993). The use of narrative in the doctor-patient encounter. *Family Systems Medicine*, 11(1), 47–53. doi:10.1037/h0089128.

Shorter, E. (1985). *Bedside manners: The troubled history of doctors and patients*. Simon and Schuster.

Simonigh, C. (2011). *L'immagine-spettacolo*. Bonanno.

Sobchack, V. (2004). *Carnal thoughts: Embodiment and moving image culture.* University of California Press.

Sontag, S. (1977). *On photography.* Dell.

Stern, D. N., Sander, L. W., Nahum, J. P., Harrison, A. M., Lyons-Ruth, K., Morgan, A. C., Bruschweiler-Stern, N., & Tronick, E. Z. (1998). Non-interpretive mechanisms in psychoanalytic therapy: The "something more" than interpretation. The Process of Change Study Group. *The International Journal of Psycho-Analysis*, 79 (5), 903–921.

Subini, T. (2010). Il cinema di Pasolini e la morte: tra complesso della mummia e sindrome di Frankenstein. *Altre Modernità*, 4, 67–81.

Turner, T. (2002). Representation, politics, and cultural imagination in indigenous video: General points and Kayapo examples. *Media Worlds: Anthropology on New Terrain*, 75–89.

Varela, F. (1992). The re-enchantment of the concrete. In J. Crary & S. Kwinter (Eds.), *Incorporations* (pp. 320–338). Zone Books.

Virzi, A., & Signorelli, M. S. (2007). *Medicina e narrativa. Un viaggio nella letteratura per comprendere il malato (e il suo medico).* Franco Angeli.

Wahn, B. L. (1965). *Beiträge zu seiner phaenomenologischen und daseinsanalytischen Erforschung [Delusion. Contributions to phenomenological and analytical investigations].* Pfullingen.

White, M., & Epston, D. (1990). *Narrative means to therapeutic ends.* W.W. Norton & Company.

Worth, S., & Adair, J. (1972). *Through Navajo eyes: An exploration in film communication and anthropology.* Indiana University Press.

Chapter 3

Audiovisual Therapeutic Approaches

Taxonomy and Classification

Anna Chiara Sabatino

Cinematherapy, Filmtherapy, Therapeutic Videotaping: The Patient-Spectator

The methodological and epistemological matrices of the therapeutic models that make use of the audiovisual medium – which we will discuss later – are already detected in classical film theories that attributed to moving images the ability to provide useful elements for a deeper understanding of psychic mechanisms, in order to outline a more conscious intervention in life outside the movie theater and the screen.

The early reflections of the clinical field on the interplay between cinematic universe and psyche seem to focus, rather than on individual psychic images processing, on a mapping of symptoms related to the attractive and suggestive power of film viewing (Belloi, 2001; Gunning, 1989). Divided between the mirroring of its mental image representation (Beller, 2006), the need to inhabit the real world and the desire to experience the imaginary one, the spectator viewer sometimes is enraptured, captured, and even, at times, bewitched and sickened by the movie itself. Indeed, the genesis of the scientific discourse on cinema reveals, in the descriptions of actual clinical cases, a particular focus on the study of the pathological effects of the phenomenon (Alovisio, 2013; Friedberg, 1990). Based on a paradigm that delineates film viewing as an enthralling experience in which the viewer finds her/himself involved or overwhelmed by pathology or adolescent suggestion (Alovisio, 2013), through numerous archival materials Silvio Alovisio illustrates how, in the early twentieth century, disciplines dealing with psychic phenomena confronted the new moving images' experiences. Early film spectators were attributed with the inability to distinguish reality from the audiovisual and imaginary representation of actual fact, and therefore classified, through the analogy of the psychological conditions activated while watching a film, with daydreaming or even psychic conditions (Gemelli, 1926). Cinema is, therefore, described as a suggestive experience through the same crisis of the reality principle that causes those "cinepathologies" that afflict the most impressionable viewers (Pennacchi, 1930). Nevertheless, descriptions of heterotopic experiences

DOI: 10.4324/9781003340508-4

opening corrupting and sickening world scenarios are accompanied by feeble attempts to devise an educational program through which the movie theatre may pedagogically produce effective models and teachings (De Sanctis, 1930).

Opposing critical opinions toward the "new medium's" corruptive power over "young and frail of spirit", some tendencies are outlined in favor of a positive connotation of the cinematic experience. Because of its virtue of employing an easily accessible language, cinema acquires unprecedented possibilities to intervene in the educational field (Cardillo, 1987). As Mario Ponzo (1914) wrote with respect to the didactic value of the cinematic experience, the pathogenic dangerousness of cinema corresponds to an equally (and potentially powerful) pedagogical capacity, to be cultivated and trained through specific interventions, such as commented projections within selected contexts.

In the face of a marked tendency to demonize the effects of film viewing on the spectator, possibilities of significantly beneficial repercussions do not appear to be as highly valued. If, however, some scholars have observed that cinema has no therapeutic effectiveness, despite being capable of stimulating and bringing to consciousness some of the deepest aspects of the psyche (Albano & Pravadelli, 2008; Bergstrom, 1999; Castriota, 2013), others have proposed the analogy between psychoanalytic setting and movie theatre (Boccara & Riefolo, 2002; Marinelli, 2006), since both can produce "powerful" images (mental associations or dream narratives) that act on the viewer at deep levels. The attraction exerted by the cinematic apparatus on human beings is justified, on the one hand, by the technology's peculiar ability to capture attention and solicit perceptual activity, acting first and foremost physiologically, perceptually and emotionally on the viewer (Trifonova, 2014), and, on the other hand, by the power of the cinematic machine, which employs a shareable though structurally complex language.

Indeed, cinema can exert a political "therapeutic" function by following a twofold direction, diversifying from the grayness of everyday life, and training humans in the operation of the cinematic machine (De Gaetano, 2012). In employing spectacular forms that modify, through technique, the perceptual and sensory apparatus, cinema acquires therapeutic potential – prophylactic and curative – toward the social body it addresses (Benjamin, 2008). Images on the screen acquire the power to re-orient the experience itself, particularly when physical and psychic sides, which are opposite and complementary, meet and mingle, interacting and infecting each other, thus exerting the power to reshape and re-imagine the world outside the representation (Balázs, 2011). Such a theoretical and pragmatic aspect is crucial, because it allows, also on the heuristic level, a preliminary methodological transition to therapeutic and clinical operative fields. Indeed, it is in this context that Embodied Simulation Theory (Gallese & Guerra, 2019) can determine a more precise delineation of a patient-spectator as peculiar kinesthetic subject.

While a therapeutic function has already been attributed to the cinematic viewing experience, as it emerges from a literature review on the psychotherapeutic approaches that have used cinematic but also audiovisual techniques and language (Fatemi, 2021), it is also clear that the configuration of a *sui generis* cinematic dispositive is in order, considering its relocation a therapeutic setting. Cinematherapy (Berg-Cross et al., 1990; Sharp et al., 2002; Tyson et al., 2000) and Filmtherapy (Hérbert & Neumeister, 2001; Moreno, 1944; Wedding & Niemiec, 2003) have been historically counted among the art therapies (Malchiodi, 2012, 2018; Rubin, 1999), facing the common tendency of being assimilated into each other.

Understood as processes of self-awareness and self-transformation that trigger while and after watching a movie, the two therapeutic approaches have been found to activate regressive, amplifying, and identifying mechanisms that facilitate the path of knowledge and inner growth (Ciappina & Capriani, 2007). While some scholars focus on beneficial aspects stimulated by the viewing experience (Eğeci & Gençöz, 2017; Marsick, 2010), it is not uncommon to detect a tendency to systematize movies into lists subdivided by themes and therapeutic goals (Mastronardi, 2005; Peske & West, 1999).

Great attention must be paid, however, to technical, methodological, and patients' position/role variations between Cinematherapy and Filmtherapy. It seems appropriate to start, with the aim to outline substantial differences, from Francesco Casetti's definition of "relocated cinema" (Casetti, 2015, pp. 37–39). We propose to distinguish Cinematherapy and Filmtherapy according to *setting* and *delivery* operations criteria (Casetti, 2015, pp. 58–70). According to the *setting* processes, the "viewing environment brings [the spectator] back to the canonical cinematic experience through a resemblance. […] We are dealing with a thing that stands for something else, but which in substituting it, recuperates its essence" (Casetti, 2015, p. 70); in the case of *delivery* processes, it is the object of vision, the movie itself, that puts the spectator "back in contact with cinema: in watching it, I reconnect with the history and the modalities of cinematic presentation" (Casetti, 2015, p. 70). In this regard, the contribution of Erich Feldmann (1956), who describes cinematic experience ritual behaviors, is particularly useful: from the spectator's entry into the hall, upon payment of a ticket, as a desiring or needing subject and as a member of a collectivity, part of the composite audience with which, although not coming into contact, s/he constitutes an apparent unity. When the lights dim and the projection begins, her/his situation drastically changes: the world around her/him dissolves, giving way to the story projected on the screen before her/him and losing contact with the surrounding reality.

Taking such processuality into account, Cinematherapy can be classified as a setting process, through which the therapist works for recreating the cinematic environment into the therapeutic setting, involving the patient in a collective viewing together with other patient-spectators. In addition to recreating the main characteristics of a movie theatre vision, Cinematherapy may consist of using the movie theater itself as an actual therapeutic setting, so as to realize the original viewing experience, as in the recent case of Medicinema (Medolago Albani, 2017), as well as in the model we will describe below. Thanks to the *setting* process, on the therapeutic setting the patient-spectator experiences an external, but internalizable space, in which s/he is immersed and from which s/he is on the verge of being completely absorbed, despite experiencing the movie from a "safe" and codified position: the inner and narrative spaces entertain reciprocal relationships, both configured as an enlargement of the patient-spectator's living space. Filmtherapy, on the other hand, is configured as a delivery process, in which the therapist addresses targeted disorders through specific movies, selected with respect to the pathology being treated and their purpose within the psychotherapeutic process. Through the therapist's guidance, the movie thus becomes a reservoir of characters and events with which to identify, an instrument of introspection and awareness.

While the viewer's participation in the events told on the screen is solicited by the film's story, the movie itself also triggers projection and identification processes that are the basis of the viewing experience: a movie spectator mobilizes her/his imagination to such an extent that the world represented by the film may take on a status of reality that can be witnessed and even participated in. Although the movie may present unreal or unrealistic events, the viewer forgets the actual situation in which s/he finds her/himself and lives imaginatively in the illusory world, believing him/herself to be truly present with her/his subjective participation (Feldmann, 1956). However, the spectator appears to be restrained in her/his desire to closely adhere to the representation, since an unconscious inhibition usually represses the natural impulses to mimicry and the longing to intervene in the film's events (Morin, 2005). The circumstances of fruition further prevent her/him from acting as if s/he were at the actual site of action, making her/his participation incomplete. It is this inhibition to participation that, in our view, Filmtherapy makes use of: if the movie events correspond to a predetermined storyline in which the spectator can never fully participate, at the end of the projection, in a reality in which, instead, s/he acts and can intervene, s/he will be more predisposed to respond and react to the situations that are similar to those experienced while watching the movie and which, thanks to the selection and mediation of the therapist, pertain to the therapy targets.

In both Cinematherapy and Filmtherapy, the patient coincides with the traditional spectator. In the Cinematherapy, just as at the movie theatre, the patient finds her/himself in an immersive condition thanks to the proposed or recreated setting; during the Filmtherapy, the patient turns her/his attention to the projected event, the storyline and the selected movie. The viewing experience makes the patient-spectator the privileged recipient of the effects produced by a double dispositive, doubly pre-constituted and external: from one side, the cinematic apparatus, capable of affecting the relations between a sighted subject and the object of her/his viewing through the specific components of which this apparatus is composed; from the other side, the therapeutic setting, constituted, in the case of Cinematherapy, by the modes and the viewing environment, and, in the case of Filmtherapy, by the choice of the film to be viewed and later commented on, through patients' biographies and characters' vicissitudes overlapping that helps both therapist and patient to dialogue and reflect on the targeted disorder.

But if film viewing is not infrequently used in the context of integrated psychotherapeutic approaches (Lampropoulos et al., 2004; Portadin, 2006; Powell, 2008; Prados, 1951), videotaping technologies have been found, in therapeutic contexts, since its origins: firstly, in relation to the study of the film projection effects on viewers; secondly, to document psychotherapy sessions for educational purposes (Hankir et al., 2015). The use of video for didactic purposes not only consisted in videotaping and reviewing sessions by students of psychiatry and psychotherapy, but was also successfully employed in some re-educational treatments toward patients (Kenney, 1982). Based on the vicarious learning principle, which comes into play whenever the subject is in the presence of a model with whom to compare and, above all, to imitate in attitudes or behaviors (Bandura, 1986; Halliwell, 2002), audiovisual modeling makes use of audiovisual techniques focusing mainly on supervision and theoretical application for psychiatrists' and psychotherapists' training (Giusti & Montanari, 1992). The study of group interactions also proposes the use of the audiovisual tool, in terms of self-review through the video-replay strategy (cf. Giusti, 1999), in order to facilitate the identification of inner processes during interactions and stimulate self-observation, increasing one's level of awareness (Dufour, 2000). The audiovisual language and technology may be, in short, useful research tools in the study of psychological events, as well as a valid support for the training and improvement of interpersonal skills between teachers and students, therapists and patients. Through the Therapeutic Videotaping of observed phenomena, many disciplines aim to review and interpret audiovisual records, besides collecting for cataloging and dissemination (Grasseni et al., 2021; Iedema et al., 2006).

In this context, within the mental health studies field, numerous scholars have underlined the use of audiovisual recording devices in the therapeutic setting (Berger, 1978; Brown, 1980; Heilveil, 1983; Hirschfeld, 1968): this tendency toward videotaping, rather than the therapeutic content of the film or the sanctity of the cinematic setting, makes use, in fact, of the recording technologies rather than the cinematic apparatus.

In psychotherapy, as in counseling and psychiatry, videotaping techniques may concern not only training but also the anamnestic, diagnostic, and evaluative phases (Giusti & Proietti, 1995), especially in creating a video archive to document progress of psychiatric patients (Giusti, 1999). But the use of audiovisual tools in psychotherapeutic practice has led to a number of creative practices that are easily contextualized and applied within the therapeutic setting. We limit ourselves to recalling the main ones.

Primarily, *Video-Confrontation* is a technique that eliminates the gaze of others during the confrontation and allows the participant to connect directly with her/himself through a screen: filmed by a camera, s/he is guided by the voice of the therapist who, although present, does not intervene on the image, controlled instead by an operator who mainly follows the patient's directions and the direction of the discourse between the interviewers (Berger, 1971; Thénot, 1989). Secondly, the *Psycho-Videoclip* involves a fixed framing that delimits the field of action of the participant who, based on the therapist's directives, "inhabits" the scene, improvising in the manner of a theatrical performance, controlling the static image through her/his own movements, moving closer to and further away from the lens; at the end of the sequence recording, therapist and patient review the footage for commentary. This technique, which can also be used in group sessions, is not dissimilar to *Video-Drama*, which is aimed at facilitating the patient's expression of a traumatic experience: if, as with Video-Confrontation, Video-Drama can be experienced live or delayed, in this case the participant has the power to decide to show the recording to others or delete it (Giusti, 1999, p. 88).

Creative practices that make use of the audiovisual medium within the therapeutic setting are certainly not limited to those listed (Giusti, 1999; Rossi, 2009), but some common assumptions that govern its use and functioning within psychotherapeutic treatments can be highlighted.

The audiovisual medium is configured first and foremost as a third element that, by inserting itself within the therapeutic relationship and setting, can foster in the patient the acquisition of an autonomous system of self-representation (Giusti, 1999). Triggering a processes of self-confrontation, the video image allows subjectivity to be observed objectively, materializing outside of oneself, externalizing a point of encounter with oneself in such a way as to connect fantasy (attachment to the mother and the desire to remain in her gaze) with reality (one's own autonomous image).

The Lacanian mirror phase, then, aligns in the three poles that organize it (the child, the mirror, and the parent's gaze) with those of video use (the patient, the screen, and the psychotherapist) (Bléandonu, 1986): it is through such correspondence that one can identify in the audiovisual medium an effective tool of mirroring, not just projective, but also actual, of and in one's own image, especially for patients who cannot feel "seen" and suffer from being without mirrors to really see themselves. If in front of the mirror the proprioceptive feelings are directly related to the seen reflected image, during *Videotherapy* there is discrepancy between the feelings and the observed images, and it is mainly because of this discrepancy that therapeutic work becomes possible.

At this point, it is important to highlight the differences and similarities with respect to the environment and the subject of vision. As we have already pointed out, the subject of vision is the patient involved in the videotherapeutic journey, a patient who, at this given stage of treatment, is above all a spectator, hinged within the double dispositive we have already described, simultaneously therapeutic and cinematic. If Cinematherapy and Filmtherapy can be defined as circumscribed manifestations of the cinematic dispositive within the therapeutic one, in which the act of viewing is limited to a series of spectatorial practices that make the patient entirely a spectator but return her/him entirely to the therapy as soon as the lights come back on and the movie ends, for *Therapeutic Videotaping*, understood as a set of techniques that make use of videotaping during the psychotherapeutic session, this enmeshment is broken.

Not to be confused with *Filmed Videotherapy*, with documentary and didactic purposes, Therapeutic Videotaping is quite different from Cinematherapy and Filmtherapy: these ultimately summon the patient to cognitive and emotional participation, the one through the dark room and the collective vision, the other through the events and characters in the film. Therapeutic Videotaping, on the other hand, requires not only active attention and listening from the patient, but also a participatory creative presence, a utilization of one's own verbal and mental content rather than a fruition of others. It is the discrepancy between the mental self-image and the image of one's own existence and acting on the screen, between image and picture in short, that constitutes the activating nucleus of therapeutic experiences for the patient, who confronts with her/himself when placed in front of her/his autonomous image. Being a main character, and no longer just a spectator of the images being viewed, and a co-creator, together with the therapist, of certain "creative" choices – the camera movements during the Video-Confrontation, the body movements that s/he stages and represents in the Psycho-Videoclip, the fate of the Video-Drama Recording – radically change the position of the patient, no longer conventionally seated, but possibly mobile, dynamic, active in the dual therapeutic and cinematic dispositive. In making use of Therapeutic Videotaping techniques within its therapeutic space, psychotherapy triggers situations not easily circumscribed, in which cinematic and therapeutic aspects, instead of alternating, hybridize until, at times, they coincide.

The therapeutic setting begins, in this way, to include the film set, which is "relocated" by transferring the modalities, procedures, dynamics, and roles that compose it, thanks above all to the mediation of those narrative tools that unite it with the therapeutic dispositive. Both "disciplined" by the liminal and heterotopic character of the experience to which they provide access, they hybridize reciprocally thanks to the recognizability and applicability of certain rules that allow them to function: the patient-spectator, welcomed into a double space, safe and perimetered, which the 'outside world cannot access except through her/his own narratives, uses a series of tactics that allow her/him to "appropriate" useful and beneficial elements to tailor her/his own experience. Faced with the "objective" figuration – always mediated by the medium and context, and from a tacitly given and voluntarily assumed institutional and hermeneutic framework – of her/his own subjective gaze, the patient-spectator behaves, in fact, like a bricoleur (Lévi-Strauss, 1966), selecting and identifying, with the therapist's guidance, what is useful to her/him among the multiple pieces of her/himself, in order to deal with the targets of therapy, and, finally, to reconfigure and recount and differently perceive her/himself.

Beginning with Therapeutic Videotaping, an interesting contamination of the dual narrative dispositive, the patient starts to experience an increasing level of participation in her/his own therapeutic path, being less and less a "spectator" and bringing into play the script of her/his own life (Rossi, 2009) within a "set-ting" that allows her/him to critically and creatively intervene, through her/his own narratives, on her/his own disorder.

Documentary Videotherapy: The Patient-Actor

Until this point of our reflections, we have proposed theoretical frameworks explicitly instrumental to the focus and methodological protocol that is the subject of this book, illustrating techniques and methods that use the audiovisual tool as a technological support and epistemological supplement to psychotherapy so far.

If biography, content-wise and stylistically, is about Aboutness, identifying its privileged object in the main character's life events, in a patient-centered, medical narrative framework, autobiography seems to be therapeutic only under certain conditions (Demetrio, 1996, p. 47). Such soothing conditions, what Demetrius calls the analgesic and restorative "powers" of biography, emerge and manifest themselves within a very peculiar therapeutic setting, which includes and incorporates the self-narrative iconic agency functioning which we have previously illustrated. But let us now propose an example that, in this direction and for this purpose, seems particularly emblematic.

In 2007, a group of Italian researchers proposed a videotherapeutic protocol following an agreement between Cineteca di Bologna and ASP Giovanni XXIII: a team made up of filmmakers and health professionals was formed to employ the use of audiovisual language in the treatment of pathologies and diseases concerning memory loss. The idea had come in 2004 to Eugenio Melloni, an Italian screenwriter who created for his father, who suffered from a memory disorder, a short movie to be viewed independently at any time of the day, with the hope of restoring references to him with respect to the places and times (past and present) of his own personal history.

Starting from Melloni's intuition, the project's research team, named Memofilm, launched a five year (2007–2012) trial in the Bologna area with a target group of patients (from 64 to 95 years old) with cognitive impairment and dementia diagnoses of varying degrees, associated with behavioral and psychological disorders. Seventeen Memofilms were produced from 2008 to 2012, aiming to counteract the psychic fragmentation caused by the disease, improve adaptive behaviors, and stimulate memory through the use of targets related to individuals and specific symptoms. Together with clinical data collected by physicians and nurses, direct and indirect testimonies of patients' daily life, and photographic material provided by family and friends, the director and psychologist worked to develop a unique and customized audiovisual product. Such an individualized person-centered therapy intervention (Kitwood, 1993) involved the use of a video camera, a small crew, and the regular projection of the customized video for that single spectator, in order to bring her/him into direct relationship with the images of her/his unique and singular story (Grosso, 2013).

In the emblematic case of Alberta, with a very serious clinical profile – major memory disorders associated with episodes of mental confusion, spatiotemporal disorientation, and delusions of persecution and misidentification (non-recognition of the family home, built together with her children) – the team chose to film her describing the house where she lived, starting from the patient's obsessive and distressing search for home, with the aim of using the Memofilm to convince her that her search had no real utility. During the filming, the granddaughter, turning to her grandmother, asked if that is her home, prompting her to reply that "home" is "a big word", which became the title of her Memofilm. In reconsidering the woman's life and past, devoted to working in the fields and lovingly caring for her family, the research team used archive materials provided by her family members, together with her own description of the house – and also filmed the unfolding of a family lunch with her entire family, providing Alberta gifts and expressions of great affection toward her as mother and grandmother. Alberta's Memofilm has then been administered to her every day for a month, with the effect of extinguishing the obsessive houseseeking disorder.

Memofilm is, therefore, a truly emblematic example of *Documentary Videotherapy*, revealing new elements with respect to the audiovisual therapeutic methodologies and practices examined thus far and their instrumental use of a therapeutic and cinematic dispositive interweaving. Aimed at dealing not only with disorders treatable through psychotherapy or psychiatric tools, but with neurological deteriorations, this model of Videotherapy personalizes the nosographic and etiological approach into a radical ideographic vision, whose relevance and effectiveness are built and verified not so much on the dialogical therapeutic relationship consisting in the comment during and after the viewing about self-viewing, but mostly on pragmatic and behavioral acts and re-enactments happening outside the canonical therapeutic setting. The actions and repetition compulsions of one's ordinary life are reinserted within a biographical documentary framework scripted and shot *ad hoc* within what we might call the *Therapeutic Set*, which specifically allows a holistic and gestalt-like self-revision by the patient. Thanks to the set established and bounded by the audiovisual dispositive, here strongly relational and narrative, the therapeutic dispositive spills over into reality, transforming it into a safe space, a "home" to be inhabited and in which to recognize and confront the disorder to be treated. The patient, watching a short movie that watches her/

him back, working as a refunctionalizing mirror image would do, literally becomes a spectator of her/his own unedited story, a renewed biographical path oriented by her/his subjective gaze (Starobinski, 1989), now put in conditions of flipping that subjective perspective into an objectively possible and auspicable scenario which audiovisual narrative dispositive can stage and display.

But the audiovisual dispositive this time is not summoned within its singular function as in all the methodologies we previously described: not only in the evocative ritual of accessing the movie theater and collectively experiencing the film viewing (Cinematherapy), nor in the storyline or the represented characters (Filmtherapy), but it is the audiovisual language itself, by means of documentary genre and rhetorics employed in light of the therapeutic-narrative goal. In this perspective, directorial choices, from the use of close-up to the editing style (linear, complex, alternating), are formulated to totally adhere to the pathology treatment in its peculiar specificity. In the analysis of structural recurrences among the various Memofilms, *thematic images*, understood as vehicles of immediate meaning and the main stimulus for eliciting patients' reactions, are common. Producing immediate mental associations, such images act on residual memory by summoning the patient's main emotional source; *reinforcing images*, on the other hand, evoke the patients' past and storyline and amplify thematic images' scope, being their temporal counterpoint. In the case of the absence of particular mental representations, the *restorative images* are able to induce new ones; finally, the *support images*, as the glue between the previous ones, act iterating the fundamental contents for memory stimulation (Bencivenni, 2016). Attention to forms and editing modes is determined, therefore, as an essential component for the assembly of the short movie, which totally originates from the life, perceptual, and emotional experience of patients suffering from dementia.

Within Memofilm documentary narratives, the essential element is therefore not verbal mediation of the therapist, who guides Memofilm administration, but throughout the audiovisual language and diegetic (though biographical) universe: therefore, not only the narrative content, but also the videomaking formal choices, where the participation of the patient-spectator is a key element: the initiation of the healing process can be triggered only if the images solicit processes of integration and completion whose realization requires the active cooperation of the viewer (Casetti, 2015; Montani, 1999). In Memofilm, images do not solicit any process of completion for understanding and "participation" with respect to the experienced representation, but offer themselves as tools that trigger retrieval mechanisms of her/his own forgotten and elusive past through the reconstructed and eventually fictitious one. As early as the late 1920s, Ponzo and Rivano pointed out how certain characteristic and recurrent images in certain pathologies could, when associated with perceptually subjugating and psychically persistent film images, produce a "fantastic pseudology", an associative superposition between memories of factual events and artificial and fictitious experiences, recomposed together in a unitary mnemonic landscape although made at the same time of reality and imagination (Ponzo & Rivano, 1927); consequently, the pathogenic power of cinematic images could nevertheless be governed and converted into plastic and even pragmatic power, and finally offer the patient-spectator the possibility of realizing in actions an *analogon* of her/his own life represented on the screen.

In Memofilm, the images intervene, almost pharmacologically, on the memory, going so far as to modify not only its retrieval of the past, but even its participation in the perception of the present and, finally, its action on it, in the here and now, in the patient's present and daily experience. If Memofilm is a true exemplary case of narrative identity as mediated identity, putting before our eyes the nature of this mediation (Feyles, 2017), processes of self-identification occur not only through the mediation of linguistic signs and verbal structures but also through the mediation of intuitive experiences and representations of an "individual imagery", which corresponds to the process of recognizing oneself in a more or less coherent set of sensible representations (Feyles, 2017). With Memofilm viewing, the identity fragmented by memory disorder is recomposed through the act of seeing one's own finally functional and coherent acting, as well as through the "montage" of the patient's own idea of self, previously forgotten and crossed out by pathology, made finally visible by the audiovisual representation and also made accessible again through the experience of the entire production process in which the patient, as main character, is involved.

Through the audiovisual form of Memofilm that comes to life, first of all, through the body of the involved patient, the main character of storytelling and therapy, inescapably the patient of the secondary agency of the audiovisual product packaged for her/him, the threshold between reality and representation is suspended and the reversibility between them is activated through a symbolic exchange between pathological materiality and reconstituted immateriality, activated precisely because of the fruitional entry into an iconic universe that positively reverberates on the condition that the patient passively undergoes.

The transformation of the therapeutic "safe space" from setting to set in the Memofilm case is accompanied by two fundamental elements. First, the dissolution of the boundaries of the setting and the contamination of the living and experienced space by the effects of the therapeutic treatment; second, the presence of the spectator's own body, which, in reliving the film-making experience by its viewing, is reconveyed in direct and reciprocal communication with her/his own representation as an inseparable unicum of body and mind.

The pathic subject which is the cinematic spectator experiences the movie by simultaneously situating her/himself on and off the screen through embodied vision and crossmodal sensory activity (Sobchack, 2004). But if every movie is essentially grounded in the action and interaction of characters who act realistic stories before spectators' eyes, in Memofilm it is the real life representation to be experienced by that single spectator for whom Memofilm is conceived, who accesses a plot determined by a dual authorial instance, regulated by pathology and its corresponding therapeutic strategy. In this sense, Memofilm is a product of agency not only by its main character, at the center of the therapeutic narrative, but also and especially by the therapeutic team that selects and assembles meaningful and suitable elements to constitute a renewed representation as the outcome of an effective audiovisual therapy. The rehabilitative value of a movie that summons body and mind, involving present and past, then lies in its role as an interactive selector of images at the service of intersubjective memory and imagination, exactly like Memofilm, which exceeds the limits of the screen and places the image in a much closer exchange relationship with reality. Even more closely intertwined, the narrative of reality and the reality of the narrative meet, in this first phase, on the *Therapeutic Set* constitutively centered on the patient-spectator: in the same way as a social actor, object of the gaze and storytelling *raison d'être*, the patient begins to take the first steps toward an enfranchisement from spectatorial immobility. Such a spectatorial profile, made possible by the shift from static to performative spectatorship, is only the first step in an audiovisual therapeutic methodology that is patient-centered, instead of being illness-centered, progressively involving her/him in a process of construction of a customized therapeutic strategy.

Therapeutic Filmmaking: The Patient-Author

On the Therapeutic Set described so far, the Cinematherapy and Filmtherapy patient-spectator, evolving into a more participating one when involved in Documentary Videotherapy, during *Therapeutic Filmmaking* is involved in an even more performative narrative process (Arnott & Gushin, 1976; Cohen et al., 2015; Jakubowska & Michałowska, 2017; Muller & Bader, 1972). According to this audiovisual therapeutic approach, which involves, in addition to first-person hermeneutic participation, an increasingly creative activity of the participant, the patient is not engaged in a therapeutic setting, nor just plays as a social actor in a documentary field, but finally puts her/his own hands on her/his own stories of illness and treatment.

This operative and productive mode, inscribed, we may recall, in the collaborative video and the ethnographic narratives of shared anthropology, developed in the late 1960s with the pioneers of the *Fogo Process*, initiated by Don Snowden for the Memorial University of Newfoundland (Snowden, 1983). Participatory video manifests itself in many forms, from collaborative video, in which the camera remains in the hands of the facilitators – think of Harald Prins and Sarah Elder's projects in North America – to the Navajo Project (Worth & Adair, 1972), in which participation is more substantial – we are referring to

Vincent Carelli's *Video in the Villages* in 1987 and Terence Turner's *Kayapo Video Project* in 1990. However, such representational approaches, referable to visual ethnography (cf. Ginsburg et al., 2002; Marano, 2007), are redeclined and transferred from their disciplinary field of origin to other contexts and forms of use (Pink, 2007). In this sense, the Fogo Process, understood as a process of participatory filmmaking and community intervention, consisted of the production of 28 short documentaries, with the goal of representing a shared image of life on the island through the involvement of residents (Crocker, 2003; Ginsburg, 2016; MacLeod, 2004; White, 2003).

The salient point of this process is the centrality of the community worker at the expense of the documentary filmmaker, who assumes an exclusively instrumental role, since portable audiovisual recording equipment becomes a tool to accelerate the process of self-help and learning, and serves as catalyst for community action, intervening in human pathologies as well as describing them (Snowden, 1983). With therapeutic purposes and in therapeutic domains, the participatory model is then declined by Shaw and Robertson (1997): participatory video-therapeutic productions, characterized by a strong focus on the production process, are seen, when based in their constructions on the social and emotional needs of the participants, as a powerful aid in overcoming trauma and treating disorders, as well as in cultivating and realizing each individual's potential. Describing a relational model of therapy, Shaw and Robertson elaborated an approach that involved the active participation of the beneficiaries, well aware that they were working for themselves, with their own hands on the equipment and with full ownership, control, and right of choice regarding the represented content. In this type of participatory video, self-narrative proves to be the starting point of the transformative intervention: the footage and the act of filming it provides participants with a pretext for playing a role during the process rather than having relevance as a product itself.

In this regard, as Moraldi punctually points out, narrative interest in atypical categories has been instilled in documentary cinema over the past two decades. The common and salient aspect concerns the different degree of awareness with respect to the situation of representation in which their act takes place, an awareness that is expressed in a manner peculiar to each of them. For different reasons that can be traced to physiological or biological factors, children, animals, and the mentally ill relate to the act of filming with different degrees of awareness, and this confers quite peculiar characteristics to their performative acting (Moraldi, 2015, p. 207). Not only does this particular relationship to the act of filming connote a specific response to the directorial gesture, but also it may come to influence the creative gesture itself, when contextualized within agentive and therapeutic self-representative practices.

From this perspective, the methodological approach of Therapeutic Filmmaking aims at teaching the patients the fundamentals of filmmaking, in order to enable them to adopt its language and, indirectly, to creatively intervene in their trauma or disorder through audiovisual storytelling, which is co-constructed together with the members of a therapeutic team formed by the psychotherapist and at least one professional filmmaker. The patient is, thus, guided toward a participatory creation of the audiovisual product inherent in her/his own personal experiences, to the point of making a movie that has their Self as the object and the point of view of the narrative, with the goal of finally activating a reversibility between spectator, main character, and filmmaker roles (Sabatino et al., 2021; Saladino et al., 2020). The stages that mark the proposed path are:

1   development, which consists of conceiving and scripting the audiovisual narrative;
2   pre-production, which involves organizing and structuring the story by first drafting outlines and storyboarding, then developing a work schedule;
3   the shooting, the actual filming of the movie scenes;
4   editing, which includes audiovisual editing and post-production;
5   the projection of the final product.

While in Documentary Videotherapy exemplified by the Memofilm case the importance of the whole productive experience during and after the viewing of the final video is highlighted, in Therapeutic Filmmaking the production process is the most important part of the therapeutic treatment. Indeed, it is through the writing, rewriting, exploration, and visual storytelling, along with the continuous "processing" and analysis of the film, that the therapeutic goals are centered. The patient-author, by making use of an audiovisual language during filming that allows her/him to translate her/his pathological story into images, acquires the technical and creative skills to reinvent, rewrite, and convert it into another, functional, positive, and restructured version.

Therapeutic Filmmaking is also distinguished by a further significant difference with other therapeutic models that make use of the visual arts: unlike photography, which uses documentary materials selected or produced by the patient and family members, and, by not admitting time, becomes like painting, according to the most canonical of modern definitions, that of Lessing's Laocoon, an "art of space" (Greenberg, 1940; Lessing, 1984), video, in contrast, seems to possess the intrinsic and paradoxical condition of being timeless or, more precisely, of being marked by repetition and difference. While being, therefore, capable of allowing repeated and discontinuous viewings in heterogeneous and diverse contexts, the audiovisual product is time-based, since it concerns and represents the circumscribed performance of the patient, being equally considered among the "timeless" arts, due to its ability to crystallize and immortalize a single moment in time (cf. Auerbach, 2000; Johnson, 2015).

While the patient is at work creating her/his therapeutic movie, the team follows all stages of its making by documenting every phase and collecting audiovisual materials that will be used in the next methodological step. All the members of the team, patients and filmmakers, film others and themselves, within a setting that encompasses the creative and procedural space of the set. This setting stimulates a *therapeutic agency* of the patient who is now a filmmaker, finally author of her/his own storytelling of life plot, illness, and treatment. This perspective derives from the evolution of the setting into the set, thus, in the progressive production of a self-narrative, though collective, movie made by the patient. Indeed, as Casetti observes, a mediascape, rather than being such, is constituted through *mediascaping* on the basis of circumstances and by virtue of its components, through a process that makes it so (Casetti, 2018, pp. 134–135).

In a media environment that welcomes the camera as an agent of a narrative field emergence, the presence of multiple cameras in contact with the profilmic gives rise to a contact between the rituality of the context and the rituality of the recording that is revealed and shown in the final product, whose therapeutic agency is built precisely around the presence of audio and video recording devices. Already Memofilm was able to trigger the feeling of acting in a protected territory, in which to temporarily abandon oneself to the *libido agendi*, to the desire to participate in the game (even if only in the form of an act of thought and imagination, and not necessarily as physical action), generating shared ways capable of producing a renewal of the bodily memory.

Where the director relinquishes her/his "auratic" role as author by becoming a kind of facilitator who puts her/his own skills at the service of a group to facilitate its creation process, the participants construct an audiovisual narrative oscillating between self-representational modes, stemming from a self-staging of their everyday lives, and inevitably participatory narratives.

In fact, the products created within the process of Therapeutic Filmmaking, which can hardly be attributed to a single storytelling instance, slip between the voices and gazes of all participants in a continuous exchange of roles between those who watch and those who are watched, those who tell and those who are part of the story. Constituting themselves as the material outcome of a horizontal collaboration and, at the same time, dynamic objects in which patients, physicians, and filmmakers are simultaneously producers, main characters, and spectators, Therapeutic Filmmaking takes place within a narrative field desecrated by the amateurishness of narratives, hosting a rituality that is at least double (cf. Moraldi, 2015, p. 88), or even triple, constituted as a result of the interaction between documentary field, therapeutic setting and the recording devices that trigger and transform in them.

Within a "set-ting" in constant making and becoming, the audiovisual production experience, through writing, rewriting and exploring the visual narrative, allows the patient to set aside the perspective of illness in favor of the creative possibility, and to confront, at this stage, at least two "visualizations" of the same event: the images of the memory of her/his own experience and those of the audiovisual narrative being produced. By engaging in an activity of interpretive cooperation only after having actively participated in and literally interacted with the constitution of the narrative, after having materially made her/his own movie, the patient finds her/himself in a privileged position that allows her/him to understand and feel – again and differently – what s/he has gradually composed into a unity, into a synthesis, to use an Aristotelian and classical term. Only when things are done, in the face of such a composition, and in reliving the feelings that accompanied it, the patient-author confronts an objective impersonality manifestation: as it happens in bricolage or improvisation (Bertinetto, 2013, 2017; Pelgreffi, 2018; Peters, 2017), or in those forms of artistic "making" in which one gives oneself the rules as one does, and only at the end, in the first person, does one grasp the necessity of what one has done and what one has really felt and felt in doing it (cf. Montani, 2017).

Indeed, such a narrative independently develops a dynamic through which its material, formal, stylistic, referential properties are forged (Bertram, 2019), triggering a specific action as a *reflexive object* capable of influencing in a new way the praxis of its own creator and her/his own ability to interact with others and the world in general, and also intervening, in our case, even on the pathological or traumatic state. The *amauthor*, conceived as an amateur author (Sabatino, 2022b) – considering the whole therapeutic and creative experience as an outcome of an entirely amateur authorship – sets and conceives her/his own therapeutic self-narrative, reformulating and reinventing her/his own pathological experience through a constantly performative creative process (Richardson, 2022). Adopting the conclusions reached by Bertram inspired by Kant, one can say that the activities engaged in Therapeutic Filmmaking by the patient-author acquire a strong connotation of Ehrfarung, a "dependence in independence" experience: dependence is first of all in facing the dynamic object that is being made, but also the singular and irreplaceable embodiment of the involved subject, at the same time inscribed in a situation (grounded) and immersed in a culture (embedded). Such dual dependence, is, however, constrained by the independence of thinking and imagining that the pathological subject must and can exercise.

Another philosopher, also not coincidentally starting with Kant, Pietro Montani, helps us here to focus on a delicate and difficult but decisive passage for what we are going to say about the very special articulation between narrative, interpretation, understanding, praxis, and improvisation in Therapeutic Filmmaking. Montani argues that our imagination is at the same time reproductive (a dispositive that preserves and recalls what it has preserved), productive (a dispositive that recombines, integrates, designs, and configures) and interactive (a dispositive that affects the modification of the environment by being guided by what it finds there or by what it glimpses and projects) (Montani, 2014, p. 12).

The imagination of a patient engaged in Therapeutic Filmmaking is interactive precisely in the sense proposed by Pietro Montani: not vacuous and involuted daydreaming nor reprocessing and readjusting memories, or painful shirking of the surrounding world, but rather a processual trigger to modify and act on the environment from what the "dynamic object" that the movie, in its being unfinished, open, and *in fieri*, offers and imposes: it is to exercise, in short, one's independence starting from the dependencies, that the audiovisual product place before the eyes of the patient, at once spectator, author, and then, as we shall see later, *spectauthor*.

In this perspective, Therapeutic Filmmaking can be understood as an exquisitely amateur artistic "doing" that, without specific intentions or aesthetic qualities, "struggles to generate productive determinations of human being, […] determinations of human practices – that is, determinations of perceptive, emotional and symbolic bodily practices – that affect other worldly activities" (Montani, 2014, p. 154). Such productive determinations seem capable of affecting even ordinary life practices, transforming a pathological state of hermeneutic stalemate into an ordinary revelatory engagement of the self, moving from fiction to ordinary life and arriving, only at the end of the realization of such an essentially autobiographical narrative, at the production and application of its own therapy. If, as is evident in the autobiographical genre, the author and the main character of the described events generally coincide (Lejeune, 1989), for the patient addressed by the described videotherapeutic approaches this is partly true at the beginning of the treatment, at the moment when s/he becomes familiar with narrative methodologies and audiovisual techniques, but it is lost when, during the therapeutic journey, the convergence of roles dissipates. While believing s/he is telling about her/himself as the main character of the experience, the patient gives birth to another figure who, while perhaps resembling her/him, will be another character.

The depersonalization operated by the autobiographical work thus described, contextualized in a therapeutic course that is inscribed in what Foucault defines a "Technique of the Self" (Foucault, 1988) leads the patient toward creative self-treatment through her/his own autobiographical narratives. In this sense, the patient-author's gestures are far from a mono-directional conception of her/his own authorship: if the subject has already been summoned to a social everyday performance, the same subject will enact the aforementioned *performative surplus* (Comolli, 2004) in the course of the narrative negotiations that will take place on any documentary field. On the Therapeutic Set that hosts amateur narrative practices, similarly, the patient-author narrates through the audiovisual medium a further Self, imagined and then showed, who incorporates and embodies a reconstituting and significantly therapeutic self-representation.

By becoming, in the last stage, a spectator of her/his narratives, the *spectauthor*, whom we will discuss shortly, becomes aware of the potential reversibility between the two narratives of Self, the real and pathological one, the narrated and restructured one, transforming her/himself from an ineffective subject, devoted to inaction, to a finally self-effective individual (Bandura, 1997).

Video-Pharmakon: The Patient-*Spectauthor*

In the methodological proposal discussed so far, the "things" and "people", to borrow Gell's terms, are transformed by virtue of reciprocal contact and act on each other: the elements of the Therapeutic Set – in particular the patient-*amauthor* by means of the narrative of her/his own life and illness – are mutually shaped through their existence in the medial environments and dispositives in which the mediation takes place and is situated. Thus takes shape a process of narrative construction that entrusts all the choices concerning the autobiographical fabula of plot design by the patient her/himself. Only after actively participating in and literally interacting with the constitution of the self-narrative, after having "hand-made" her/his own movie, the patient-amateur, with the appropriate guidance of filmmaker and psychotherapist, retrospectively recognizes and reconfigures the pathological manifestations through the editing process. If the artifact was defined by Alfred Gell as a system of actions such as to invest it with an almost human agency, a condensate of a form of life which actively mediates new social relations and grows over time by incorporating and creating ever new meanings (Bartalesi, 2014, p. 117), it also acts on its viewer/recipient when that subject is also the producer of that artifact. The power of self-telling is, in fact, a kind of "involuntary autobiographical narrative, which works as our daily dose of self-help" (Demetrio, 1996, p. 48).

In narrating her/his past and present as lived experience (Ricoeur, 1984, 1985), the patient thus becomes a radical medium of her/his own healing journey. Such radical mediation refers to that process whereby all bodies (whether human or non-human) are fundamentally configured as mediations, since life itself is a form of mediation (Grusin, 2015), not understanding mediation as a process which acts between already given subjects or objects, but that generates or provides the conditions for the emergence of subjects and objects, for the individuation of entities within their own world (Grusin, 2015). In our case, medial levels of Therapeutic Filmmaking methodology often remain intertwined to such an extent that no distinction can be made. On the one hand, there is the visual, participatory, and creative element of "film-making", acting on the instantaneous well-being of the patient; on the other hand, there is the therapeutic rewriting of the autobiographical narrative by the patient, in her/his here-and-now, being at the same time embodied, grounded, and embedded. These two operative and methodological elements constitute the actual "radical mediations" of the healing process. Translating what Grusin argues to the Therapeutic Set framework, it can be said that the core of Therapeutic Filmmaking radical mediation lies in its immanence, in the immediacy itself, not a transparent immediacy which would illusorily put the patient in touch with a healed scenario, but in an embodied immediacy that characterizes the event of therapeutic mediation.

In the case of Memofilm, it is precisely the movie, with its "biographical body", that restores the memory of the patient-spectator through a compensatory corporeity for the targeted missing story. In Therapeutic Filmmaking, on the other hand, it is the creative act itself, whether through the movie style – shaped by the point of view, camera movements, and editing, in short, by the language of film – or through the gestures, actions, intentions, and emotions of the filmmaker, that serves as a catalyst for change within the reality in which it intervenes.

In Therapeutic Filmmaking methodology, this specificity is located in the relationship between the narrating Self and the narrated Self, as well as in the intersection between the authorial and spectatorial Self, making the creative filmmaking performance significantly therapeutic due to the established relationships between the footage and the self-image review during all stages, and particularly retrospectively, once concluded, of the entire production process (Hasson et al., 2008; Magliano & Zacks, 2011; Sabatino, 2022a).

At the end of the Therapeutic Filmmaking process, the patient-author becomes a spectator again, confronting her/his own movie as material outcome of the whole therapeutic journey. This movie has the function and role of what we define as a Video-Pharmakon, here understood as an assemblage of audiovisual materials administered to patients with the function of intervening in the disorders at the center of therapeutic treatment (see Chapter 6). Such an audiovisual narrative, just like the Memofilm, consists of contents concerning the patient's life and is assembled for her/his own benefit alone: unlike the autobiographical narrative described by Elizabeth Bruss (1980), the Video-Pharmakon that the patient experiences at the conclusion of Therapeutic Filmmaking has no need to possess the value of truth and the value of act; it must only be aesthetically relevant to a fruition dedicated to an external spectator. In such a case of therapeutic self-narrative, the element that Bruss identifies as the cause of ineffective autobiographical filmmaking becomes the real active principle of the therapeutic process: the duplication that for Bruss undermines the value of identity for an autobiographical narrative viewer, for a patient-*spectauthor* who is also author of her/his own autobiographical narrative, determines the activation of a powerful therapeutic effect as a result of watching her/his own movie about her/himself.

This type of audiovisual product, although packaged with the assistance of a professional editor, is made exclusively of footage shot by the patient her/himself. The active role in the process of editing allows the patient to organize the conflicts and wounds of her/his personal history according to a renewed point of view, offering unprecedented possibility of manipulating her/his own self-images.

Through the patient's "making", the audiovisual footage is selected and reassembled, taking shape in terms of sequentiality and relevance, leading to a crystallization, and therefore an internalization, of the lived experience. The editing room hosts a re-enacted Therapeutic Set, in which the therapist works with the images of the feelings and emotions triggered by their viewing and productive re-viewing (Kerem, 2015).

This reversal of the relationship between *filmeur* and *filmé* is embodied in the practice of video-feedback (Marano, 2007), or counter-gift (Mauss, 2000), understood as the symbolic movie restitution to the filmed subjects. Feedback circuits, in this sense, work on awareness and the creation of empowerment as resulting from seeing one's own image on a screen, in seeing oneself reflected through video (Extension Service, 1972; MacLeod, 2004; Williamson, 1991).

We will not dwell, here, on the different economies of counter-gifting (Starobinski, 1997), but we simply recall the practice of condensing and reconfiguring peculiar symbolic spaces and of assigning, thanks to audio-visual mediation, a different status to the Self, even in the therapeutic field (Gwyn, 1972). In the wake of such models, self-narrative Video-Pharmakon,[1] administered within an actual movie theater, constitutes the culmination and crowning creative effort in the making of a real movie, thus acquiring the power to ratify the reality it narrates and enabling the patient to finally become a *spectauthor* of her/his own therapeutic course and autobiographical opera. If "seeing yourself on screen in a context of collective enjoyment pro-motes self-confidence, and, in short, a better self-image, as a combined result of seeing yourself tangibly worth listening to, and seeing yourself as others see you" (Collizzolli, 2010, p. 51; Crocker, 2008), we may well say that not only the act, but even more, seeing oneself while doing that very act, makes the Video-Pharmakon therapeutically effective: that movie that the patient "makes" her/himself is not only enjoyed, seen, and relived by her/him as a spectator of her/his protagonist self, but it is also determined as "made" in its transversely and therapeutically occurring in the patient's real life.

Such a movie is, in short, not only living in the reconstructed, restored, and re-narrated plot on-screen, but also present and acting in the lived reality and everyday life, thus acquiring a double life thanks to the counter-given feed-back (Gauthier, 2015), but also the double gestural process, both self-repre-sentational and reflexive, of creative re-appropriation of a renewed Self, finally distant from the illness and pathological condition. It is for this reason that, in addition to the self-narrative Video-Pharmakon, a different typology of Video-Pharmakon is edited by the videotherapeutic team, with the goal of preserving the progress achieved over the whole therapeutic course. Aiming at returning the patient's narrative of her/his experience, in the journey of emancipation from passive condition of patient-spectator to the active role of patient-author, the Video-Pharmakon is administered to the patient in order to show her/himself the very act of filmmaking. But unlike the self-narrative Video-Pharmakon, which was made exclusively of footage shot and selected by patients, the short movie is composed of audiovisual materials of a hybrid nature and authorship: customized for the individual patients' needs, the

Video-Pharmakon aims to deliver a synthesis, a holistic synopsis between the self-representation and the representation of self, allowing the participants to experience the narrative as a segment of lived life, as a part of self, and as a reality beyond self, at the same time carrying both familiarity and diversity.

Such an audiovisual configuration is complex, linguistically layered, oscillating between autobiographical and self-portrait forms, but also documentary and participatory: including all typologies of collected footage and showing all team members, together with the patients, the *maintenance Video-Pharmakon* – unlike the self-narrative one which coincides with the movie authored by the patient – is assembled according to intermedial editing (Montani, 2010). Such editing criteria intercept critical modes that explore the relationship between different technical formats of the image, which, interacting, reconfigure themselves determining, on the one hand, an "authentication" (Montani, 2010, p. 23) of the real, and, on the other, allowing, through the overcoming of the principle of transparency and the observational mode, a critical redefinition of it.

Through intermedial editing, the maintenance Video-Pharmakon,[2] more than the self-narrative one, is able to make the screen effectively empathic. If during the final vision of the Therapeutic Filmmaking the patient recognizes her/himself as the maker of her/his own audiovisual product, in the maintenance phase, the Video-Pharmakon sends her/him not only images of her/himself before and after the therapeutic intervention, together with the salient images of the movie s/he made, but above all images of her/himself in the act of creating her/his own movie. Through an alternation of viewpoints and focuses that significantly determine the diegetic form of the Video-Pharmakon, a narrative dispositive as described so far is configured to intervene on the pathological, biographical fabula with a therapeutic, self-narrative, and documentary interweaving. The assemblage of the autobiographical sequences s/he produces, together with the documentary sequences of her/himself in the act of filming them, is able to bring about in the patient a recognition of the complex Self – at once agnition and ratification, acceptance and constitution – not only of her/his own role, active and authorial, within the creative lived experience, but also, transitively, within her/his own life: it is, in short, the revisioning of oneself in the act of rewriting trauma or illness within the *set-ting*, the Therapeutic Set, of one's everyday life that triggers the healing process.

It seems to us, then, that the therapeutic power of the autobiographical act first emerges in the creative distancing which allows the patient-*spectauthor* to observe and analyze from the outside her/his own life in the movie s/he is making, finally creating, in that "dependence of independence" relationship that we have previously analyzed, a narrative that productively and pragmatically intervenes on the everyday, ordinary and out-of-fiction life. In the act of detaching her/himself from her/his "handmade" stories, the patient makes and witnesses a personal transformation of Self, therefore multiplying, starting from her/his imaginative and visualizing storytelling applications, her/ his identities and possible scenarios of existence, gradually conveying the belief to exist in another condition beyond disorder and pathology, a status that is shown and told on the screen without belonging to her/him anymore.

In the methodological path outlined so far, on the one hand, Cinematherapy and Filmtherapy provide for a *post hoc* high-interpretive fruition of audiovisual materials; on the other hand, Therapeutic Videotaping, Documentary Videotherapy, and Therapeutic Filmmaking propose an interactive, individual or participatory, but above all progressively performative relationship with the filmic text. Such a relationship shifts the emphasis to the processuality and gestural dimension consisting in the act of filming, an agentive narrative act because it is physically acted and fabricated by its author her/ himself, who experiences, in the re-viewing phase, all its beneficial and therapeutic effects by becoming agent and patient in a virtuous circle that is almost entirely self-produced.

Notes

1   Two examples of Self-Narrative Video-Pharmakon can be seen on the Audiovisual Storytelling Lab – Labsav (University of Salerno) YouTube channel at the following links:
    www.youtube.com/watch?v=Xc2le37m2n0&list=PLU6miEzwFS61ZUVbZlEw_ XLum3j06C8AT&index=4   and   www.youtube.com/watch?v=izhOcbla0Us&list= PLU6miEzwFS61ZUVbZlEw_XLum3j06C8AT&index=6.
2   Some Maintenance Video-Pharmakon examples can be seen on the Audiovisual Storytelling Lab – Labsav (University of Salerno) YouTube channel at the following link:
    https://youtu.be/fM2QzhqVpVs?list=PLU6miEzwFS61ZUVbZlEw_XLum 3j06C8AT.

References

Albano, L., & Pravadelli, V. (2008). *Cinema e psicoanalisi. Tra cinema classico e nuove tecnologie.* Quodlibet.

Alovisio, S. (2013). *L'occhio sensibile. Cinema e scienze della mente nell'Italia del primo Novecento.* Kaplan.

Arnott, B., & Gushin, J. (1976). Filmmaking as a therapeutic tool. *American Journal of Art Therapy,* 16(1), 29–33.

Auerbach, J. (2000). Chasing film narrative: Repetition, recursion, and the body in early cinema. *Critical Inquiry,* 26(4), 798–820.

Balázs, B. (2011). *Early film theory: Visible man and the spirit of film* (E. Carter & R. Livingstone, Trans.). Berghahn Books.

Bandura, A. (1986). *Social Foundations of Thoughts and Action: A Social Cognitive Theory.* Prentice Hall.

Bandura, A. (1997). *Self-efficacy: The exercise of control.* W H Freeman & Co.

Bartalesi, L. (2014). La fragilità dell'oggetto estetico. *Lebenswelt: Aesthetics and Philosophy of Experience,* 5, 106–119.

Beller, J. (2006). *The cinematic mode of production: Attention economy and the society of the spectacle.* Dartmouth College Press.

Belloi, L. (2001). *Le regard retourné: Aspects du cinéma des premiers temps.* Nota Bene, Méridiens-Klincksieck.

Bencivenni, L. (2016). *Memofilm a memoria d'uomo. Ricostruzione dell'identità narrativa attraverso l'utilizzo dei linguaggi audiovisivi.* [Bachelor dissertation, University of Bologna]. https://memofilmontheweb.files.wordpress.com/2016/09/memofilm-a-memoria-duomo-tesi-lisa.pdf.

Benjamin, W. (2008). *The work of art in the age of its technological reproducibility, and other writings on media.* Harvard University Press.

Berg-Cross, L., Jennings, P., & Baruch, R. (1990). Cinematherapy: Theory and application. *Psychotherapy in Private Practice,* 8(1), 135–156. doi:10.1300/J294v08n01_15.

Berger, M. M. (1971). Self-confrontation through video. *American Journal of Psychoanalysis,* 31(1), 48–58. doi:10.1007/BF01872309.

Berger, M. M. (1978). *Beyond the double bind: Communication and family systems, theories, and techniques with schizophrenics.* Brunner/Mazel.

Bergstrom, J. (1999). *Endless night: Cinema and psychoanalysis, parallel histories.* University of California Press.

Bertinetto, A. G. (2013). Performing imagination: The aesthetics of improvisation. *Klesis,* 28, 65–99.

Bertinetto, A. G. (2017). Valore e autonomia dell'improvvisazione: Tra arti e pratiche. *Kaiak,* 3, 1–17.

Bertram, G. W. (2019). *Art as human practice: An aesthetics* (N. Ross, Trans.). Bloomsbury Publishing.

Bléandonu, G. (1986). *La vidéo en thérapie: Le choc de l'image de soi dans les soins psychologiques.* ESF.

Boccara, P., & Riefolo, G. (2002). Psicoanalisi al cinema. Alcune considerazioni di metodo su cinema e psicoanalisi. *Rivista di Psicoanalisi,* 8(3), 691–705.

Brown, S. D. (1980). Videotape feedback: Effects on assertive performance and subjects' perceived competence and satisfaction. *Psychological Reports,* 47(2), 455–461. doi:10.2466/pr0.1980.47.2.455.

Bruss, E. W. (1980). Eye for I: Making an unmaking autobiography in film. In J. Olney (Ed.), *Autobiography: Essays theoretical and critical* (pp. 296–320). Princeton University Press.

Cardillo, M. (1987). *Tra le quinte del cinematografo. Cinema, cultura e società in Italia, 1900–1937.* Dedalo.

Casetti, F. (2015). *The Lumière galaxy: Seven key words for the cinema to come.* Columbia University Press.

Casetti, F. (2018). Mediascape: Un decalogo. In P. Montani, D. Cecchi, & M. Feyles (Eds.), *Ambienti mediali* (pp. 111–138). Meltemi.

Castriota, F. (2013). Psicoanalisi e cinema. In P. Carbone, M. Cottone, & M. G. Eusebio (Eds.), *Cinema, adolescenza e psicoanalisi: Comprendere gli adolescenti per aiutarli a comprendersi* (pp. 17–30). Franco Angeli.

Ciappina, G., & Capriani, P. (2007). *Manuale di cinematerapia.* Istituto Solaris.

Cohen, J. L., Johnson, J. L., & Orr, P. (2015). *Video and filmmaking as psychotherapy: Research and practice.* Routledge.

Collizzolli, S. (2010). *Il video partecipativo. Dalla comunicazione sociale alla socializzazione della comunicazione.* [Doctoral dissertation, Padua University]. https://hdl.handle.net/11577/3426590.

Comolli, J. L. (2004). *Voir et pouvoir: l'innocence perdue, cinéma, télévision, fiction, documentaire.* Editions Verdier.

Crocker, S. (2003). The Fogo Process: Participatory communication in a globalizing world. In S. A. White (Ed.), *Participatory video: Images that transform and empower* (pp. 122–145). Sage.

Crocker, S. (2008). Filmmaking and the politics of remoteness. *Shima: The International Journal of Research into Island Cultures,* 2(1), 59–75.

De Gaetano, R. (2012). *La potenza delle immagini. Il cinema, la forma e le forze.* ETS.

De Sanctis, S. (1930). Applicazione del Cinema nel campo dell'educazione dei fanciulli e dei ragazzi, in Cinematografo ed organizzazione scientifica del lavoro. *Quaderni dell'Istituto Internazionale per la Cinematografica Educativa,* 17, 183–202.

Demetrio, D. (1996). *Raccontarsi. L'autobiografia come cura di sé.* Raffaello Cortina.

Dufour, M. (2000). *Through the looking glass: The therapeutic potential of videotaping as an adjunct tool in non-directive art therapy in an object relations perspective.* [Master dissertation, Concordia University]. https://spectrum.library.concordia.ca/id/eprint/1258/.

Eğeci, İ. S., & Gençöz, F. (2017). Use of Cinematherapy in dealing with relationship problems. *The Arts in Psychotherapy,* 53, 64–71.

Extension Service. (1972). *Fogo Process in communication: A reflection on the use of film and video-tape in community development.* Memorial University of Newfoundland.

Fatemi, S. M. (2021). *Film therapy: Practical applications in a psychotherapeutic context.* Routledge.

Feldmann, E. (1956). Considération sur la situation du spectateur au cinéma. *Revue Internationale de Filmologie,* 7(26), 83–97.

Feyles, M. (2017). Immagini di sé: Un caso esemplare, il Memofilm. In S. Capezzuto, D. Ciccone, & A. Mileto (Eds.), *Dentro/fuori: Il lavoro dell'immaginazione e le forme del montaggio* (pp. 132–137). Il Lavoro Culturale.

Foucault, M. (1988). Les techniques de soi. *Dits et écrits,* 4, 783–813.

Friedberg, A. (1990). A denial of difference: Theories of cinematic identification. In E. A. Kaplan (Ed.), *Psychoanalysis and Cinema* (pp. 36–45). Routledge.

Gallese, V., & Guerra, M. (2019). *The empathic screen: Cinema and neuroscience.* Oxford University Press.

Gauthier, G. (2015). *Le documentaire: Un autre cinéma.* Armand Colin.

Gemelli, A. (1926). Le cause psicologiche dell'interesse nelle proiezioni cinematografiche: Il fondamento scientifico per la riforma del cinematografo. In S. Alovisio (Ed.), *L'occhio sensibile: Cinema e scienze della mente nell'Italia del primo Novecento* (pp. 209–220). Kaplan.

Ginsburg, F., Abu-lughod, L., & Larkin, B. (2002). *Media worlds: Anthropology on new terrain.* University of California Press.

Ginsburg, F. (2016). Indigenous media from U-Matic to YouTube: Media sovereignty in the digital age. *Sociologia & Antropologia,* 6, 581–599. doi:10.1590/2238-38752016V632.

Giusti, E. (1999). *Videoterapia. Un ausilio al counseling e alle arti terapie.* Sovera.

Giusti, E., & Montanari, C. (1992). La Gestalt della supervisione. *Realtà e prospettive in Psicofisiologia,* 3, 161–170.

Giusti, E., & Proietti, M. C. (1995). *L'anamnesi e il colloquio. Un modello integrato di cartella clinica in psicoterapia.* Quaderni Aspic.

Grasseni, C., Barendregt, B., de Maaker, E., De Musso, F., Littlejohn, A., Maeck-elbergh, M., ... & Westmoreland, M. R. (2021). *Audiovisual and digital ethnography: A practical and theoretical guide.* Routledge.

Greenberg, C. (1940). Towards a newer Laocoon. *Partisan Review*, 7(4), 296–310.

Grosso, L. (2013). *Memofilm. Creatività contro l'Alzheimer*. Mimesis.

Grusin, R. (2015). Radical mediation. *Critical Inquiry*, 42(1), 124–148.

Gunning, T. (1989). An aesthetic of astonishment: Early film and the (in)credulous spectator. *Art and Text*, 34, 31–45.

Gwyn, S. (1972). *Cinema as a catalyst: Film, videotape and social change. A report on a seminar.* Memorial University of Newfoundland.

Halliwell, S. (2002). *The aesthetic of mimesis: Ancient texts and modern problems.* Princeton–Oxford.

Hankir, A., Holloway, D., Zaman, R., & Agius, M. (2015). Cinematherapy and film as an educational tool in undergraduate psychiatry teaching: A case report and review of the literature. *Psychiatria Danubina*, 27(suppl 1), 136–142.

Hasson, U., Landesman, O., Knappmeyer, B., Vallines, I., Rubin, N., & Heeger, D. J. (2008). Neurocinematics: The neuroscience of film. *Projections*, 2(1), 1–26. doi:10.3167/proj.2008.020102.

Hébert, T. P., & Neumeister, K. L. S. (2001). Guided viewing of film: A strategy for counseling gifted teenagers. *Journal of Secondary Gifted Education*, 12(4), 224–235. doi:10.4219/jsge-2001-669.

Heilveil, I. (1983). *Video in mental health practice: An activities handbook.* Springer.

Hirschfeld, A. G. (1968). Videotape recordings for self-analysis in the speech class-room. *The Speech Teacher*, 17(2), 116–118. doi:10.1080/03634526809377660.

Iedema, R., Forsyth, R., Georgiou, A., Braithwaite, J., & Westbrook, J. (2006). Video research in health. *Qualitative Research Journal*, 6(2), 15–30.

Jakubowska, M., & Michałowska, M. (2017). Filmmaking as therapy: Between art therapy and resilience theory. *Panoptikum*, 18, 227–236. doi:10.26881/pan.2017.18.14.

Johnson, J. L. (2015). Vision, story, medicine: Therapeutic Filmmaking and first nations communities. In J. L. Cohen, J. L. Johnson, P. Orr (Eds.), *Video and Film-making as Psychotherapy* (pp. 55–66).Routledge.

Kenney, B. L. (1982). Audiovisuals in mental health. *Library Trends*, 30(4), 591–611.

Kerem, Y. (2015). Felt sensing video art therapy. In J. Cohen (Ed.), *Video and Film-making as Psychotherapy* (pp. 181–201). Routledge.

Kitwood, T. (1993). Towards a theory of dementia care: The interpersonal process. *Ageing & Society*, 13(1), 51–67. doi:10.1017/S0144686X00000647.

Lampropoulos, G. K., Kazantzis, N., & Deane, F. P. (2004). Psychologists' use of motion pictures in clinical practice. *Professional Psychology: Research and Practice*, 35(5), 535. doi:10.1037/0735-7028.35.5.535.

Lejeune, P. (1989). *On autobiography*. University of Minnesota Press.

Lessing, G. E. (1984). *Laocoön, or On the limits of painting and poetry* (1766). Johns Hopkins University Press.

Lévi-Strauss, C. (1966). *The savage mind: The nature of human society series*. University of Chicago Press.

MacLeod, P. (2004). *Participatory filmmaking and video: Building on the legacy of the Fogo Process*. Symposium on Communication for Social and Environmental Change, University of Guelph, October 5.

Magliano, J. P., & Zacks, J. M. (2011). The impact of continuity editing in narrative film on event segmentation. *Cognitive Science*, 35(8), 1489–1517. doi:10.1111/j.1551-6709.2011.01202.x.

Malchiodi, C. (2012). Art therapy materials, media and methods. C. Malchiodi (Ed.), *Handbook of art therapy* (pp. 27–41). Guilford Publications.

Malchiodi, C. (2018). Creative art therapies and arts-based research. In P. Leavy (Ed.), *Handbook of arts-based research* (pp. 68–87). Guilford Press.

Marano, F. (2007). *Camera etnografica: Storie e teorie di antropologia visuale.* Franco Angeli.

Marinelli, L. (2006). Screening wish theories: Dream psychologies and early cinema. *Science in Context*, 19(1), 87–110.

Marsick, E. (2010). Cinematherapy with preadolescents experiencing parental divorce: A collective case study. *The Arts in Psychotherapy*, 37(4), 311–318. doi:10.1016/j.aip.2010.05.006.

Mastronardi, V. M. (2005). *Filmtherapy: I film che ti aiutano a stare meglio.* Armando.

Mauss, M. (2000). *The gift: The form and reason for exchange in archaic societies.* W. W. Norton & Company.

Medolago Albani, F. (2017). MediCinema: Quando il cinema diventa terapia. *Economia della Cultura*, 27(2), 253–264. doi:10.1446/87278.

Montani, P. (1999). *L'immaginazione narrativa. Il racconto del cinema oltre i confini dello spazio letterario.* Guerini e associati.

Montani, P. (2010). *L'immaginazione intermediale. Perlustrare, rifigurare, testimoniare il mondo visibile.* Laterza.

Montani, P. (2014). *Tecnologie della sensibilità. Estetica e immaginazione interattiva.* Raffaello Cortina.

Montani, P. (2017). *Tre forme di creatività: tecnica, arte, politica.* Cronopio.

Moraldi, S. (2015). *Questioni di campo. La relazione osservatore/osservato nella forma documentaria.* Bulzoni.

Moreno, J. L. (1944). Psychodrama and therapeutic motion pictures. *Sociometry*, 7(2), 230–244. doi:10.2307/2785414.

Morin, E. (2005). *The cinema, or, the imaginary man.* University of Minnesota Press.

Muller, C., & Bader, A. (1972). Therapeutic art programs around the world IX. Filmmaking in a Swiss psychiatric hospital. *American Journal of Art Therapy*, 11(4), 185–189.

Pelgreffi, I. (2018). *Improvvisazione.* Mimesis.

Pennacchi, F. (1930). *Cinema e adolescenza con speciale rapporto alle malattie nervose e mentali.* In S. Alovisio (Ed.), *L'occhio sensibile. Cinema e scienze della mente nell'Italia del primo Novecento* (pp. 244–277). Kaplan.

Peske, N. K., & West, B. (1999). *Cinematherapy: The girl's guide to movies for every mood.* Dell.

Peters, G. (2017). *Improvising improvisation: From out of philosophy, music, dance and literature.* The University of Chicago Press.

Pink, S. (2007). *Visual interventions: Applied visual anthropology* (Vol. 4). Berghahn Books.

Ponzo, M. (1914). Il valore didattico del cinematografo. In S. Alovisio (Ed.), *L'occhio sensibile. Cinema e scienze della mente nell'Italia del primo Novecento* (pp. 168–172). Kaplan.

Ponzo, M., & Rivano, F. (1927). La realizzazione nell'azione di un decorso rappresentativo Onirico. *Archivio di antropologia criminale psichiatria e medicina legale*, 67(2), 185–201.

Portadin, M. A. (2006). *The use of popular film in psychotherapy: Is there a "Cinematherapy"?*Massachusetts School of Professional Psychology.

Powell, M. L. (2008). *Cinematherapy as a clinical intervention: Theoretical rationale and empirical credibility.* University of Arkansas.

Prados, M. (1951). The use of films in psychotherapy. *American Journal of Orthopsychiatry*, 21(1), 36–46. doi:10.1111/j.1939-0025.1951.tb06084.x.

Richardson, J. F. (2022). *Art as a language for autism: Building effective therapeutic relationships with children and adolescents.* Routledge.

Ricoeur, P. (1984). *Time and narrative (Temps et récit)*, Vol. 2. Seuil.

Ricoeur, P. (1985). *Time and narrative (Temps et récit)*, Vol. 3. Seuil.

Rossi, O. (2009). *Lo sguardo e l'azione. Il video e la fotografia in psicoterapia e nel counseling.* Edizioni Universitarie Romane.

Rubin, J. A. (1999). *Art therapy: An introduction.* Brunner/Mazel.

Sabatino, A. C. (2022a). Audiovisual means to therapeutic ends: The cinematic dispositive within medical humanities. *Cinéma & Cie. Film and Media Studies Journal*, 22(39), 53–68. doi:10.54103/2036-461X/17748.

Sabatino, A. C. (2022b). L'amautore. Note sull'autorialità amatoriale. *Imago*, 25, 109–128.

Sabatino, A. C., Fimiani, F., Pastorino, G. M., Petruccelli, F., Saladino, V., Verrastro, V., … & Coppola, G. (2021). Therapeutic Filmmaking, strategic psychotherapy and autism spectrum disorder: An integrated approach. *Journal of Psychological & Educational Research*, 29(2), 56–89.

Saladino, V., Sabatino, A. C., Iannaccone, C., Giovanna Pastorino, G. M., & Verrastro, V. (2020). Filmmaking and video as therapeutic tools: Case studies on autism spectrum disorder. *The Arts in Psychotherapy*, 71, 101714. doi:10.1016/j.aip.2020.101714.

Sharp, C., Smith, J. V., & Cole, A. (2002). Cinematherapy: Metaphorically promoting therapeutic change. *Counselling Psychology Quarterly*, 15(3), 269–276. doi:10.1080/09515070210140221.

Shaw, J., & Robertson, C. (1997). *Participatory video: A practical approach to using video creatively in group development work.* Routledge.

Snowden, D. (1983). *Eyes see; ears hear.* Memorial University, St. John, Newfoundland.

Sobchack, V. (2004). *Carnal thoughts: Embodiment and moving image culture.* University of California Press.

Starobinski, J. (1989). *The living eye.* Harvard University Press.

Starobinski, J. (1997). *Largesse* (J. M. Todd, Trans.). University of Chicago Press.

Thénot, J. P. (1989). *Vidéothérapie. L'image qui fait renaître.* Greco.

Trifonova, T. (2014). *Warped minds: Cinema and psychopathology.* Amsterdam University Press.

Tyson, L., Foster, L., & Jones, C. (2000). The process of Cinematherapy as a therapeutic intervention. *Alabama Counseling Journal*, 26(1), 35–41.

Wedding, D., & Niemiec, R. M. (2003). The clinical use of films in psychotherapy. *Journal of Clinical Psychology*, 59(2), 207–215. doi:10.1002/jclp.10142.

White, S. A. (2003). *Participatory video: Images that transform and empower.* Sage.

Williamson, A. H. (1991). The Fogo Process: Development support communications in canada and the developing world. In F. L. Casmir (Ed.), *Communication in development* (pp. 270–288). Ablex.

Worth, S., & Adair, J. (1972). *Through Navajo eyes: An exploration in film communication and anthropology.* Indiana University Press.

Chapter 4

Art-Based Therapy in the Digital Age

A New Form of Participation

Valeria Saladino

Toward a Definition of a Participatory Art-Based Therapy

Carl Gustave Jung provides a definition of therapy as a form of creativity derived from experience. According to his vision, individuals should learn psychology from both books and experience. Indeed, psychologists possess their personal experience, which enriches their understanding of the phenomenon and its inner substance (Jung, 1967). Art-based therapy considers creativity and direct experience as the basis of the therapeutic process. These types of therapies provide tools that activate through creative stimulation and individuals' feelings and emotions. Art-based therapy focuses on the creative experience and on the emotional interpretation of the content, translated into functional behaviors. This process activates the emotional area and reaches memorization, leading individuals to learn more quickly. At a neuroscientific level, this process is explained by the proximity to the limbic area of the insula, amygdala, and hippocampus respectively involved in the sense of disgust, emotions, and memorization (Blonder, 1999).

From a historical point of view, the origins of art as a valid process for human communication can be found in the Middle Ages, where magical thinking and superstitions substituted medical cures for psychic distress. During the Renaissance art was considered power in curing individuals with psychic disorders: painting, music, and sculpture became "moral therapies". In the twentieth century, with Freud and Jung, art was considered an expression of the unconscious and sublimation of primary instincts. According to Freud, art sublimes the sense of dissatisfaction derived from a renunciation imposed by reality (Freud, 1920). Freud emphasizes that the power of art derives from the product rather than the process and defines the artist as a person who detaches her/himself from reality since s/he cannot adapt to it and realizes her/his desires in fantasy. The creative product, therefore, represents a privileged means to access the unconscious emotional content, understood as a mirror reflecting the inner world of the subject (Freud, 1920). Jung, on the other hand, considers creativity as an instinct along with hunger, and sexuality, referring to it as the element that characterizes humans by

DOI: 10.4324/9781003340508-5

differentiating them from other living species (Jung, 1967). According to the author, creativity allows the expression of spirituality through the production of symbols. Creativity creates contact with inner experiences and recovers unconscious images through an artistic code that makes them intelligible to all.

The acceptance of the use of art in therapy was not immediate, as explained by Elinor Ulman, who founded The Bulletin of Art Therapy in 1961. According to the author, anything called art therapy should include art and therapy (Wolf, 1977). This process describes the dynamic interplay between several variables that may change over time, such as the setting and duration of treatment, the client's background, abilities, and interests as well as clients' needs, the resources of context, the theoretical orientation, and the experience of the art therapist. Therefore, it is not a comparison between performing portions of art or therapy, but the incorporation of both into a single process. For instance, a sound, a color, or a scent can stimulate sensations or emotions that evoke certain memories or traumatic events leaving vivid or even still ongoing emotions difficult to translate into an organized and rational process. In this case, a repertoire of sounds, images, or gestures, by creativity-enhancing work, can enable the expression or description of feelings and actions. Moreover, through the stimulation of auditory, visual, tactile, or kinesthetic senses, traumatic memories can be recovered by allowing the connection between feelings and explicit memory (Appleton, 2001). In this sense, art therapy is defined as a form of "sensory" therapy.

Damasio explained this mechanism of interaction between mind, body, and emotions (1995), emphasizing the role of individuals as thinking and emotional machines. Nonverbal exploration through sensory experiences including touch, movement, sight, and sound can enable individuals to regulate themselves easily. An art-based therapy process also involves and integrates the brain's sides and its functions. During the artistic and therapeutic process, through specific sensory activities, the left and the right brain are involved in showing their components together. Respectively, rationality and creativity. Art therapy integrates fear-evoking emotions with positively connoted ones, giving a feeling of relief. Indeed, direct experiences of emotions translated into graphic or musical form can be revelatory or even sensational. Individuals can graphically express negative feelings while balancing emotional activation within the therapeutic process (Schouten et al., 2014).

Firstly, the procedure in arts therapies involves communication through nonverbal channels, using drawings, gestures, and sounds to stimulate communication. This could be beneficial, especially among children or compromised individuals, such as those with disabilities or language disorders (Bailey, 2015). These creative tools promote and facilitate relationships with others and the outside in a dialogic construction. The main purpose of working through art therapy derives from the recognition and understanding of others, through the creative process (Stevenson & Orr, 2013).

According to Vygotskij (2004), creativity leads to projecting into the future through a process of imagination. This process creates a connection between the present and the future of a person. Basically, art therapy refers to different theoretical approaches such as cognitivist, psychoanalytic-psychodynamic, systemic, and gestalt. All these approaches aim to promote self-acceptance and contact with emotional conflicts through the therapeutic relationship. Along this line, Arieti (see Werman, 1979) addresses the concept of creativity as a human capacity that contributes to progress by allowing the individual to access images connected to the unconscious, defined as "extraordinary creativity". This concept is different from "ordinary" creativity which enhances life by making it full and satisfying.

According to the definitions described, creativity can be considered a process of awareness that enriches our knowledge. Indeed, arts therapies are based on the process of "mirroring" that characterizes the therapeutic relationship. During the therapeutic process, the art therapist conveys confidence to the clients, recognizing their ability to express themselves through the medium of art. Clients introject these learnings within the therapeutic relationship and experience them in daily relationships with greater awareness and adaptation. In this perspective, the success of the therapy is influenced by the feeling of trust and mirroring between the client and the therapist, who has the responsibility to contain the difficulties of the clients and stimulate them to continue the creative process (Knol et al., 2020). As in all kinds of therapy, the process can drop out due to the fear of the client in dealing with difficulties. Sometimes the dysfunctional situation represents a "safe harbor" for the client, who prefers to maintain the difficulty rather than face the change. Art therapists can use different tools to promote awareness among clients, such as visual or tactile. The visual experience represents personal perceptions of what surrounds the person, while the tactile experience is focused on the projection of the internal world in the image. In fact, communication between therapists and clients is characterized by the verbal and nonverbal channels that intersect with each other at different levels. Firstly, the therapist observes the creative expression between the client and the images, then the therapist focuses on the image produced by the clients to create a bridge of creative-symbolic expression with the patient, and finally, the therapist moves to the interactive-analytic expression (Weir, 1987). This process acts in a specific setting, characterized by essential equipment, such as pencils, tempera, markers, and other tools.

The setting is also a physical and relational place in which clients can express themselves. The artistic product could be considered through the setting analysis as tripolar. The image represents the third object and the silent partner of the art therapist (Dilawari & Tripathi, 2014). In the therapeutic setting, the therapist promotes the transition from concrete to symbolic images, in favor of expressiveness that leads to the integration and harmonization of opposites, and the dialogue with images to achieve self-awareness

(Dilawari & Tripathi, 2014). For instance, Milner (see Stefana, 2019) refers to the art of drawing as a process based on symbolic representations that project through the creative process the deeper psyche of the client. Through identification with the drawing, the person externalizes feelings and other psychological elements, translating the symbol into a real product and giving new meanings. Like dreams, drawings can reveal the incommunicability of certain contents. The first images produced are the first level for the therapist, who uses active listening to read and transform it into communications and readable tools for the patient (Jung, 1967).

Mostly, art therapies have in common an "instrument" that resonates internally and allows the expression of emotions and internal states. Patients participate with body and mind, perceiving the process and the development of her/his personal evolution of meaning.

For instance, in music therapy, music is used as a "prescription" to improve the patient's quality of life and to support a change in communicative, emotional, and intellectual conditions (Pèrez-Eizaguirre & Vergara-Moragues, 2021). Rhythm, melody, and harmony resonate within the body by stimulating internal vibrations and allowing the individuals to emerge (even if at first not consciously) and then attribute meaning because of a psychotherapeutic process. The use of musical language involves the patient's mind, body, and soul together with the music therapist who sets the rhythm. Rolando Benenzon (2007) considers music therapy as a psychotherapeutic technique that uses sound, music, and movement to determine a bond between the therapist and the patient or groups of patients, to improve the quality of life and reduce the symptoms of the patient. Music therapy promotes the relationship between sound and human beings and uses musical instruments as stimuli to observe body and mind changes (Benenzon, 2007). According to Benenzon, music therapy allows the patient to deal with past frustrations, reinforcing rewarding experiences (Benenzon, 2007).

Dance-movement therapy is another commonly used art therapy and focuses on the reading of the body in movement (Kawano & Chang, 2022). The body has a "subjective" value (Lauffenburger, 2020) and it is considered a relational representation of the patient. The scientific literature in the field of psychopathology confirms the absolute relevance of the body in several mental disorders, recognizing a discomfort that originates from the perception of the body as disturbing, connected to feelings of distress and disgust. For instance, the family rejects the sexual body (Leijssen, 2006). Moreover, dance has always been associated with the expression of culture, and identity expression (Brosius & Polit, 2020). According to the American Dance Therapy Association, dance therapy is the therapeutic use of movement to help individuals to regain psycho-body communication. Dance-movement therapy aims to rediscover "functional pleasure", associating satisfaction with the pleasure of movement. This therapy redefines psychomotor functions, allowing the person to rediscover functional pleasure from a perceptual and physical level, through play, rhythm, coordination, and precision of movements involving various muscle groups within a well-defined space. Movement can stimulate emotional reactions through the body, expressing conflicts and leading to a "body symbolization". According to Winnicott (1971), dance is a transitional space in which the movement of the body is the protagonist, and it is supported by the relationship with the therapist who acts as a mirror.

The arts therapies represent support for expressiveness. The movement of the body, of the hands to make a drawing or melody composition, becomes an essential channel of communication with the person or within a group to deliver the possibility of expression. Thus, art therapies can be integrated into a therapeutic process to promote nonverbal communication and to create a different setting for a specific target of clients.

Today, the increment in technology use in every aspect of our routine and in the management of mental health is noted. Mediated communication using electronic devices and technology has radically changed habits and perceptions of individuals' participation in daily life. Children and adolescents especially may express themselves and develop their sense of identity using social networks and online applications. Teenagers are immersed in the tendency to show their life (what they do, and where they go), ready to immediately view the latest message and to continuously check their notifications due to the fear of missing out (Przybylski et al., 2013).

Recently the provision of numerous services, including therapeutic programming, has drastically grown. As a result, online therapy and online art therapy practices received greater attention from technological developers and clinicians. This constant attention has led researchers and professionals toward a more careful analysis of the use of remote or technologically mediated art therapy and the methods of use by clients, specifically of the study of the online therapeutic setting, of the impact that this modality of use has on patients and of the practical applications for specific problems.

Online Therapy, Art-Based Therapy, and Technology

As mentioned in the previous paragraph, the new language of the digital age involves psychotherapy and art-based therapy and is included in the traditional methodological framework of clinicians and practitioners. Indeed, the analysis of recent literature on the topic suggests the effectiveness of online psychological intervention and the possibilities of integration with traditional counseling and therapy in several contexts of applications (Saladino, Alegri et al., 2020).

The evolution of technologies leads to significant changes in managing relationships between individuals and in psychological interventions. The term "online therapy" includes any type of professional and skilled therapeutic interaction that uses the medium of the internet to connect mental health professionals and services (Bloom, 1998; Rochlen et al., 2004). Online therapy can include several types of interactions, such as videoconferencing, which allows for synchronic communication, or chat and e-mail, which is asynchronous (Suler, 2000). Some studies highlight the potential role of online therapy in empowering the patient, who has an active role, to be more autonomous in daily life (Levy et al., 2018; Spooner et al., 2019).

The main difference between online and in-presence therapy is the setting. This is characterized by the following elements: (a) reduction of distances; (b) optimization of time; (c) immediate support; (d) reduction of prejudices; (e) confidentiality, derived from the absence of waiting rooms; (f) ease of use through the device, that allows the therapist to better manage documents, and organize and schedule appointments (Saladino, Alegri et al., 2020). A Canadian study (Gibson et al., 2009) specifically examined the views of mental health professionals who work in rural and distant settings toward using digital tools (mostly videoconferencing) for mental health. The study concentrated on the opinions and perceptions about the usefulness and appropriateness of the technology in a clinical setting, such as the perceived benefits and drawbacks, and the obstacles in usage. Data show that 10% of respondents used teleconferencing at least once per week. Most people agreed that videoconferencing is convenient and useful, but they also thought that some services, especially psychotherapy, were less suitable for delivery via videoconferencing than others. Other client groups, such as small children, people exhibiting psychotic symptoms, or uneasiness with digital tools, may perceive videoconferencing as less suited. In addition, 81.8% of the respondents mentioned difficulties in using technological tools due to the lack of access or technical know-how, issues with privacy and confidentiality, as well as the expense of buying applications or specific tools. The authors' conclusion emphasized the importance of providing mental health workers with proper training on how to use technology properly.

Along the same line, this process of technological development of psychotherapy involves art-based therapy. Multimedia art therapy has become a new set of applications that includes technology and its tools with new creative and exploratory potentialities to experience the Self and others. The use of technology complements the classical areas of art therapy (graphic-plastic-painting, theater therapy, music therapy, and dance therapy), enriching creativity and contributing to the conscious and active use of multimedia tools. Over the past three decades, art therapists have integrated computer technology into their clinical work (Gussak & Nyce, 1999; Hallas & Cleaves, 2016; Parker-Bell, 1999; Thong, 2007). The concept of digital art therapy is related to the use of computer-generated content and digital media in the therapy practice. For instance, digital photography (Atkins, 2007), animation (Austin, 2009), collage making (Diggs et al., 2014), and art-making apps (Choe, 2014). Delivering art therapy services and art therapy online, instead, was introduced two decades ago with studies by Collie (1998; and with colleagues: Collie & Čubranić, 1999; Collie & Čubranić, 2002; Collie et al., 2016).

Mostly, multimedia art therapy uses cell phones and free applications as intervention tools to explore psychological issues and intervene early. An example of art therapy mediated by technology is Videotherapy, which refers to activities that use video as an artistic mediator in expressive therapies. In the Videotherapy process, image production becomes the means of fostering knowledge and self-awareness. The camera is the essential element that provides a language through which individuals can express their voice and develop creativity by standing behind and in front of the lens, experiencing different roles and responsibilities during the process. According to the participatory approach, video is used as a tool for individuals and groups to be part of the therapeutic process. The use of digital images is proposed to encourage participants to express themselves creatively, develop self-confidence and self-esteem, manage anxiety and depression, and solve psychological issues through the creative instrument (Brazzale et al., 2018).

Also, online music therapy presents some differences from face-to-face music therapy. For instance, the setting is constituted by the virtual room of the screen and the musical instruments become "domestic" and used only by the client in her/his room, changing perspective and participation from sharing to intimate. The sounds produced by the clients are the only mediators of the sessions. Ahessy (2021) evaluates the experiences and viewpoints of parents with children who suffer from visual impairment, and who participated in online music therapy. Mostly (95%), parents thought their child had a good experience with the telehealth program, 73% saw positive behaviors immediately following the sessions, and 82% said the program was a great family resource that encouraged engagement and bonding. Four themes emerged from the qualitative data through inductive reflexive thematic analysis: positive benefits, interactive family resources, school commitment, and obstacles.

Regarding dance-movement therapy, applications for cell phones and computers are used at educative, rehabilitative, and therapeutic levels. Dance therapy is a method that contributes to the development of individuals using movement as a medium for exploring the Self, body, and expressiveness abilities. An example of an application for dance movement therapy (DMT) is the iPad software called Marking the Moves, created to evaluate and collect data on DMT programs. The authors (Dunphy et al., 2016) create this application in the Framework for Dance Movement Assessment to study the effectiveness of DMT among clients with disabilities. Specifically, two pilot studies were conducted, both on dance programs for special needs kids to ascertain the apps' utility and functionality for DMT practice. Therapists monitor, through the app use, developments in the areas of physical, cognitive, emotional, interpersonal, and personal growth, obtaining positive results in incrementing deficit domains among the children involved and in using and collecting data among therapists. Susana Garcia-Medrano (2021), instead, conducted a study on online DMT, showing nine months of online work, in which participants improve their embodied empathy and bodily awareness.

Specifically, the author develops DMT group sessions, called Spontaneous Movement, with the aim to promote well-being and health and to encourage participants to follow their impulses or needs. A specific playlist characterizes each session. Firstly, participants receive an explanation and are asked to present themselves to the rest of the group. After this participants creatw specific and intense movements to express their emotions and physical tension, and finally, they are asked to share with the group their feelings about the session (García-Medrano & Panhofer, 2020). Some participants can feel nervous due to the camera. However, at the end of the session they are involved in the music and in the feelings of experimenting through their body, and they forget about the camera. The author reports some words used to describe participants' feelings after the session: "harmonised, without anxiety, increased body awareness, enjoyment and warmth, synchrony with the group, vibrant energy, relaxation, energising, novelty, connection with the group, liberating" (Garcia-Medrano, 2021, p. 70). As emerged from the mentioned studies, art-based therapy mediated by technology assists people in feeling less alone, encouraging a sense of belonging. Especially, in group sessions, a sense of synchronisation is established – participants start to feel others through their bodies, despite the distance (Sletvold, 2014), and the medium of the camera becomes part of the experience, like in the Videotherapy framework.

Another example of online art-based therapy is the digital photocollage by Keisari et al. (2021) with participants aged from 78 to 92 years old who adhere through Zoom teleconferencing software. During the online sessions, participants create their own photocollage, representing their personal narratives, through a shared screen in the platform. They focus on the following themes: significant life events and turning points; the continuity between their past and their future, their values and personal bonds; and future concerns and perspectives regarding the end of the life. Sometimes, participants use other methods to contact therapists, such as WhatsApp or email, to share personal information and materials useful for their photocollage, creating a bridge between the online therapeutic setting and their routine, mostly related to the therapeutic office in face-to-face therapy. During each session, a collection of photographs was presented to the participants with the aim of stimulating emotions and thoughts associated with their life experiences (Weiser, 2004). Participants should choose photographs that mostly are related to their personal themes of life and store the collected photos on the screen. During this therapeutic experience, patients were the director of their creative process, while the therapist monitored the activity, helping participants in creating the photocollage with PowerPoint, and sending the completed collage by the end of the session. This computer software facilitates the digital creative process, using all the technical functioning to cut, position, and title the collage, according to the main perception of the participant.

As inferred by the literature research, digital art therapy involves other components of creativity and establishes a connection between the private and social perception of the Self, empowering the principal characteristics of art therapies and reaping the benefits of online therapy. Online instruments integrated into specific therapeutic frameworks could be well-used and translated into effective resources.

Digital Art Therapy and Therapeutic Setting

Art therapists support an individual or group of individuals in promoting self-expression using the artistic medium. This form of psychotherapy employs artistic creation for integrative personality processes and is an effective tool for psychological well-being and in the treatment of clinical syndromes. The art therapy setting involves three elements, which are interdependent and in a constant and reciprocal relationship: the patient who creates the artistic product, the product that encompasses the personal and deep messages of the patient and activates the experiences and feelings of the therapist, and finally the therapist who responds to the patient and the artistic product.

In art therapy, the therapeutic relationship is related to the artistic product, resulting from the client's capacity for thought and imagination. Communication between client and therapist takes place through the exploration of the patient's and therapist's subjective setting and transformation into a common, transactional space. This communication is mediated by multiple elements, for example, empathic and non-empathic responses, transference and countertransference mechanisms, and emotional resonances. In this synergy, a "container" is co-constructed that allows the therapist and patient to release their inner world.

Digital arts allow new forms of expression for art therapy. The characteristics of the experience produced by the virtual world are enriched by the new possibilities for artistic expression and therapeutic possibilities (Malchiodi, 2011).

This mode of expression allows people to generate their own personalized setting in the therapy process. Thus, bypassing possible limitations of some approaches to digital psychotherapy, the implementation of an inclusive therapy of a current and virtual mode of expression can generate a therapeutic environment that can be well adapted to several clinical needs. The application of technology and digital media is included in art therapy and is equally relevant to face-to-face practice as online communication technologies. Extending the range of therapeutic tools that encompass digital arts media could expand the art therapy tools and increase access for specific types of clients. Online art therapy has the potential to broaden the scope of therapy to include new target groups. The development of technological solutions for supporting art therapy practice is an important point of discussion among art therapists, designers, and developers. For instance, art therapists who incorporate the digital aspect into their art-based practice can choose the use of painting apps that are not necessarily suitable for art therapy. For this reason, digital devices suitable for art therapy are needed. This integration needs input from art therapists at the technical stage to implement the process with digital devices and technologies.

An ongoing debate is also derived from the lack of materials and tactile stimuli in online art therapy, an aspect that can impact the client's commitment to the therapy, together with the therapeutic relationship in the online setting. Art therapists support the patient in engaging in creative processes to gain psychological benefit. On the one hand, due to the incorporation of art created within the therapeutic process and the key role of the triangular therapeutic relationship between the therapist, client, and artwork (Haywood & Grant, 2022), art therapy practice could be more difficult to interpret and translate into online situations. On the other hand, art therapy is particularly well suited for online delivery due to the ease of sharing images through online channels and the non-reliance on verbal communication, and because of the handling of symbols, metaphors, and projections, which can be shared regardless of the medium used (Linesch, 2013; McNiff, 1999).

Despite debates about the usefulness of digital technology for art therapy practice and conflicting opinions, practitioners have argued for the possibility of adding the digital aspect to the therapeutic process by reinforcing the growing and permanent role of technology in art therapy (Kapitan et al., 2011; McNiff, 1999). Some studies show a positive impact of online art therapy on the development of the therapeutic alliance (Levy et al., 2018; Spooner et al., 2019).

Also, the digital aspect of therapy could reduce patient resistance to therapy and/or art creation (Cook & Doyle, 2002). The therapist considers the client's home a useful setting to create and establish more immediate trust (Levy et al., 2018). A case study of a female veteran pointed out and confirmed that her progress was greatly facilitated by being able to "host" art therapy in her home (Spooner et al., 2019) more easily.

In the field of art therapy, recent research has focused on the adaptation and connection of the technological environment and the therapeutic environment for general use and specifically for adolescents (Hacmun et al., 2018; Kaimal et al., 2019; King & Kaimal, 2019). Bellani et al. (2011) examined digital media's interactive and sensory aspects and noted differences between the sensory experiences provided by digital technology and more traditional creative materials. According to their results, digital media can be a viable alternative that can contribute to self-expression and therapeutic change.

Digital art therapy can be considered a kind of collage, in which images or selected parts of images are used, cut, and attached to new content, allowing the expression and reconnection of different components of the psyche (Zubala & Hackett, 2020). For instance, in the application for adolescents, the product can accommodate and contain typical teens' feelings, such as anger, guilt, and confusion, and allow the expression of mechanisms of disengagement and dissociation. Chandra (2016) pointed out that daily life moves simultaneously within two primary spaces: interpersonal and digital. Online art therapy could be for adolescents a familiar way to interact with their feelings and experiences, due to the association with their daily virtual communication (Prensky, 2001). Indeed, "Digital natives" are that group of children who already, at preschool age, use digital devices almost like an adult. They tend to use the internet and social networks as the main medium of communication (Casale et al., 2015; Tolokonnikova et al., 2020). Autry and Berge (2011) conducted a survey on adolescents' relationship with technology in their learning environment. The authors show how adolescents are less resistant to sharing their feelings by sending a photo or video than externalizing intimate content through a conversation. However, it can be difficult to establish a therapeutic relationship with adolescents who do not collaborate during art therapy sessions. In this frame, the encounter between the art world and the online world creates a bridge of communication between the therapist, the adolescent, and the digital artwork. The presence of traditional art materials and virtual art materials in the therapy setting allows patients the opportunity to take part in a visual creative experience that utilizes their imagination and enables the symbolic and nonverbal expression of unconscious content (Case & Dalley, 2014). For example, some digital elements allow 360° visual fields, and by tracking the participant's head movements, promote a sense of presence (Slater & Sanchez-Vives, 2016). The sense of presence and modifiable environments in virtual reality enable transformations of the sense of self (Rognini et al., 2013; Slater et al., 2010).

The creative digital medium for art therapy can offer a creative and playful space between fantasy and reality, laying the foundation for a conducive environment for therapy. In addition, the client's separation from the real world generates a sense of privacy and detachment from the outside. This private, dreamlike space embedded in an immersive, inactive environment shows great potential for enhancing the effectiveness of art therapy.

Along the same line, Lucy Shaw described a scientific work on anorexia nervosa and art-based treatment (2020) "'Don't look!' An online art therapy group for adolescents with anorexia nervosa", showing an interesting and introspective experience of patients with their body image through web camera use. This research demonstrated the level of safety that clients can perceive in an online art-based therapy setting. The art therapy process is focused on the relationship between the internal and external world and the ability to mentalize personal perceptions about self and other. Specifically, a group of adolescents aged 12 to 17 years old with a diagnosis of anorexia nervosa was involved in art-based online treatment using Microsoft Teams. The art therapist asked the participants to produce drawings to express their feelings, using several materials they had at home, such as pencils and colors and a sketchbook. Through artworks it was possible to analyze the emotion of self-criticism and feeling of the smallness of some participants, and relate to their sensation of not being able to realize a drawing. Through this activity, participants show the negative perception of their body. In this frame, the therapeutic group becomes a container, contributing in elaborating their feelings. The web camera creates, as the therapy room, an "emotive container". The therapist's office is a physical container, while the therapist is a mental container. Similarly, the camera and the video link for the session can become a virtual container that solves the same function of the physical and mental setting that characterizes in-presence therapy (Case & Dalley, 2014). Indeed, the reflected image on the screen represents for the clients a way to express in a safe contest their emotions, perceiving themselves protected from the unconscious material.

Shaw (2020) underlines in her study the important aspect of the feeling of connectedness, analyzing the art-based online setting. One of the participants reports she felt less nervous at home with her family, preferring to follow the service and to share her feelings online, rather than at the clinic. Another element of reflection concerns the therapist's ability to detach her/himself from the traditional setting, flexibly projecting into the online context. For instance, communication between the facilitators of the group becomes part of the group itself, due to the difficulty in eye contact. So, the process of therapy is more transparent among the members of the group (Coles et al., 2019).

Finally, a further element is the perception of control over what you see and what you want to show. For example, one of the participants started crying after a drawing. The participant decided to turn off the camera so as not to show herself, excluding the others from her pain and pretending the group was not present. Furthermore, sometimes the participants refused to show their drawings in front of the camera and limited themselves to a description, making the therapist feel helpless. However, these mechanisms reveal the importance of the therapeutic process and not of the image represented by the drawing. The description of the artwork creates a direct line with the mental representation of the patient, beyond what it is possible to see.

According to the studies reported, most participants experimented with positive experiences in the online setting. This seems to be true for both young and old participants. Children and adolescents have a good relationship with online and adults and the elderly can be successfully involved in online platforms and software, despite the lack of basic skills.

Moreover, participants create an intimate and positive alliance with the therapist, often forgetting about the camera and showing a feeling of safety and emotional containment. The online setting promotes a sense of control for both participants and therapists due to digital media enabling simultaneous storage of artworks by the client and the therapist. According to Benoit (2020), this evens out the power dynamics between the client and the therapist and gives the client a sense of empowerment by putting them in control of their artwork. Also, the therapist develops greater flexibility in listening to and perceiving the artistic and therapeutic process, not focusing solely on the element of the artworks but observing the process and what it delivers – painting, drawing, composing a song, shooting a video – in the patient.

The artworks represent the way in which the patient interacts with her/himself and with others. In producing the artistic subject, the patient elaborates on personal contents which include her/his past, present, and future with a view to self-representation. The same mechanism is activated in a traditional psychotherapy setting, in which the dialogue and the behaviors acted out in the session describe the patient's interpersonal dynamics.

Through reading these dynamics, the therapist establishes a mental connection with patients, and the online medium does not preclude the creation of this rapport, but rather can often facilitate it.

Art-Based Therapy Process and Application: Some Reflections

Art-based therapy works with specific materials of intervention to support patients with psychological issues, to prevent disorder or malaise, to treat diseases, and in education in the school context. Art-based therapy in-person or mediated by the technological medium stimulates connection between people and with their inner world. The creative process influences the personal perception of our image, evoking the integration of several parts of our identity. Indeed, during the art therapy process, clients re-create and re-build, using tools such as dry, liquid, and malleable materials or/and new media like photographs and videos to recreate their internal and external world (Zubala et al., 2021). Specifically, a narration of one's feelings is performed with the use of a visual language, through lines, shapes, colors, lights, and shadows capable of translating into images, objects, and scenes slices of life belonging to the person who is performing the narration, bringing content to a conscious level, overcoming the barrier of defense mechanisms.

The materials and techniques should be chosen according to the person and according to a specific area of intervention: cognitive, emotional, bodily, or imaginary. Specifically, dry materials (chalk, Indian ink, charcoal, markers, oil pastels, pencils) act on the cognitive area and logic, incrementing the technical skills of participants with physical and intellectual disabilities and in elderly patients. For instance, Datlen and Pandolfi (2020) introduced the use of online art therapy group support among young adults with learning disabilities during COVID-19. The online sessions involved the group working with art therapists using the social media platform WhatsApp to reduce the sense of isolation and loneliness. In this virtual art therapy studio, participants could share artworks realized with pastels, pencils, and other similar materials, using all the forms of communication of the platform, such as text messages, photo, video, vocal messages, emojis, and calling. This mode of communication created a feeling of togetherness among the members, maintaining unity and holding the group, and reducing negative feelings related to isolation.

Also, art-based therapy is useful among elderly patients, such as in preventing cognitive decline or dementia. Indeed, creative artwork engages attention and cognition and improves mood and positive feelings. As shown by Lee et al. (2019), two organized elements of art therapy are the actual making and the analysis of artworks. According to the authors' results among a sample of participants with mild cognitive impairment, cognitive function on neuropsychological tests revealed notable memory domain improvements maintained after nine months of art therapy, together with visuospatial ability, attention, working memory, and executive function.

Liquid materials (acrylics, tempera, watercolors), instead, activate the emotional area and moods to decrease anxious and depressive symptoms, post-traumatic disorder, and improve quality of life in patients with the illness. Along this line, Zhang et al. (2021) conducted a study on a group of patients with mild and moderate depression, using Chinese flower and bird painting art therapy intervention, showing a decline in symptoms. This art therapy intervention acts on emotions related to depression and on the pessimistic mental state of patients. Indeed, participants were asked to select a painting object, such as colorful flowers, and reproduce it independently under the guidance of the therapist. Other studies (Bosman et al., 2020) underlying the use of art-based therapy among people with depression and anxiety related to cancer. For instance, Geue et al. (2013) described an intervention divided into three stages: learning to draw with an artist's help, self-guided watercolor painting, and making a personal book to convey emotions. The patients decide how to organize and structure their artwork elaborating on the emotional contents related to cancer.

Finally, sculptural materials act on the body area for patients with psychological issues related to their body image, such as anorexia nervosa. Johnson (2021) works with a group of women with eating disorders to investigate efficacy in mindfulness experience through art therapy. During the art therapy sessions, participants created art on river rocks with the aim to express the feelings associated with their bodies. Participants were involved also in a group sculptural process using their art rocks. After the period of the creative process, participants increase their experience of mindfulness and the level of emotional awareness related to their disorder.

Art therapy mediated by technology and new media materials (collages, photographs, videos) stimulate the imagination, fantasy, projections, and dreams, overcoming unconscious defenses and could be applied to a broad type of clients, especially children and adolescents in the educational context (Saladino et al., 2021).

The product of the art therapy process is expressions and containers of meanings, relational and personal contents, states of mind, reorganized thoughts, regulated emotions, and modulated conflicts, as a mirror of internal and external experiences.

Regarding the influence of digital and technological development, due to the spread of social networks, there is an easy and constant production and sharing of photos, videos, and multimedia documents. Photos and video could be used in art therapy as expressive mediators of knowledge and awareness (Despenser, 2006). Photographs in art therapy are used for the evocation of feelings, thoughts, and memories and vary according to who is translating them, on a subconscious level, and the meaning each person projects into them. Photographs or images (postcards, newspaper, magazine pages, and posters) communicate something about the person and the attributed meaning that motivated their preservation, as reported in the study on photocollage with elderly patients (Keisari et al., 2021) described in this chapter (see the section "Online Therapy, Art-Based Therapy, and Technology").

Self-portraits reflect the desirable perception of others. From self-portraits emerge beliefs, values, personal judgments, self-esteem, and self-evaluation. In addition, it is possible to perceive the hidden part of the Self. Further art therapy techniques make use of multimedia tools such as video, photomontage, storytelling, and digital comics, which explore interpersonal and intrapersonal relationships, developing emotional regulation, creativity, and expressive skills.

For instance, in the participatory video the camera is used to represent people's thoughts, develop creativity, and experiment with different roles. The participatory practice provides a tool for growth, individually and in groups, as participants are encouraged to express themselves creatively, control anxiety, develop self-esteem and self-confidence, counter depression, and gain critical awareness (Cohen et al., 2015).

In comics and digital photo storytelling or superhero therapy, individuals are guided to the construction of a comic book using images and the creation of evocative settings. Storytelling that uses images with the accompaniment of written words is simple, immediate, and effective and, at the same time, can transfer deep content and address sensitive issues (Robin & Pierson, 2005).

In digital storytelling, the process of storytelling used also in Therapeutic Filmmaking (see Chapter 3) is carried out with digital tools that allow the telling of stories with the combination of different elements, such as text, images, audio, and video (Saladino, Sabatino et al., 2020).

The audiovisual expressive languages can be applied for education, rehabilitation, and promotion of individual well-being. The goal of multimedia art therapy is to foster the process of self-definition: photography and video act as a mirror and are used to stimulate reflection and the development of a stable sense of self and one's role in relational contexts such as group, work, and family. A further goal concerns the development of self-determination and the development of the ability to take initiative, analytical skills, observation, evaluation, drive to action, and responsibility.

From these assumptions, it emerges that these tools can be used for several contexts, such as cyberbullying, gender-based violence, school dropout, depression, disabilities, grief processing, self-esteem, post-traumatic stress disorder, anxiety and panic attacks, substance and behavioral addiction, autism spectrum disorder, eating disorders, and emotional psychoeducation.

As described, artworks empower the therapeutic setting, amplifying the emotional states, reflections, dialogues, and perceptions that are established and enrich the therapeutic relationship.

References

Ahessy, B. (2021). "Boom boom in the Zoom Zoom room": Online music therapy with children and adolescents with visual impairment. *British Journal of Visual Impairment*, 41(1), 143–161. doi:10.1177/02646196211029342.

Appleton, V. (2001). Avenues of hope: Art therapy and the resolution of trauma. *Art Therapy*, 18(1), 6–13. doi:10.1080/07421656.2001.10129454.

Atkins, M. (2007). Using digital photography to record clients' art work. *International Journal of Art Therapy*, 12(2), 79–87. doi:10.1080/17454830701538410.

Austin, B. D. (2009). Renewing the debate: Digital technology in art therapy and the creative process. *Art Therapy*, 26(2), 83–85. doi:10.1080/07421656.2009.10129745.

Autry, A. J., & Berge, Z. (2011). Digital natives and digital immigrants: Getting to know each other. *Industrial and Commercial Training*, 43(7), 460–466. doi:10.1108/00197851111171890.

Bailey, K. (2015). Art therapy and developmental disabilities. In D. E. Gussak & M. L. Rosal (Eds.), *The Wiley handbook of art therapy* (pp. 317–328). Wiley. doi:10.1002/9781118306543.ch31.

Bellani, M., Fornasari, L., Chittaro, L., & Brambilla, P. (2011). Virtual reality in autism: State of the art. *Epidemiology and Psychiatric Sciences.*, 20(3), 235–238. doi:10.1017/s2045796011000448.

Benenzon, R. O. (2007). The Benenzon model. *Nordic Journal of Music Therapy*, 16 (2), 148–159. doi:10.1080/08098130709478185.

Benoit, S. (2020). Online art therapy. News briefing Summer 2020, British Association of Art Therapists.

Blonder, L. X. (1999). The emotional brain: The mysterious underpinnings of emotional life. *The Quarterly Review of Biology*, 74(4), 505–505. doi:10.1086/394219.

Bloom, J. W. (1998). The ethical practice of web counseling. *British Journal of Guidance & Counselling*, 26(1), 53–59. doi:10.1080/03069889808253838.

Bosman, J. T., Bood, Z. M., Scherer-Rath, M., Dörr, H., Christophe, N., Sprangers, M. A., & Van Laarhoven, H. W. (2020). The effects of art therapy on anxiety, depression, and quality of life in adults with cancer: A systematic literature review. *Supportive Care in Cancer*, 29(5), 2289–2298. doi:10.1007/s00520-020-05869-0.

Brazzale, R., Maddalena, Y., Cozzi, A., & Brazzale, L. (2018). New pathways of intervention for adolescents at clinical high risk of psychosis: Improving meta-representation skills and strengthening identity with video-confrontation techniques. *Adolescent Psychiatry*, 8(2), 121–132. doi:10.2174/2210676608666180605092604.

Brosius, C., & Polit, K. M. (2020). *Ritual, heritage and identity: The politics of culture and performance in a globalised world*. Taylor & Francis.

Casale, S., Fiovaranti, G., & Caplan, S. (2015). Online disinhibition. *Journal of Media Psychology*, 27(4), 170–177. doi:10.1027/1864-1105/a000136.

Case, C., & Dalley, T. (2014). *The handbook of art therapy*. Routledge.

Chandra, A. (2016). Social networking sites and digital identity: The utility of provider-adolescent communication. *The Brown University Child and Adolescent Behavior Letter*, 32(3), 1–7. doi:10.1002/cbl.30107.

Choe, S. N. (2014). An exploration of the qualities and features of art apps for art therapy. *The Arts in Psychotherapy*, 41(2), 145–154. doi:10.1016/j.aip.2014.01.002.

Cohen, J. L., Johnson, J. L., & Orr, P. (2015). *Video and filmmaking as psychotherapy: Research and practice*. Routledge.

Coles, A., Harrison, F., & Todd, S. (2019). Flexing the frame: Therapist experiences of Museum-based group art psychotherapy for adults with complex mental health difficulties. *International Journal of Art Therapy*, 24(2), 56–67. doi:10.1080/17454832.2018.1564346.

Collie, K. (1998). *Art therapy online: A participatory action study of distance counselling issues*. A thesis submitted in partial fulfillment of the requirements for the degree of Master of Arts in the Faculty of Graduate Studies, Department of Counselling Psychology. University of British Columbia.

Collie, K., & Čubranić, D. (1999). An art therapy solution to a telehealth problem. *Art Therapy*, 16(4), 186–193. doi:10.1080/07421656.1999.10129481.

Collie, K., & Čubranić, D. (2002). Computer-supported distance art therapy: A focus on traumatic illness. *Journal of Technology in Human Services*, 20(1), 155–171. doi:10.1300/j017v20n01_12.

Collie, K., Prins Hankinson, S., Norton, M., Dunlop, C., Mooney, M., Miller, G., & Giese-Davis, J. (2016). Online art therapy groups for young adults with cancer. *Arts & Health*, 9(1), 1–13. doi:10.1080/17533015.2015.1121882.

Cook, J. E., & Doyle, C. (2002). Working alliance in online therapy as compared to face-to-face therapy: Preliminary results. *CyberPsychology & Behavior*, 5(2), 95–105. doi:10.1089/109493102753770480.

Damasio, A. R. (1995). On some functions of the human prefrontal cortex. *Annals of the New York Academy of Sciences*, 769(1), 241–252. doi:10.1111/j.1749-6632.1995.tb38142.x.

Datlen, G. W., & Pandolfi, C. (2020). Developing an online art therapy group for learning disabled young adults using WhatsApp. *International Journal of Art Therapy*, 25(4), 192–201. doi:10.1080/17454832.2020.1845758.

Despenser, S. (2006). Photographs and therapy: The quest for meaning, *Psychodynamic Practice*, 12(1), 90–97. doi:10.1080/14753630500307214.

Diggs, L. A., Lubas, M., & De Leo, G. (2014). Use of technology and software applications for therapeutic collage making. *International Journal of Art Therapy*, 20(1), 2–13. doi:10.1080/17454832.2014.961493.

Dilawari, K., & Tripathi, N. (2014). Strategies to improvise teacher tasking for children suffering from attention deficit hyperactive disorder (ADHD). *International Journal on Disability and Human Development*, 13(1), 19–24. doi:10.1515/ijdhd-2013-0016.

Dunphy, K., Mullane, S., & Allen, L. (2016). Developing an iPad app for assessment in dance movement therapy. *The Arts in Psychotherapy*, 51, 54–62. doi:10.1016/j.aip.2016.09.001.

Freud, S. (1920). *A general introduction to psychoanalysis*. Horace Liveright. doi:10.1037/10667-000https://doi.org/10.1037/10667-000.

Garcia-Medrano, S. (2021). Screen-bridges: Dance movement therapy in online contexts. *Body, Movement and Dance in Psychotherapy*, 16(1), 64–72. doi:10.1080/17432979.2021.1883741.

García-Medrano, S., & Panhofer, H. (2020). Improving migrant well-being: Spontaneous movement as a way to increase the creativity, spontaneity and welfare of migrants in Glasgow. *Body, Movement and Dance in Psychotherapy*, 15(3), 189–203. doi:10.1080/17432979.2020.1767208.

Geue, K., Richter, R., Buttstädt, M., Brähler, E., & Singer, S. (2013). An art therapy intervention for cancer patients in the ambulant aftercare – results from a non-randomised controlled study. *European Journal of Cancer Care*, 22(3), 345–352. doi:10.1111/ecc.12037.

Gibson, K., Simms, D., O'Donnell, S., & Molyneaux, H. (2009). *Clinicians' attitudes toward the use of information and communication technologies for mental health services in remote and rural areas*. National Research Council Institute for Information Technology. Paper presented at the Paper presented at the Canadian Society of Telehealth Conference, Vancouver, October 3–6.

Gussak, D. E., & Nyce, J. M. (1999). To bridge art therapy and computer technology: The visual toolbox. *Art Therapy*, 16(4), 194–196. doi:10.1080/07421656.1999.10129478.

Hacmun, I., Regev, D., & Salomon, R. (2018). The principles of art therapy in virtual reality. *Frontiers in Psychology*, 9. doi:10.3389/fpsyg.2018.02082.

Hallas, P., & Cleaves, L. (2016). "It's not all fun": Introducing digital technology to meet the emotional and mental health needs of adults with learning disabilities. *International Journal of Art Therapy*, 22(2), 73–83. doi:10.1080/17454832.2016.1260038.

Haywood, S., & Grant, B. (2022). Reimagining art therapy for the digitally-mediated world: A hexagonal relationship. *International Journal of Art Therapy*, 27(3), 143–150. doi:10.1080/17454832.2022.2084124.

Johnson, A. A. (2021). *A mixed methods study of eco-art therapy and mindfulness in women with eating disorders*. A thesis submitted in partial fulfillment of the requirement for the Master of Arts in Art Therapy degree.

Jung, C. G. (1967). *The spirit of man in art and literature* (R. F. C. Hull, Trans.; 1st ed.). Routledge.

Kaimal, G., Carroll-Haskins, K., Berberian, M., Dougherty, A., Carlton, N., & Ramakrishnan, A. (2019). Virtual reality in art therapy: A pilot qualitative study of the novel medium and implications for practice. *Art Therapy*, 37(1), 16–24. doi:10.1080/07421656.2019.1659662.

Kapitan, L., Litell, M., & Torres, A. (2011). Creative art therapy in a community's participatory research and social transformation. *Art Therapy*, 28(2), 64–73. doi:10.1080/07421656.2011.578238.

Kawano, T., & Chang, M. (2022). Applying critical consciousness to dance/movement therapy pedagogy and the politics of the body. *Social Justice in Dance/Movement Therapy*, 97–118. doi:10.1007/978-3-031-19451-1_7.

Keisari, S., Piol, S., Elkarif, T., Mola, G., & Testoni, I. (2021). Crafting life stories in Photocollage: An online creative art-based intervention for older adults. *Behavioral Sciences*, 12(1), 1. doi:10.3390/bs12010001.

King, J. L., & Kaimal, G. (2019). Approaches to research in art therapy using imaging technologies. *Frontiers in Human Neuroscience*, 13. doi:10.3389/fnhum.2019.00159.

Knol, A. S., Huiskes, M., Koole, T., Meganck, R., Loeys, T., & Desmet, M. (2020). Reformulating and mirroring in psychotherapy: A conversation analytic perspective. *Frontiers in Psychology*, 11, 1–12. doi:10.3389/fpsyg.2020.00318.

Lauffenburger, S. K. (2020). "Something more": The unique features of dance movement therapy/psychotherapy. *American Journal of Dance Therapy*, 42(1), 16–32.
doi:10.1007/s10465-020-09321-y.

Lee, R., Wong, J., Lit Shoon, W., Gandhi, M., Lei, F., … Mahendran, R. (2019). Art
therapy for the prevention of cognitive decline. *The Arts in Psychotherapy*, 64, 20–
25. doi:10.1016/j.aip.2018.12.003.

Leijssen, M. (2006). Validation of the body in psychotherapy. *Journal of Humanistic
Psychology*, 46(2), 126–146. doi:10.1177/0022167805283782.

Levy, C. E., Spooner, H., Lee, J. B., Sonke, J., Myers, K., & Snow, E. (2018). Tele-
health-based creative arts therapy: Transforming mental health and rehabilitation
care for rural veterans. *The Arts in Psychotherapy*, 57, 20–26. doi:10.1016/j.
aip.2017.08.010.

Linesch, D. G. (2013). *Art therapy with families in crisis: Overcoming resistance
through nonverbal expression*. Routledge.

Malchiodi, C. A. (2011). *Handbook of art therapy* (2nd ed.). Guilford Press.

McNiff, S. (1999). The virtual art therapy studio. *Art Therapy*, 16(4), 197–200.
doi:10.1080/07421656.1999.10129484.

Parker-Bell, B. (1999). Embracing a future with computers and art therapy. *International Journal of Art Therapy*, 16(4), 180–185. doi:10.1080/07421656.1999.10129482.

Pèrez-Eizaguirre, M., & Vergara-Moragues, E. (2021). Music therapy interventions in
palliative care: A systematic review. *Journal of Palliative Care*, 36(3), 194–205.
doi:10.1177/0825859720957803.

Prensky, M. (2001). Digital natives, digital immigrants Part 1. *On the Horizon*, 9(5), 1–
6. doi:10.1108/10748120110424816.

Przybylski, A. K., Murayama, K., DeHaan, C. R., & Gladwell, V. (2013). Motiva-
tional, emotional, and behavioral correlates of fear of missing out. *Computers in
Human Behavior*, 29(4), 1841–1848. doi:10.1016/j.chb.2013.02.014.

Robin, B., & Pierson, M. (2005). A multilevel approach to using digital storytelling in
the classroom. In C. Crawford, R. Carlsen, I. Gibson, K. McFerrin, J. Price, R.
Weber & D. Willis (Eds.), *Proceedings of SITE 2005 – Society for Information
Technology & Teacher Education International Conference* (pp. 708–716). Association for the Advancement of Computing in Education (AACE). www.learntechlib.
org/primary/p/19091/.

Rochlen, A. B., Zack, J. S., & Speyer, C. (2004). Online therapy: Review of relevant
definitions, debates, and current empirical support. *Journal of Clinical Psychology*,
60(3), 269–283. doi:10.1002/jclp.10263.

Rognini, G., Sengül, A., Aspell, J. E., Salomon, R., Bleuler, H., & Blanke, O. (2013).
Visuo-tactile integration and body ownership during self-generated action. *European Journal of Neuroscience*, 37(7), 1120–1129. doi:10.1111/ejn.12128.

Saladino, V., Algeri, D., & Auriemma, V. (2020). The psychological and social impact
of COVID-19: New perspectives of well-being. *Frontiers in Psychology*, 11, 1–6.
doi:10.3389/fpsyg.2020.577684.

Saladino, V., Sabatino, A. C., Iannaccone, C., Giovanna Pastorino, G. M., & Verrastro, V. (2020). Filmmaking and video as therapeutic tools: Case studies on autism
spectrum disorder. *The Arts in Psychotherapy*, 71, 101714. doi:10.1016/j.
aip.2020.101714.

Saladino, V., Sabatino, A. C., & Sola, C. M. (2021). Therapeutic Filmmaking and
autistic spectrum disorder: A case study. *Ricerche Di Pedagogia E Didattica:*

Journal of Theories and Research in Education, 16(1), 97–103. doi:10.6092/issn.1970-2221/10704.

Schouten, K. A., De Niet, G. J., Knipscheer, J. W., Kleber, R. J., & Hutschemaekers, G. J. (2014). The effectiveness of art therapy in the treatment of traumatized adults. *Trauma, Violence, & Abuse*, 16(2), 220–228. doi:10.1177/1524838014555032.

Shaw, L. (2020). "Don't look!" an online art therapy group for adolescents with anorexia nervosa. *International Journal of Art Therapy*, 25(4), 211–217. doi:10.1080/17454832.2020.1845757.

Slater, M., & Sanchez-Vives, M. V. (2016). Enhancing our lives with immersive virtual reality. *Frontiers in Robotics and AI*, 3, 1–47. doi:10.3389/frobt.2016.00074.

Slater, M., Spanlang, B., Sanchez-Vives, M. V., & Blanke, O. (2010). First person experience of body transfer in virtual reality. *PLoS ONE*, 5(5), e10564. doi:10.1371/journal.pone.0010564.

Sletvold, J. (2014). Embodied empathy in psychotherapy: Demonstrated in supervision. *Body, Movement and Dance in Psychotherapy*, 10(2), 82–93. doi:10.1080/17432979.2014.971873.

Spooner, H., Lee, J. B., Langston, D. G., Sonke, J., Myers, K. J., & Levy, C. E. (2019). Using distance technology to deliver the creative arts therapies to veterans: Case studies in art, dance/movement and music therapy. *The Arts in Psychotherapy*, 62, 12–18. doi:10.1016/j.aip.2018.11.012.

Stefana, A. (2019). Revisiting Marion Milner's work on creativity and art. *The International Journal of Psychoanalysis*, 100(1), 128–147. doi:10.1080/00207578.2018.1533376.

Stevenson, M., & Orr, K. (2013). Art therapy: Stimulating non-verbal communication. *Nursing and Residential Care*, 15(6), 443–445. doi:10.12968/nrec.2013.15.6.443.

Suler, J. R. (2000). Psychotherapy in cyberspace: A 5-dimensional model of online and computer-mediated psychotherapy. *CyberPsychology & Behavior*, 3(2), 151–159. doi:10.1089/109493100315996.

Thong, S. A. (2007). Redefining the tools of art therapy. *International Journal of Art Therapy*, 24(2), 52–58. doi:10.1080/07421656.2007.10129583.

Tolokonnikova, A., Dunas, D., & Kulchitskaya, D. (2020). Social media and adolescents: Possibilities for satisfying psychological needs. Results of in-depth interviews with Russian pupils and university students. *World of Media: Journal of Russian Media and Journalism Studies*, 1(4), 36–55. doi:10.30547/worldofmedia.4.2020.2.

Vygotskij, L. S. (2004). Imagination and creativity in childhood. *Journal of Russian & East European Psychology*, 42(1), 7–97. doi:10.1080/10610405.2004.11059210.

Weir, F. (1987). *The role of symbolic expression in its relation to art therapy: A Kleinian approach. Images of art therapy (psychology revivals)*. Routledge.

Weiser, J. (2004). Phototherapy techniques in counselling and therapy – Using ordinary snapshots and photo-interactions to help clients heal their lives. *Canadian Art Therapy Association Journal*, 17(2), 23–53. doi:10.1080/08322473.2004.11432263.

Werman, D. S. (1979). Silvano Arieti: Creativity: The magic synthesis. *Art Journal*, 38 (3), 224. doi:10.1080/00043249.1979.10793508.

Winnicott, D. W. (1971). *Playing and reality*. Penguin Books.

Wolf, R. (1977). Elinor Ulman and Penny Dachinger (eds.), *Art Therapy in Theory and Practice. Art Journal*, 37(2), 188–190. doi:10.1080/00043249.1978.10793416.

Zhang, B., Chen, J., Huang, X., & Xu, W. (2021). Chinese flower and bird painting: A new form of art therapy for depression. *Sage Open*, 11(2), 215824402110021. doi:10.1177/21582440211002186.

Zubala, A., & Hackett, S. (2020). Online art therapy practice and client safety: A UK-wide survey in times of COVID-19. *International Journal of Art Therapy*, 25(4), 161–171. doi:10.1080/17454832.2020.1845221.

Zubala, A., Kennell, N., & Hackett, S. (2021). Art therapy in the digital world: An integrative review of current practice and future directions. *Frontiers in Psychology*, 12, 1–20. doi:10.3389/fpsyg.2021.600070.

Chapter 5

Strategic Psychotherapy and Audiovisual Language

Valeria Saladino

Strategic Approach and the Therapeutic Relationship

The origins of strategy therapy (ST) are conventionally placed in the 1950s. However, this approach has undergone a succession of definitions over time. Some of the main elements of strategic psychotherapy derived from the Zen philosophy and Sophist theory and were later reformulated in the perspectives of constructivism (Petruccelli & Verrastro, 2012). Indeed, ST includes a range of interventions inspired by the systemic approach and studies the interactions of individuals in their relationship with themselves, others, and the environment (D'Amario et al., 2015). According to the strategic school, psychotherapists actively act on the patients' cognition, using communication and prescriptions, and promoting alternative behaviors. ST focuses on the resolution of symptoms and problems related to specific psychological issues exhibited by the patient. According to this definition the term "strategic" involves the use of action plans called "strategies", focused and tailored to patients' needs. In this line, these strategies of interventions are not applicable to all patients with the same problem or disorder but are centered on the specificity of the individual (Nardone & Watzlawick, 2005). ST considers the uniqueness of the individual suffering and strengthens the resources and skills of the client. Indeed, the patient is considered a client who requires service and actively participates in the therapeutic process. According to this construct the identity of the patient is not exhausted in the symptoms shown in therapy. On the other hand, the psychotherapist creates the setting to promote the process of change (Secci, 2005).

Strategic psychotherapy derived from the scientific contribution of the ethnologist Gregory Bateson, the engineer John H. Weakland, and the scholar of communication Jay Douglas Haley. They created a research group, the Palo Alto School in California, a foundation for future scientific and clinical developments in the strategic approach. The Palo Alto School led to the constitution of the Mental Research Institute and the Brief Therapy Center, research centers for the study of communication in psychotherapy (Watzlawick & Weakland, 1976). Bateson and other important exponents of these

DOI: 10.4324/9781003340508-6

studies, focused on the influence of paradox in interpersonal relationships, reconsidering communication from an interdisciplinary perspective. Specifically, cybernetics played a key role in this new conception of human communication, including concepts such as "system", "homeostasis", and "feedback" (Hoffmeyer, 2008). The integration of these constructs into the study of human communication represented "a Copernican revolution in the field of psychology" (Secci, 2005, pp. 4–5). Indeed, from the general systems theory, Bateson redefines scientific causality by recognizing the mutual influence between the observer and the observed subject (Bateson, 1972). The construction of reality and its interpretation are mediated and influenced by the relationship between the individuals and their system. Bateson argues that all behavior has communicative value (Bateson, 1972). This principle is recognized and applied by Haley, who studied schizophrenia as an example of paradoxical communication, shifting his focus from the patient's intrapsychic variable to the study of their relational dynamics within the family system (Haley, 1977; Hoffman, 1981). This approach emphasizes the communicative value of the symptoms, instead of diagnostic categorization and patient labeling (Haley, 1977; Haley & Hoffman, 1967).

In this framework, the psychotherapist aims to show the function of the problematic behavior in the family system, to guide the patients in changing their familial interactions, facilitating the transition from a vicious to a virtuous cycle (Minuchin et al., 2006). Thus, the therapy should involve not only the patient, who is defined as the "designated patient" and the exclusive protagonist, but the entire family system. Moreover, according to Haley, schizophrenia is the product of dysfunctional communication and might be treated with the use of communication (Sechehaye, 1951).

The Palo Alto group was joined by the psychiatrist Donald deAvila Jackson who has developed a research project on family homeostasis. The psychiatrist defines the family as the primary context of learning and the major source of pathology. Indeed, the family maintains the dysfunctional homeostasis of its system by protecting it from change (Minuchin et al., 2006). Strategic psychotherapy aims to modify the learned patterns in the system (family and otherwise), that maintain dysfunctional behavior and pathology. This interpretation considers psychological issues in the relationship with the systemic interaction of individuals and their environmental and interpersonal context, differentiating from psychiatry and psychoanalysis, which consider mental distress mostly as a product of the intrapsychic world (Freud, 1942; Eagle, 2011; Jung & Hinkle, 1916; Jung et al., 1960). From such reflections and from the encounter with Milton Hyland Erickson (1964; Erickson & Rossi, 1980a), one of the most important exponents of hypnosis, the Palo Alto group enriched its knowledge by studying the therapist's hypnotic techniques and learning the fundamentals that constitute the strategic approach: (a) using a non-pathologizing theoretical-application model; (b) underlying the enhancement of the patient's strengths; (c) accommodating the communication content and the patient's modes of expression; (d) activating the patient by behavioral prescription, promoting a systematic work outside the psychotherapeutic setting; (e) designing personalized action plans tailored to the patient's peculiarities (Secci, 2005). Erickson also illustrated the strategic approach in his work, "Special techniques of brief hypnotherapy" in 1954, focusing on the patient's symptoms and the use of hypnotic communication in the therapeutic process.

Through the analysis of Erickson's techniques, Bateson notes the similarities between the influence produced by hypnotic communication and the schizophrenic influence of the mother figure, formulating the theory of the "double bind". This theory is based on the analysis of the conflict between the content of the communication (what the individual says) and the relationship expressed through the communication (nonverbal and behavioral attitude of the individual in the communication). An example could be a mother who asks their children for a hug, maintaining a rigid posture in the meanwhile, generating confusion in the request. Mostly, this incongruence may lead to psychopathologies and interpersonal distress in adulthood (Bateson et al., 1956).

Along the same line, a second Palo Alto group was formed with the collaboration of Paul Watzlawick, who formalized the strategic approach and its techniques in *Pragmatics of Human Communication: A Study of Interactional Patterns, Pathologies, and Paradoxes* (Watzlawick et al., 1967). In his work, Watzlawick enunciates the axioms of communication, a construct that constitutes therapeutic dialogue used in the ST.

According to the author, psychotherapy is an effective and efficient pathway, focused on problem understanding and aimed at the patient's psychological well-being. The therapeutic relationship guides patients in new reality interpretation to decrease the level of distress associated with symptoms. The second Palo Alto group is characterized by a constructivist conception of reality, derived from the belief in the interrelationship between humans and the environment (D'Amario et al., 2015). This conception leads the clinical approach to disregard the so-called "objective" interpretation of reality and to favor a "subjective" view (Bateson, 1972; Bateson et al., 1956; Nardone & Watzlawick, 2005). Indeed, Watzlawick distinguishes two types of reality: a first-order reality, which constitutes the physical one; and a second-order reality, derived from a subjective interpretation. In first-order reality, individuals interpret a situation by considering the (believed and assumed as) objective elements; while in second-order reality, the meaning with which individuals endow situations and elements derives from personal understandings. Psychological distress or discomfort is generated by a conflict between these two realities, which leads the person to live in an oscillation between the first and second order (Watzlawick, 1977).

Moreover, first-order reality can be interpreted according to the observer's perspective. The glass of water which could be half full or half empty is a well-known example of this mechanism. According to first-order reality, the object remains the same; while, in second-order reality, the observed object may have two identities or controversial meanings. The strategic approach also focuses on mental attributions and not on underlying motivations, aspects investigated by psychoanalysis instead. Thus, "how" and not "why" is important (Verrastro, 2004). Answering this question and investigating the functioning of the process leads to a solution. This conception goes against a deterministic and dualistic epistemology, based on knowledge of the cause as the main form of solution to the problem and the right/wrong dichotomy in the interpretation of psychopathology (Nardone & Watzlawick, 2005). The Palo Alto School experiments with new forms of the therapeutic relationship, breaking the rigidity provided by deterministic models and considering a circular perspective (Secci, 2005). Strategic psychotherapy is a creative approach, based on new learnings in a shared and empathetic setting (Petruccelli & Verrastro, 2012). From a systemic perspective, strategic psychotherapy aims to replace the patient's dysfunctional perception of reality with a more functional one, focusing on the present rather than on the past (Watzlawick, 1984; Watzlawick et al., 1974). Moreover, the therapeutic process involves a progressive internalization of positive relationships and related emotions (Watson et al., 2011).

Therapeutic communication stimulates confrontation with social dynamics, leading patients to co-define their identity mutuality with others (Verrastro, 2004). Strategic psychotherapy restructures the patient's worldview, provides corrective emotional experiences, uses symptoms and psychological resistance in a positive manner, and stimulates insights. All these elements change the individual's perceptual-reactive system, modifying the patterns of action and reaction that encompass the person in rigid and dysfunctional behaviors (Petruccelli & Verrastro, 2012).

Strategic psychotherapy is an interactive game between two actors, the patient and the therapist, in which the relationships between the observed system and the observing system play a key role. In this process of change, the therapist follows a circle that guides her or him from the first clinical assessment of the question. Therapy performs the function of accepting a request for help that is not always clear and explicit by the patient. The psychotherapist deciphers not only the content of the question but more importantly the ways in which the person, family, or couple perceives and symbolizes reality (McGee et al., 2005). The symbolization represents the mode through which the patient expresses and ascribes a different meaning to a situation, person, or discomfort experienced.

During the first analysis of the request of the patient, the therapist explains and defines the clinical setting to avoid emotional collusion with the patient. This represents the first step in building the therapeutic alliance with the patient, also called "rapport". According to Richard Bandler and John Grinder (1975a), rapport is defined by the degree of agreement between two individuals and their ability to reciprocally mirror. The therapeutic relationship consists of four stages: (a) "matching", in which the therapist traces the verbal, nonverbal, and para-verbal communicative modes, through a selection of expressions presented by the patient in session; (b) "pacing", in which the therapist replays the patient's movements, also defined as matching in movement; (c) "recast", that represents the sum of the previous two phases, in which a therapist mirrors the patient's behavior, showing closeness and understanding; (d) "guidance", in which the therapist checks the therapeutic rapport, by operating practice trials in the session that consist of slightly changing her/his communication patterns to evaluate if the patient mirrors her/his behavior (Bandler & Grinder, 1975a).

The focus of the strategic therapist is based on four elements:

1   interaction of the individuals with themselves, others, and the environment;
2   functioning of the problem within its system;
3   study of the strategies of the individual to solve the problem;
4   application of useful techniques to effectively modify the problematic situation.

From these elements, the psychotherapeutic intervention will lead to a reduction in symptoms and a progressive change in the perception of the patient. The patients will change the rigidity of their perceptual-reactive system toward greater flexibility in interpreting the situations and the behaviors. This change in perspective also affects their ability to solve the problem and produces increased self-esteem and self-efficacy. The therapeutic process involves concrete actions and facilitates positive experiences that change patients' perception of reality in daily life (Goffman, 1959; Watzlawick et al., 1974).

Strategic psychotherapy is structured according to possible, concrete, and verifiable goals (Bandler & Grinder, 1975a; Petruccelli & Verrastro, 2012), focused on decreasing the distress related to the problem (Chevalier, 1995; De Shazer et al., 1986). An example that explains this concept is the anecdote of the drunk who looks for lost keys in unlikely places. This anecdote illustrates how what makes a situation problematic is not the event, but the reaction or solution enacted. In fact, losing keys is an entirely normal and common occurrence but the fact that the person looks for the keys under a lamppost or in a non-usual place makes the behavior "pathological" and therefore dysfunctional, generating malaise. From this anecdote, it is possible to infer that in strategic psychotherapy, although the techniques are well defined, it is not entirely possible to separate the assessing of the problem from the intervention, since the procedures acted during the first phase of the therapy could be interpreted as part of the intervention. Therefore, the process and procedures that characterize the strategic approach define a single system of clinical practice and point to a fundamental principle: it is the therapy that should adapt to the patient and not the patient to the therapy (Nardone & Watzlawick, 2005).

Self-Representation and Audiovisual Medium

Strategic psychotherapy is based on the concept of representation, a term defined as "making present" or "exposing before the eyes". According to the language of visual culture studies mental representation or images (Belting, 2005; Mitchell, 2005) consists of evoking an object, person, or entity that is not present, including an intermediary or medium, whose iconic content is recognized as similar (Bruner et al., 1956; Verrastro, 2008). According to this conception, memory assumes an important role in mental representation. Indeed, even in the absence of the memory image of the represented subject, the representation can still exist, unintentionally or intentionally reactivated, and constructed in the individual's mind. In psychotherapy, words become emotional catalysts that, through the evocative power of sounds and images, create or recall mental representations. Images are not definitive and satisfying constructs, but open cognitive projects, structured through images and visions, linked together by mental associations. Mental images and words influence each other creating the individual's subjective reality (MacLuhan, 1964; Saladino & Ricapito, 2020).

Strategic psychotherapy uses a peculiar language, called strategic dialogue, such as metaphors, aphorisms, and paradoxes characterized by using mental representation as an agent of reflection and change. For instance, metaphor, literally "transposition", is a rhetorical figure that describes the meaning of a word according to implicit or explicit similarity and not based on its proper or literal characteristics. Metaphors make it easier to understand abstract concepts or situations and evoke feelings and emotions. Paradox, instead, emphasizes an absurdity and refuting, with the force of the figural and cognitive shock, the logic of a linear and deductive discourse, promoting reflection by the interlocutor, who will be led to question her or his beliefs.

The strategic dialogue is based on a sharing – implicit or explicit – of a mental representation between sender and receiver or therapist and patient. This mental representation within the therapeutic context is continuously redefined and renegotiated. The patient reprocesses the framework introduced by the therapist and reworks it with new meanings and images (Mozdzierz et al., 1976).

The representation of self through words and images, as an individual in connection with others and the context, creates a vision in the interlocutor's mind, consisting of colors, sounds, smells, and emotional, relational, and contextual content.

For this vision to reach the patient, three principles should be considered: (a) the patient's attention is attracted especially by the expression level of communication rather than the content; (b) the effectiveness of words derives from accuracy in what words are chosen rather than from quantity; (c) the communication used is in line with the actions (Mozdzierz et al., 1976).

Words can be interpreted as pictures enunciated by a singular individual in a specific phonation and intonation. These contents are received in a pragmatic context and interiorized in an existential, cultural, and social frame. As such, words are the vehicle of change and can modify mental representations and internal reality, generating a perceptive, cognitive, and behavioral transformation. In describing the concept of mental representation or image, reference is made to words, or verbal pictures, that involve the individuals' visual experience and culture, which involves visual perception and imagination. This correspondence between mental representation and visual experience emphasizes the power of images, which become activators and vehicles of a sense-making process that characterizes the therapeutic relationship. The strategic psychotherapist engages patients in their own narrative, playing with images and the senses. This mechanism allows the patient to realize what was thought or felt inwardly, according to the principle that if we can imagine something, we can also achieve it.

The ability to stimulate the individual's imagination through senses, memories, and mental associations makes the use of imagery functional. Moreover, for the psychotherapist, it may be easier to act on the imagination rather than on reality. Also, a therapist can stimulate imagination and guide it in the desired direction to produce a change. Imagination is an "as if" translated into concrete actions during the therapeutic process. Imagination allows the patient to project her/himself into a possible reality in which s/he has a greater power of action and can modify attitudes and behaviors, by differently acting and living in daily life. The word becomes the instrument conveying the images, which describe the experiential background of the person who evokes, creates, and shapes internal or mental realities, first unconsciously and gradually more consciously. The therapist catalyzes such linguistic and imaginative power guiding the patient toward real change. This is characteristic of psychotherapy in general, however, it is particularly pronounced in the strategic approach because of the prevalent use of communication and language. Indeed, the well-known strategic psychotherapists were primarily skilled communicators (Erickson et al., 1976; Haley, 1977; Watzlawick et al., 1967). The therapeutic process helps patients in imagining themselves in an alternative way, change their self-representation as well, and promote the so-called "functional self-deception" (Nardone & Watzlawick, 2005). The transition from dysfunctional to a more functional self-deception is associated with the modification of the patient's "perceptual-reactive system" and with the involvement in the therapeutic process. Patients are no longer passive spectators who observe, nor victims of their discomfort but a protagonist of their self-representations, that in turn influence and are influenced by the relationship with the context. Thus, mental representations are co-constructed in an interpersonal weave, consisting largely of reciprocal images shared by each person.

Ronald David Laing studied interpersonal relationships in his medical-psychiatric practice. Specifically, the author focused on the effect of projection and introjection mechanisms on generational transmission in friendship, couple, and family relationships. Laing showed communicative constraints underlying relational conflicts and individual distress, called "knots". This construct is built on individual representations of reality that disregard or falsify the relationship with the Other, creating communicational impasses that are inadvertent and tacit "deadly dialogues and meta-dialogues that underneath destroy relationships" (Laing, 1972, p. 7). Everyone elaborates an image and a subjective idea of the Other and the related behavior, which becomes a pragmatic and relational picture of the affective interpersonal communication and relationship. The pictures reflect, as in a mirror, the contradictions of the intersubjective relationship. The Self and the Other are constantly mutating, changing in conjunction with and in relation to the relationship.

The individual is considered as a "subject in situation" and that situation is lived and embodied, communicational, and pragmatic, and consequently culturally rooted and associated with implicit pre-understandings and shared beliefs. As for the family dynamics of schizophrenic patients, Laing introduces a key concept to understanding relational difficulties by proposing a basic interpretive code based on the interplay of infinite representations of Self and Other. According to Laing individuals experiment with a conflict between what they would like to be and what they would like others to be. The dialectic between these two levels of mental representation assumes an important role in psychotherapy and in familial and interpersonal relationships, which are always inscribed in a social and cultural frame. To date, society is characterized by an increasing and systematic focus on the image, an interest that distinguishes a different kind of communication no longer attentive only to the values of encounter and exchange, but more aware of the social logic of appearance and the construction and negotiation of identities (Mirzoeff, 2016; Verrastro et al., 2018). Virtual and technologically mediated representations, such as through smartphones, personal computers, digital machines, and webcams, contribute to the creation of multiple self and relational images (Gunthert, 2013), that have an impact on both the producer and the observer (Eleuteri et al., 2017). The modern reality is a visual context that communicates through images, fueled by social consensus and positive feedback on idealized and shared representations.

Photography is the favorite tool capable of capturing the image so it can be repurposed in different times and spaces. In this way, individuals can look at and interpret their images transformed (Barthes, 1980). According to French philosopher and semiologist Roland Barthes, a person in front of the photographic lens becomes an image and expresses the desire to exist. This interpretation stimulates reflections on idealized representations and self-referential modes, used in our century to show oneself and display the best image as an ego-image (Barthes, 1980) or the so-called "selfie" (Barry et al., 2017). The selfie is comparable to portraying oneself in a mirror (Fontcuberta, 2016). The reflected image is trapped, fixed, and deprived of the dynamism that instead characterizes the individual as a subject constantly transformed by the context and "in situation" (Laing, 1972). The photographic medium is an art of space and not of time and implements the principle of crystallization or "mummification" (Bazin & Gray, 1960) by fixing elements of the individual and context in a specific moment (Berman, 1993; Weiser, 2004).

In the proliferation of technological tools and audiovisual media, which are increasingly accessible and have more and more habitual uses, amateur audiovisual products are perhaps the best example (Verrastro, 2015). Moreover, the video realized with a smartphone represents the individual in the process in relation to a given situation.

In contrast to the photo, the video does not show only a static image but also the person's language and behavior, which represent their modes of interaction (Bateson et al., 1956; Berger, 1971), or a "dynamic mummification" (Bazin & Gray, 1960).

Technological development influences our daily lives, also increasing the use of audiovisual tools in mental health, especially in therapeutic approaches based on a systemic and patient-centered focus (Brentano, 2014; Wheeler, 1991). Referring to the already discussed audiovisual techniques (see Chapter 3), such as Filmtherapy, involves the patient watching a series of movies selected by the therapist and then commenting on the contents and the emotions related (Sabatino & Saladino, 2018). This therapeutic methodology focuses on cognitive, emotional, and psychophysical processes related to the creative skills of the individual. The undisputed sensitive and evocative power of audiovisual language activates a process of introspection and awareness that reconfigures and re-signifies the trans-modal and multisensory impact on the patient (Dumitrache, 2013, 2014; Saladino, 2015). The therapist selects movies or specific sequences aimed to stimulate the patient's feelings and to re-structure them according to a personal interpretation. The patient is a viewer who is not passive in front of the screen but moves to an active and participatory position that engages the person through mechanisms of identification and projection with the main characters (Rossi, 2009). In fact, one of the goals of the Filmtherapy process is the exploration of the Self in an open and creative setting, in which it is easier to contact personal fears and awareness. This concept is related to the so-called "daydreaming" or "daydreaming functioning" – the association between dreamlike thinking and the waking state produced by the altered state of consciousness of the individual while watching a movie. According to classical theories of cinema as an ideological dispositive (see Chapter 1), during this state, like a dissociative status, the patient contacts parts of the Self which represent beliefs and perceptions. The therapist guides the patient toward reflection on elements of her or his biography. Those patients observed in the film and the characteristics of the protagonists could stimulate a reworking of self-representation that ranges from selective and analytical viewing to imagination and reflective comparison, and finally to greater self-awareness.

Cinematherapy, instead of Filmtherapy, involves a setting like a movie theater, which both isolates and amplifies the experiences and perceptions of the patient, who change her/his cognition of time and space, finding her/himself in another reality, or in a double heterotopia – the theater and the screen on which memories and thoughts are projected (Mangin, 1999). The device-cinema and the fictionality of the narrative allow the individual to be involved in a true existential process, in which s/he feels her/himself differently. In the Cinematherapy setting patients can process complex emotional content, reduce symptoms related to anxious and phobic states, and rediscover key elements of their own well-being. The first processing is mental and imaginative, concerning the individual sensory and psychic plasticity with which patient viewers create images for themselves, while a second reworking, more complex and articulated, can be facilitated by the intervention of the therapist (Powell, 2008). The filmic images stimulate the psychological and physical components of the person, totalizing the external and internal, proprioceptive, and reflective attention and the process of internalization from the perceptual and affective to the reflective and the cognitive, from the sensitive to the hermeneutic elements (Solomon, 2001).

A different tool from Filmtherapy and Cinematherapy is Therapeutic Videotaping (Berger, 1971; Giusti & Iannazzo, 1998; Giusti & Montanari, 1992), which is characterized by the comparison, through a camera and recorded pictures of the sessions, of the images, of the patient's mental representations, and of their intra and interpersonal relationships. This form of therapy involves several techniques. For instance, in the "deferred video confrontation", the patient is filmed during sessions and after s/he comments on the recorded materials together with the therapist. The sessions may be shown in their entirety or only selected sequences, either by the patient ("selected video comparison") or by the therapist ("stimulus video comparison"). Such images promote awareness of patients' behaviors and attitudes. Also, the therapist can select and use the most significant sequences of the sessions, showing the patient the results obtained in therapy ("control video comparison") (Berger, 1971; Giusti, 1999; Rossi, 2009). The Documentary Videotherapy, instead, contrasts with Therapeutic Videotaping because it involves the recording of the patient's behaviors in their daily context, outside the therapeutic setting and "in situation" (Laing, 1972). This approach is characterized by the documentation of biographical aspects considered relevant to the history and the development of the therapeutic process of the patients. The audiovisual tool, and specifically an appropriately shot and edited video, can have a treatment function, acting on the patient's disorder or issue, guiding the viewing experience and the hermeneutic activity (Sabatino & Saladino, 2018). Through this process of reviewing, the image captured by the video becomes autonomous and showed to the patient the temporal discrepancy between what happened in the session and what is happening at the time of reviewing. This mechanism underlines the difference between the patient's mental image and the image projected on the screen, between the image and the picture of the Self (Starobinski, 1989). This audiovisual tool has a therapeutic potential based on the emerging reflection between the memory of the lived experience in session and the observable narrative on the recorded video; between the potential, imaginary, and unreflective, an auto-biographical account of the Self and the Self narrated concretely in and by images. Patients dialogue with themselves using the video as a medium and perform, following the indication of the therapist, a series of actions, aimed to experience a reconfiguration of the self-narrative. For instance, patients could remove the audio or image from the video, bring specific sequences forward or backward, pause, etc. These technical interventions stimulate the comparison between the "here and now" and the "there and then", between old and new representations of the Self, both material and mental. Such manipulation of the audiovisual product allows patients to recognize themselves in new skills in an interaction with a technical object and promotes a sense of agency (Gell, 1998). The video facilitates the detachment between individuals and their disorders by the agentive mediation of the artwork (Rossi, 2003). In the mode "live video confrontation", patients can manage the camera shots and have a direct confrontation with themselves during the therapeutic sessions. Moreover, the "localized video confrontation" directs patients' attention to certain actions or attitudes that they unconsciously enact or that characterize their dysfunctional behavior (Giusti, 1999; Thénot, 1989). In the Videotherapy process, the camera assumes an identity, becoming part of the setting as a "person" and no longer a "thing", citing the theory of Alfred Gell (see Chapter 2). Also, the camera communicates the representations of the patient, and their images both material and mental, which become more manageable (Rossi, 2004; Rossi & Rubechini, 2004). Bateson already used to videotape the family interactions of some schizophrenic patients to show them the "double bind" of the system (Bateson et al., 1956). According to Bateson, explicitly showing family patterns to the members allows the therapist to construct the best-suited strategy for the patient and the system (Bateson et al., 1956).

Another audiovisual technique is Therapeutic Filmmaking, characterized by the participation of the patient in the process of shooting and creating a personal video (Cohen et al., 2015). In Therapeutic Filmmaking, the process consists of the co-construction of an audiovisual product by the patient, with the support of the therapist. This aspect ensures a co-participation in psychotherapy that emphasizes the active role of patients, empowering them about the change and the goals set together (Harvey et al., 2000). Therapeutic Filmmaking is based on procedure and process, on a set of rules and actions, such as writing a storyboard or script, the choice of a fictional or auto-biographical plot, protagonists, and locations, and the filming and editing of the audiovisual product. This arts-based technique combines practical work with creative and expressive actions, constituting the therapeutic process. This creative process also involves flexibility, open-mindedness, memory associations, and reworking past and present mental representations. In Therapeutic Filmmaking, the patient is the protagonist and author of the therapeutic process. The patient-author imagines, designs, and communicates a vision of reality and images, reinventing her/his story and constructing it as a picture, adding or removing relevant narrative elements. The patient can also reproduce reality, which becomes an autonomous product. The potential of this tool is evident in making a narrative that modifies rigid beliefs and stereotypical behaviors. Therefore, individuals decrease symptoms related to her/his dysfunctionality. Psychotherapy could have greater effectiveness and efficiency on the patient's identity through the dynamic and expressive use of storytelling – fictional or biographical. Creativity in the context of moving image construction supports an understanding of the pragmatic, imaginative, and cognitive activity, activates ideas and emotions, and stimulates memories and future projects, allowing for a reconfiguration of reality and greater assertiveness of the Self. Therapeutic Filmmaking is based on self-efficacy and on improving the individual's cognitive and emotional adjustment from reflection to action (Johnson & Alderson, 2008; LePage & Courey, 2011).

Audiovisual integration into the psychotherapeutic process leads the patient to construct a new identity, endowing with a different meaning the images of an incomplete Self.

In this integrated context, the therapist represents an anchor, a catalyst, and a stabilizer since it enables the patient not to disperse but to restructure seemingly disconnected elements. These elements are projected on the protagonist of the film and reviewed in psychotherapy sessions or incorporated into the personal script of the patients. The space-time of the Therapeutic Videotaping creates a situation that is both realistic and fictional, leading the individual toward a real splitting into two different images and exploring a suspension of the threshold between outside and inside, given world and inner world, real and perceived, objective and subjective, first-order and second-order reality. The video and the self-representation are represented as a second psychic skin (Anzieu, 1989) and allow, under the guidance of the therapist, projected contents to be processed and re-introjected (Bion, 1962; Giusti, 1999).

Strategic Psychotherapy and Audiovisual Techniques

Audiovisual tools have an important and functional role in psychotherapy disciplines (Rossi, 2009). According to strategic psychotherapy, the audiovisual medium is part of the process of change. From the ST perspective, regardless of the tools and techniques used, the therapeutic intervention should involve specific planning and the identification of shared, concrete goals to be accomplished during therapy. Indeed, the use of techniques devoid of a therapeutic hypothesis produces the same results as the attempted solutions of the patient and could lead to conflict and resistance. Centered on the uniqueness of the person, the therapist's strategies are contextualized to support a treatment hypothesis.

According to the logic of the "subject in situation" (Laing, 1972), therapy is based on the specific understanding of the individual, and not only on applying pre-established or predetermined techniques and tools. The psychotherapist studies the available elements and works through hypotheses and strategies, acting heuristically in the function of promoting the patient's well-being (Petruccelli & Verrastro, 2012). Intuition is one of the most important tools of the strategic psychotherapist aimed to empower alternative interpretations of the patient's behaviors. Also, intuition is oriented toward activating and enacting a change in the patient from a different view, such as the metaphor of the individual changing the lenses through which s/he views the world, things, others, and self. This perspective could be compared to artistic activity, characterized by inventiveness, improvisation, and the absence of an objective interpretation of reality (Bertram, 2019).

Psychologists are human and fallible, they are not omnipotent "subjects of knowledge", and patients create a therapeutic relationship, recognizing such fundamental points, and sharing trust and responsibility. The actors of the process – therapists and patients – have a reciprocal commitment in aiming to achieve the planned goals.

The interpretation of patient resistance is another principle of the strategic approach. Resistance could be a sign of non-functional therapeutic intervention and can stimulate a revision of the process. From this perspective, resistance can represent resources (De Shazer et al., 1986).

ST focuses on the practicality of the intervention and on the active involvement of the patient. The smart goals model (Bandler & Grinder, 1975a) represents a landmark of this perspective and ensures planning punctuated by goals characterized as follows: (a) "specificity", it should be described in concrete and not abstract form; (b) "verifiability", it should be measurable and quantifiable through actions or examples that represent its achievement; (c) "attainability", it should be adapted to the condition in which the individual lives or operates; (d) "realism", it should be applicable and possible; (e) "scheduling over time", it must have a defined timing. For translating this theoretical model into intervention strategies requires the ability on the part of the therapist to "mirror" the patient's communication patterns, placing her or him as if in front of a mirror (Bandler & Grinder, 1975b; Zeig, 1985). The technique aims to build a solid therapeutic alliance and greater compliance with treatment (Petruccelli & Parziale, 1999), facilitating patients in reviewing interpersonal dynamics, and producing an effect like in-session exposure to the video camera. Videotherapy concretely allows patients to revise themselves in a material, tangible, and modifiable, thus technical and actionable, way during the therapeutic process. In this confrontation between the person and the video, self and self-image, a paradoxical process is triggered whereby the observer is also the observed subject, interpreting her/himself as transparent because of the mediation of the audiovisual tool (Bolter & Grusin, 1999; Giusti, 1999). The patient, recorded by the camera and observed by the therapist, communicates and expresses through verbal and nonverbal communication aspects that describe her/his functioning, showing behavioral dynamics and allowing strengths and criticalities to emerge.

The technique of tracing applied by the therapist is like the training of actors and, in general, of relational performance. The practitioner learns to manage the communication style and expressions, both verbal and behavioral, adapting to the interlocutor, appearing spontaneous and not contrived. This also represents an exercise in mental elasticity that involves a greater ability to swing from one point of view to another, from one perceptual reality to another. Likewise, the therapist helps the patient to see more alternatives of interpretation to her/his problem and to reason possible solutions, learning complexity. As mentioned earlier, audiovisual tools have been used and integrated into several approaches, especially relational systemic and gestalt, and more generally by psychotherapies with a creative background (Rossi, 2009; Shaw & Robertson, 1997).

This interaction is made possible by sharing the systemic rules of feedback and circularity (Hoffmeyer, 2008), based on which there is a relationship of interdependence between individuals involved in a system. According to the strategic approach, the individual is part of a system defined as "living" since it is capable of self-regulation based on shared roles. Therefore, pathology or distress is the result of a systemic disease, of which the patient is a "messenger". In detail, we move on to illustrate the possible parallels between the techniques of the strategic approach and the audiovisual medium.

Filmtherapy stimulates the patient's inner motions and works on both first-order (objective, physical) and second-order (subjective, mental) reality (Watzlawick et al., 1967). The psychotherapist places her or his attention on what emerges in the second-order reality, in which emerged the dynamics and behavioral patterns of the person. As already illustrated, watching a film facilitates reflection thanks to projection and identification mechanisms with the story and the main characters, focusing on "what" is represented. Patients feel understood and welcomed in a therapeutic setting where they can be inside or outside the scene.

Cinematherapy, on the other hand, acts on the resistances and deep perceptions of the patient within the ritual frame of the film experience, tuned to the "how" of the environmental conditions of viewing (Casetti, 2015). Cinema creates a third-order reality (Watzlawick et al., 1967) due to its attractive power. In this third-order reality, elements of objectivity (first-order reality) and subjectivity (second-order reality) converge. This convergence, thanks to the remediation of the cinematic device (Bolter & Grusin, 1999) structures the therapeutic approach.

Therapeutic Videotaping and Documentary Videotherapy act on the defense mechanisms, bypassing them thanks to the experience of reviewing the self in a portrait audiovisual in motion, documented and recorded, live and not analyzed in vitro and retrospectively. In the Videotherapy process, in fact, patients revise themselves through a live or delayed confrontation mediated by the camera and guided by the therapist. During the application of Videotherapy techniques, the camera plays a fundamental function of mediation (Bolter & Grusin, 1999) and assumes both a passive and active role. On the one hand, it records without directly interacting with its interlocutor, almost a foreign body in the intersubjective situation; on the other hand, it produces a phenomenon of communicative "transparency" in which it is as invisible as a technical object and participatory as a "thing-person" (Gell, 1998). Thanks to this mechanism the patient feels a sense of disclosure in communication. If the therapeutic relationship is based on a play of roles, "up" and "down", in which the therapist manages the relationship (Petruccelli & Verrastro, 2012), guiding the patient, in the Videotherapy setting the camera acts as a fundamental and neutral third party. The camera allies with the therapist and the patient and – in this complex and articulated intersubjective and intraobjective relationship, in this agentive dynamic between "people" and "things" (Gell, 1998) – communicates in the first person a representation of reality different from that known and imagined by the patient and therapist (Bateson, 1972; Watzlawick et al., 1967).

Therapeutic Filmmaking adds another piece to the therapeutic relationship. This technique enables the sharing of a story, imagined, planned, and realized as an audiovisual self and all biographical that is a narrative together of the "self that is" and "the self that would like to be". The process of Therapeutic Filmmaking allows the patient to record, preserve, and reproduce her or his daily life in images, and to externalize and reappropriate the emerged contents, exploring alternative realities.

The audiovisual techniques can be integrated into the strategic method, as follows:

Amplification. This technique is used to emphasize specific aspects, situations, or characteristics reported in session by the patient, who tends to underestimate or overestimate her/his problems. The therapist can downsize what is reduced or exaggerated through specific questions or by re-proposing an alternative version of the content reported by the patient (McGee et al., 2005). Such restitution may elicit positive or negative reactions in the patient, structured in a rigid self-image. Amplification means mirroring the patient's answers by placing greater or lesser emphasis on the contents, either through a paradoxical use of language or by following the patient's logic (Bandler & Grinder, 1975a). Audiovisual tools are amplifiers of emotional states. According to the Videotherapy perspective, the patient is aware of being filmed but unaware that s/he is an actor and co-director of the session. Contents filmed by the camera will become valuable materials and can be used to illustrate the behaviors and attitudes of the patient. The therapist shows to the patient a selection of sequences important for the personal evaluation of the problem and explores the contents. Filmtherapy, instead, emphasizes through images and fictional characters underestimated or overestimated aspects, which are more accessible to the patient thanks to the projection and identification mechanisms (Schneider, 2002). In both cases, the patient reduces her/his resistance related to the therapeutic process (Eğeci & Gençöz, 2017) and perceives the therapist as a neutral intermediary (Bolter & Grusin, 1999), not an interpreter but the figure who presents the objective reality of a Therapeutic Videotaping session (Videotherapy), or fictional film sensitive for the patient (Filmtherapy and Cinematherapy).

Concretization. Patients often share in psychotherapy abstract problems, whereas the strategic approach involves a pragmatic focus on the issue. For that reason, the therapist can use the concretization technique by stimulating the individual to construct a practical and verifiable idea, for instance, recall the smart goals model (Bandler & Grinder, 1975a). This model requires purposes with the following characteristics: specificity, verifiability, realism, and scheduled in a defined time. Concretization leads the patient toward a greater awareness of the problem and a recognition of her or his true potential. "Concretizing" also means acting on the problem through the guidance of the therapist, who helps the patient control and modify mental representation and self-image. Therapists can use the concretization technique during a session supported by the audiovisual medium. For example, through live Videotherapy (Giusti, 1999), in which the person communicates the concrete aspects of the symptom and her or his attempts to solve it to the camera, which becomes a real interlocutor, a "thing-person" (Gell, 1998). The construct of "to be concrete" can become a therapeutic prescription (Nardone & Watzlawick, 2005) to be carried out through the audiovisual medium. This prescription leads the patient to progressive awareness and planning through "doing concrete actions" and interaction with the medium. For example, the therapist might formulate the following task: "From now until the next time we meet, I want you to record three videos: a three-minute video in which you list all the features of the problem you told me about, a three-minute video with all the attempted solutions to the problem, and a three-minute video with all the solutions you have not yet attempted".

Externalization. This technique enables patients to distinguish themselves from their symptoms through a process of redefinition of psychological issues. The process of externalization promotes the observation of a problem's functioning and stimulates the imagination of possible alternatives and solutions. Externalizing means effectively working on oneself (White & Epston, 1989). Discomfort symbolically becomes an enemy to be fought or a problem to be solved. This perspective strengthens the therapeutic alliance and connects the patient and therapist toward the achievement of a common goal. In addition, the patient gains a greater capacity for self-observation. This technique could be more effective with the support of the audiovisual medium, which facilitates observation of the problem from the outside, in an immediate and transparent manner, and makes faster the patient's ability to separate themselves from their disorder. For instance, externalization could be acted out through Videotherapy by showing and illustrating live or delayed elements of the problem and analyzing them.

Positive redefinition of the disorder. This technique shows patients the "benefits" of the experienced symptoms, allowing them to perceive themselves as the protagonist of their issues and of change. Also, this technique can be applied and facilitated by Videotherapy by showing the patient the symptom from another point of view. The following case may be an example: a patient complains of feeling neglected by his wife and distressed by her possessive overcontrol. However, in recounting this, the patient smiles. In a classical setting, the therapist would emphasize explicitly the inconsistency between verbal and nonverbal communication. The use of the Videotherapy technique allows the patient to see himself again as he talks about what is causing his discomfort and to directly recognize his real mental states without the mediation of the therapist. In this case, by observing his nonverbal communication, he may realize that the possessiveness of his wife is a source of gratification for him, instead of mortification. The patient may conclude that what makes him feel bad is not the woman being overly controlling but the fear of losing her. In this example, the therapist stimulates reflections using the video which becomes an objective tool that observes without interpreting. The patient endows what s/he sees with meaning, guided or supported by the therapist.

As if. This technique consists of leading the person to fantasize and hypothesize a different reality, other than the one experienced, in which the individual can behave in the absence of the psychological issue or problem. The therapist asks the patient to imagine what s/he would do or how s/he would behave if no longer afflicted by the disorder. The "as if" is a flexible technique useful to stimulate a process of exploration of self and personal goals, or to overcome difficulties through alternative solutions. Filmtherapy is comparable to the "as if" technique because it stimulates a projection of the Self into fictional characters. The viewers perceive themselves differently, placing themselves as the protagonist or antagonist or any character or story with which s/he finds connections. This technique shifts the focus from "how I am" to "how I could be", leading to a reflection on personal change. The "as if" technique acts according to the "self-determining prophecy" (Sabatino & Saladino, 2018; Watzlawick, 1977; Wolman, 1965). This concept assumes that our actions are influenced by thoughts that contribute to realizing them. When these thoughts are consciously acted on, this mechanism can become a daily exercise that progressively shapes the patient's rigid patterns. Therapeutic Videotaping and Documentary Videotherapy can accelerate and enhance the effectiveness of this technique, observed concretely in the actions performed by the patient in sessions. The following is an example of a prescription that includes the "as if" technique used with a couple during a

Videotherapy session: "I will now show you a video with some sequences from our previous session and ask you to observe yourself as if you were your partner. So, the lady will observe the video as if she were her husband and the gentleman will observe the video as if he were his wife. When the video is finished, in turn, I want you to tell me, always thinking as if you were your partner, what you feel now and what you think the other person felt in the video you just watched".

Miracle question. This technique, like the "as if", is based on stimulating the patient's imagination and creativity. The miracle question (De Shazer, 1988, 1994) leads the patient toward a greater awareness of the goals s/he wants to achieve in psychotherapy. There are many forms of miracle questions that the therapist can construct based on the specific situation. The important aspect is the management of the patient's responses, which should be directed toward concrete and achievable statements (De Shazer et al., 2007). One form of miracle question often used is the "magic wand", i.e., asking the patient what s/he would change about her or his situation if s/he had a magic wand, keeping the focus on the problem. The miracle question is in fact a solution-centered technique and can easily be applied to Therapeutic Filmmaking by asking the patient to construct an autobiographical or fictional self-representational story and suggesting elements of daily life and wishes for the future. In creating the storyboard, the therapist focuses on the future and alternatives to the problem. The storyboard becomes the concrete representation of the patient's goals and solutions. The therapist can use the miracle question by asking the patient to create a story in which s/he is the protagonist, converging the imaginative technique of "as if" and problem-focusing with the creative process of Therapeutic Filmmaking. After, the therapist may suggest the patient create a video in which s/he reproduces the process of problem-solving, following the resolution of the issue. This second video is intended to consolidate the goals achieved and to make the patient aware of alternatives to the disorder, analyzing the first-order reality and stimulating a reflection of the second-order reality, which involves a change in imagery and in real life.

Scaling. This technique involves the creation of an intersubjective scale used by the patient and therapist to measure achievement, symptom reduction, and motivation to change (De Shazer & Berg, 1992). After identifying the aspects to be measured and monitored, the therapist asks the patient to rate them on a scale from 0 to 10 in their current position, where 0 is the minimum level and 10 is the maximum level. For example, if the scale is used to measure the patient's anxiety, which carries a level equivalent to 8 in the first session that is reduced to 5 after three sessions, scaling helps the patient to recognize her or his changes and the therapist to monitor the process (Ruini & Fava, 2009). Therapeutic Videotaping makes this technique even more effective by showing the patient's self-assessments on video. The comparison through the video from the first session which reports a level of anxiety equivalent to 8 and that of the third session which reports a level of anxiety equivalent to 5 allows the therapist to observe the characteristics of anxiety, differences in verbal and nonverbal communication, and attitudes. In addition, through the therapist's guidance, the patient can act on the video and realize her/his actual improvement. Similarly, if the patient cannot recognize her or his improvements, the video shows them and can be a valuable tool for the therapist to encourage the patient to recognize the positive outcome of her/his efforts.

Diary. The diary, like scaling, is a technique used to monitor the therapy and act on the patient's awareness. It is a notebook in which the patient notes the progress of therapy and the developments of the problem (Nardone & Watzlawick, 2005). This technique allows the therapist to gather information about the symptom and shifts the patient's focus from the problem to the task, producing a reduction of symptoms (Watkins, 1992). This technique can also be carried out in the form of a video diary, maintaining the same function as the paper diary. The video diary is structured as a live video confrontation in the absence of the therapist. The patient films her/himself while performing the task and adjusts the framing and elements needed for the recording, implementing an immediate comparison with the video. In addition, the video diary is a form of deferred video confrontation, like the Therapeutic Videotaping and the Documentary Phototherapy techniques. During this process patients can observe themselves again, in the presence of the therapist in session, confronting a second time. Finally, the video diary, potentially constituting a record of the progress made in therapy, can be used by the therapist as video maintenance (Sabatino & Saladino, 2018), with the aim of positively reinforcing the patient outcomes.

Letter writing. Like the diary technique, writing letters stimulates patients' awareness and helps the therapist in monitoring the treatment (Erickson & Rossi, 1980b; Schafer, 1992; White & Epston, 1990). There are various forms of writing letter prescriptions. For example, the patient could write to the therapist, strengthening the therapeutic alliance and promoting a positive emotional atmosphere related to the association between epistolary exchange and relationships of friendship and intimacy (White & Epston, 1989). The therapist can indicate the exact time when these letters should be written, the length, and the type of paper to be used or may give fewer rigid directions. In addition, the therapist may choose to write to the patient to reinforce certain positive outcomes or to ask questions (Rossi & Rubechini, 2004). This technique, like the diary, can be translated into audiovisuals through video letters, verbal messages, or monologues recorded by the patient and addressed to the therapist, to a third party, or to herself or himself. The video letter amplifies the emotional impact on the sender and the receiver, by the suggestive power on the person who records and receives the message. The video letter could be used, for example, as a means of communication to promote open dialogue. This communication involves the multisensory level, as the person feels observed by the camera and is simultaneously aware that s/he can review the images, building her or his own video archive. This technique is a useful tool for monitoring the progress in therapy and reinforcing positive outcomes (Giusti, 1999).

Restructuring. This tool allows the therapist to redefine the perception that the person has of her/himself and the problem (Nardone & Watzlawick, 2005; Watzlawick et al., 1974). The therapist avoids labeling the person as pathological but works on the meanings brought by the patient and creates alternatives to the patient's perspective. Each alternative provided by the therapist is characterized by several possible scenarios that have in common one element: problem resolution. The strategic therapist stimulates the patient to adopt new points of view by providing keys that shape the patient's rigid patterns. Indeed, restructuring also means providing guidance and prescriptions, enabling the patient to practically see ways to change her/his reality. The tool of restructuring is based on producing change through a creative act that upsets the logic followed by the patient.

According to strategic psychotherapy (Watzlawick, 1977), reality is composed of first-order and second-order. All the videotherapeutic techniques discussed act on the second-order reality. Filmtherapy helps the imaginative process of identification; Documentary Videotherapy shows a part of objective reality. Finally, through the process of Therapeutic Filmmaking, instead, patients configure themselves as a co-constructor of their reality, the architect of a shared restructuring with the therapist.

Behavioral prescriptions. Prescriptions are behavioral indications that the therapist provides in session. The patient should perform these tasks between sessions or during the session itself. In strategic therapy, prescriptions are concrete methods to act on dysfunctional behaviors outside the therapist's office (Nardone & Watzlawick, 2005). The absence of the therapist allows the patient to improve their skills with a concrete experience. Prescriptions can be direct, indirect, and paradoxical.

In the first case, these are clear indications about actions that the patient should perform aimed at achieving a specific goal shared in the session. Cooperative patients benefit from this type of prescription (Haley, 1977; Watzlawick, 1978). Indirect prescriptions, on the other hand, are injunctions of behavior that conceal their true goal from the patient and circumvent the individual's resistance. These prescriptions are more suitable for those who have higher resistance. The therapist shifts patients' attention from the problem to other elements that reduce the tension related to the discomfort, allowing them to neutralize the problem through a communicative technique called "the bald-faced lie", also referred to as "beneficent deception". This technique implicitly acts on the problem. Therefore, the person enacts a given behavior without realizing it. Finally, paradoxical prescriptions, e.g., symptom prescription, involve the use of symptom or resistance as actions to be voluntarily enacted to increase the patient's perceived level of control over a situation. For instance, if the patient suffers from anxiety, the therapist might prescribe to feel the symptoms of anxiety at a specific time in daily life, or might prescribe increased anxiety, and both actions will be voluntarily enacted. Prescriptions are more effective if communicated in hypnotic and injunctive methods. Following the prescription performed the therapist reinforces the results obtained, redefining the situation, and gratifying the patient (Haley, 1977).

The prescription can be integrated with the videotherapeutic process or be part of the process itself. For example, patients might be instructed to review themselves on video during a session and identify the defining characteristics of "how I am", "how I should be", and "how I would like to be" with respect to their attitude toward the therapist, realizing the interpersonal pattern that distinguishes their behavior, the level of motivation to change or other aspects of Self. When patients observe themselves in the presence of the therapist, they emphasize certain aspects of the recorded session and pay attention to one image rather than another, experiencing a role reversal in which patients lead the session, creating three poles of observation: the camera, the therapist, and the patient. The paradoxical prescription can be applied through Film-therapy and Therapeutic Filmmaking. In the former case, the therapist can give patients a series of thematic films focused on their disorder, asking them to watch at a specific moment of the day. For example, the therapist might give a paradoxical prescription to her/his patient relative to her/his disorder (watch movies for a specific time per day or select a sequence of scenes). Therapeutic Filmmaking can be used in the same way, asking the patient to start from her/his disorder to construct the story s/he wants to portray. The story will have an autobiographical character, through a creative process of disidentification.

Paradoxical prescription in Therapeutic Filmmaking leads patients to be actors and directors of their products, writing a script based on the reality of their symptoms and creating a plot enriched with places, people, and events. The process of filmmaking becomes a peculiar space-time, a "scene" in which elaborate symptoms neutralize the paralyzing effect of the disorder. The eclecticism that distinguishes strategic psychotherapy allows this approach to use and integrate audiovisual tools and languages into clinical practice, increasing its effectiveness.

The Dynamic and Relational Setting of Strategic Psychotherapy

The setting is a fundamental component of the psychotherapeutic process, constituted by a set of physical and relational elements, and shared rules, which characterized the therapeutic relationship and alliance. The setting, in its classical interpretation, is a physical and temporal space delimited by the roles and functions of the patient and the therapist. In humanistic and patient-centered psychotherapies, the setting is flexible and is based on the contextual and situational variables that constituted the therapeutic process (Haley, 1973). In strategic psychotherapy, the setting defines the therapeutic process and fosters the agency and self-efficacy of the patient (Saladino, 2015).

The therapist adapts her or his strategies to the patient's characteristics. In this way, the patient is gradually guided by the therapist to rediscover her or his potential and possible alternative solutions to the problem. This aspect is made possible by active and constant listening and using the contents that emerged in therapy (Secci, 2005). Indeed, the therapist uses the information shared by the patient as useful and effective strategies to produce change. Mostly, therapeutic approaches share a common definition of a setting as a safe place. This definition represents a physical place – such as a furnished room, or the presence of windows, curtains, or other objects – and a relational place – such as the presence of the therapeutic alliance and the professional and personal characteristics of the therapist (Bandler & Grinder, 1975a).

Firstly, the setting is the place that structures the therapeutic relationship and alliance. The setting is a container of emotions that allows the patient to disclose in a neutral place. The setting definition through explicit and implicit rules promotes a sense of protection and a sharing of the therapist's and patient's dynamics and worldviews.

This encounter influences the therapeutic interaction and is characterized by perceptions, feelings, emotions, opinions, beliefs, thoughts, and behavioral attitudes. In the therapeutic setting, the professional investigates the psychological and behavioral dynamics of the patient based on two dimensions of communication: the "content" – the information reported by the patient – and the "relationship" – the interpersonal exchange between the two actors in the conversation. This generally occurs in any common interaction, verbal and nonverbal. However, what distinguishes the therapeutic from the daily setting is the fact that the former consists of a therapeutic deal, in which the patient and the therapist parallelly act toward a single goal.

Moreover, a positive therapeutic setting is facilitated by the patient's motivation and the therapist's empathic skills. The setting is a clinical tool constituted of external and internal components. Aspects related to the place of the therapy are part of the external setting. There are individual and collective images associated with the idea of psychotherapeutic context. These external characteristics are important elements of influence in the therapeutic relationship since human beings attribute specific characteristics to others based on impressions and non-rational beliefs. Similarly, the patient might attribute characteristics to the therapist and choose whether to pursue therapy due to their impressions related to the place.

The internal setting, instead, is composed of the therapist's mental organization and is built through therapeutic alliance and rapport. In fact, the therapist structures the treatment process by involving patients, who become an active part of the setting (Bandler & Grinder, 1975a). The following elements characterize the internal setting and guide the strategic therapist in her/

his practice. Firstly, the therapist and patient interact in the present condition of the setting (De Shazer, 1975). The patient shows the relational dynamics enacted in her/his daily life, while the therapist collects impressions on the reactive perceptual system of the patient (Petruccelli & Verrastro, 2012), a system that describes the person's functioning and the modality to perceive and react to events. The strategist therapist focuses on the current interaction of the session since the sides connected to the patient's past emerge because of the same interaction. Mostly, this behavior also describes past interactions and attempted solutions applied by the patient.

Moreover, the focus on the present increases the sense of control of the patient and her/his self-efficacy in resolving difficulties expressed in therapy and dealing with past dynamics.

A second element is the acceptance of the contents of the patient. According to this principle, all materials, such as memories, descriptions, and feelings described during the therapy are useful to the therapeutic relationship and to understand the patient's functioning (Fish et al., 1983). Indeed, the act of "telling the story" has a therapeutic function for the patient and allows the psychotherapist to use that narrative to achieve the purposes of the therapeutic process. The therapist accepts content to restructure its meaning and transform it into a resource.

Another characteristic of the strategic setting is its flexibility and adaptability to the context and to the needs of the patient (Nardone & Watzlawick, 2005). For instance, Milton Erickson (Zeig & Geary, 1990) reshaped and managed the setting and the relationship with the patient, not fixing specific external elements. The author interprets the rigidity of the setting as a form of immaturity, adapting it to the needs of the patients, often receiving them in unusual places. This flexible attitude fosters the therapeutic process and relationship. The therapist is not solely concerned with the external factors of the setting, i.e., holding sessions in the same place, but rather in adapting to the situation. This mechanism avoids forcing the patient into an inappropriate rigidity that evokes relational difficulty.

Therapist and patient act on two interpretive levels: the first-order reality, characterized by the place and events of therapy; the second-order reality, consisting of the meanings they both attach to the same space and events (Watzlawick, 1977). These two levels constantly interact, restructuring the patient and the therapist's perceptions.

Moreover, the flexible setting interprets uncertainties as potential opportunities. As in improvisational performance, in strategic psychotherapy the therapist's uncertainty is a useful element for the therapeutic process, to understand whether the therapy needs restructuring. Breakdowns in the setting also assume a relational meaning. Indeed, the therapist should not provide easy solutions, but s/he should create the basis for working together with the patient toward a shared aim. The therapist should be experienced as human and fallible, not as omnipotent. This attitude promotes higher responsibility in patients.

Another element of the setting is the prescription of behavior that allows for continuity in the therapeutic setting, creating a connection between sessions (Haley, 1977). This is one of the most representative aspects of strategic psychotherapy and cognitivist approaches. The goal of the strategic therapist is to enable the development and increase of autonomy of the patient, who gradually learns to challenge her/himself and act, through specific tasks, on her/his problem. The patient is constantly involved in the therapeutic relationship, and prescriptions emphasize this constant commitment.

Time management also could be flexible in the strategic approach. Indeed, although the frequency of sessions usually equates to once a week and the session lasts 60 minutes, there is no rigid interpretation of this rule. Time and its management have a therapeutic value and can change according to the specificity of the situation (Secci, 2016). The setting is organized in time frames and the therapist uses time within a flexible framework, emphasizing the progression of the process, session by session.

Another element of the setting is creativity, which leads to recognizing the person as a unique subject and adapting the best solution for the patient. Being creative means using intuitions, experiences, and suggestions that derive from one's personality and background, integrating them with the techniques. Another creative use by the therapist is to welcome the patient's aptitudes without prejudice to reuse and apply them to the psychotherapeutic context (Haley, 1973, 1985; Perls et al., 1951). For example, a patient might be passionate about writing or prefer practicality and movement; in that case, a non-rigid but creative use of techniques and setting might allow for greater adaptation to the patient's modalities, promoting therapeutic compliance.

An element associated with creativity is experimentation. Therapists act referring to psychotherapeutic techniques interpreted in a personal manner. This principle was structured within Gestalt psychotherapy (Perls, 1969; Perls et al., 1951), which considers the therapeutic techniques as experiments applicable to the setting (Mann, 2010). Moreover, creative and expressive therapies and art therapies lead the therapist to confront and actively work with other disciplines. Comparison with other disciplines and professionals stimulates creativity and flexible thinking, which are fundamental aspects of problem-solving and decision-making in the therapeutic context. Confrontation and integration of personal aspects and other disciplines become a resource for the therapist, who increases her or his expertise and knowledge, and for the patient, who gains new perspectives and resources (D'Amario et al., 2015).

The setting in strategic psychotherapy assumes dynamic and ever-changing significance and is suitable for the integration of different techniques and tools. The use of the audiovisual medium in psychotherapy is a clear example of resource, integration, and experimentation in the clinical setting. Indeed, audiovisual tools are based on adaptation to the patient's functionality rather than theoretical and conceptual rigidity. The setting in ST could be used in a creative manner, maintaining its structural elements but in a flexible therapeutic framework. In Videotherapy, for example, the element integrated into the setting is the camera, which is inserted as a third party, as well as in other situations in which the setting is modified through the insertion of a specific technique, tool, process, or other interlocutors besides the therapist. The principle that underlies the above elements is the perception of the diversity of patients. This aspect leads to considering each therapeutic intervention as peculiar and as a creative act. This perception is extensively illustrated and explored in the next chapter, containing an experimental therapeutic model based on the integration of audiovisual tools in a setting of strategic psychotherapy.

References

Anzieu, D. (1989). *The skin ego*. Yale University Press.
Bandler, R., & Grinder, J. (1975a). *The structure of magic* (Vol. 1). Science and Behavior Books.
Bandler, R., & Grinder, J. (1975b). *Patterns of the hypnotic techniques of Milton H. Erickson, MD* (Vol. 2). Meta Publications.
Barry, C. T., Doucette, H., Loflin, D. C., Rivera-Hudson, N., & Herrington, L. L. (2017). "Let me take a selfie": Associations between self-photography, narcissism, and self-esteem. *Psychology of Popular Media Culture*, 6(1), 48–60. doi:10.1037/ppm0000089.
Barthes, R. (1980). *La chambre Claire*. Gallimard.
Bateson, G. (1972). *Steps to an ecology of mind*. Ballantine Books.
Bateson, G., Jackson, D. D., Haley, J., & Weakland, J. (1956). Toward a theory of schizophrenia. *Behavioral Science*, 1(4), 251–264. doi:10.1002/bs.3830010402.
Bazin, A., & Gray, H. (1960). The ontology of the photographic image. *Film Quarterly*, 13(4), 4–9. doi:10.2307/1210183.
Belting, H. (2005). Image, medium, body: A new approach to iconology. *Critical Inquiry*, 31(2), 302–319. doi:10.1086/430962.
Berger, M. M. (1971). Self-confrontation through video. *American Journal of Psychoanalysis*, 31(1), 48–58. doi:10.1007/BF01872309.
Berman, L. (1993). *Beyond the smile: The therapeutic use of the photograph*. Routledge.
Bertram, G. W. (2019). *Art as human practice: An aesthetics* (N. Ross, Trans.). Bloomsbury Publishing.
Bion, W. R. (1962). *Learning from experience*. Karnac Books.
Bolter, J. D., & Grusin, R. (1999). Remediation: Understanding new media. *Corporate Communications: An International Journal*, 4(4), 208–209. doi:10.1108/ccij.1999.4.4.208.1.
Brentano, F. (2014). *Psychology from an empirical standpoint*. Routledge.
Bruner, J. S., Goodnow, J. J., & George, A. (1956). *A study of thinking*. John Wiley & Sons, Inc.
Casetti, F. (2015). *The Lumière galaxy: Seven key words for the cinema to come*. Columbia University Press.
Chevalier, A. J. (1995). *On the client's path: A manual for the practice of solution focused therapy*. New Harbinger Publications.

Cohen, J. L., Johnson, J. L., & Orr, P. (Eds.). (2015). *Video and filmmaking as psychotherapy: Research and practice* (1st ed.). Routledge.

D'Amario, B., Saladino, V., Santilli, M., & Verrastro, V. (2015). Le competenze trasversali. Teorie e ambiti applicativi. *Quale Psicologia*, 5(2), 99–114.

De Shazer, S. (1975). Brief therapy: Two's company. *Family Process*, 14(1), 79–93. doi:10.1111/j.1545-5300.1975.00079.x.

De Shazer, S. (1988). *Clues: Investigating solutions in brief therapy*. W.W. Norton & Co.

De Shazer, S. (1994). *Words were originally magic*. W.W. Norton & Co.

De Shazer, S., & Berg, I. K. (1992). Doing therapy: A post-structural re-vision. *Journal of Marital and Family Therapy*, 18(1), 71–81. doi:10.1111/j.1752-0606.1992.tb00916.x.

De Shazer, S., Berg, I. K., Lipchik, E. V. E., Nunnally, E., Molnar, A., Gingerich, W., & Weiner-Davis, M. (1986). Brief therapy: Focused solution development. *Family Process*, 25(2), 207–221. doi:10.1111/j.1545-5300.1986.00207.x.

De Shazer, S., Dolan, Y., Korman, H., McCollum, E., Trepper, T., & Berg, I. K. (2007). *More than miracles: The state of the art of solution-focused brief therapy*. Haworth Press.

Dumitrache, S. D. (2013). Cinema-therapy: The sequences of a personal development group based on movies. In S. D. Dumitrache & I. Mitrofan (Eds.), *The unifying experiential psychotherapy behind the scenes – case studies and applicative research* (pp. 71–83). SPER Publishing House.

Dumitrache, S. D. (2014). The effects of a cinema-therapy group on diminishing anxiety in young people. *Procedia-Social and Behavioral Sciences*, 127, 717–721. doi:10.1016/j.sbspro.2014.03.342.

Eagle, M. N. (2011). *From classical to contemporary psychoanalysis: A critique and integration*. Routledge.

Eğeci, İ. S., & Gençöz, F. (2017). Use of Cinematherapy in dealing with relationship problems. *The Arts in Psychotherapy*, 53, 64–71. doi:10.1016/j.aip.2017.02.004.

Eleuteri, S., Saladino, V., & Verrastro, V. (2017). Identity, relationships, sexuality, and risky behaviors of adolescents in the context of social media. *Sexual and Relationship Therapy*, 32(3–4), 354–365. doi:10.1080/14681994.2017.1397953.

Erickson, M. H. (1964). Initial experiments investigating the nature of hypnosis. *American Journal of Clinical Hypnosis*, 7(2), 152–162. doi:10.1080/00029157.1964.10402410.

Erickson, M. H., & Rossi, E. L. (1980a). *The collected papers of Milton H. Erickson on hypnosis* (Vol. 1). Irvington.

Erickson, M. H., & Rossi, E. L. (1980b). *The collected papers of Milton H. Erickson on hypnosis* (Vol. 3). *Hypnotic investigation of psychodynamic processes*. Irvington.

Erickson, M. H., Rossi, E. L., & Rossi, S. I. (1976). *Hypnotic realities: The induction of clinical hypnosis and forms of indirect suggestion*. Irvington.

Fish, R., Weakland, J. H., & Segal, L. (1983). *The tactics of change: Doing therapy briefly*. Jossey-Bass.

Fontcuberta, J. (2016). *La furia de las imagines: Notas sobre la postfotografía*. Galaxia Gutenberg.

Freud, S. (1942). Outline of psychoanalysis. *The Psychoanalytic Review (1913–1957)*, 29, 197.

Gell, A. (1998). *Art and agency: An anthropological theory*. Clarendon Press.

Giusti, E. (1999). *Videoterapia: Un ausilio al counseling e alle arti terapie*. Sovera.

Giusti, E., & Iannazzo, A. (1998). *Fenomenologia e integrazione pluralistica. Libertà e autonomia di pensiero dello psicoterapeuta.* Edizioni Universitarie Romane.

Giusti, E., & Montanari, C. (1992). La gestalt della supervisione. *Realtà e Prospettive in Psicofisiologia,* 3, 161–170.

Goffman, E. (1959). *The presentation of self in everyday life.* Doubleday.

Gunthert, A. (2013). *Viralité du selfie, déplacements du portrait.* http://histoirevisuelle. fr/cv/icones/2895.

Haley, J. (1973). *Uncommon therapy: The psychiatric techniques of Milton H. Erickson, MD.* W.W. Norton.

Haley, J. (1977). *Problem-solving therapy: New strategies for effective family therapy.* Jossey-Bass.

Haley, J. (1985). *Conversations with Milton H. Erickson, MD* (Vol. 1). *Changing individuals.* Triangle Press.

Haley, J., & Hoffman, L. (1967). *Techniques of family therapy.* Basic Books.

Harvey, A. G., Clark, D. M., Ehlers, A., & Rapee, R. M. (2000). Social anxiety and self-impression: Cognitive preparation enhances the beneficial effects of video feedback following a stressful social task. *Behaviour Research and Therapy,* 38(12), 1183–1192. doi:10.1016/S0005-7967(99)00148–00145.

Hoffman, L. (1981). *Foundations of family therapy: A conceptual framework for systems change.* Basic Books.

Hoffmeyer, J. (Ed.). (2008). *A legacy for living systems: Gregory Bateson as precursor to biosemiotics* (Vol. 2). Springer Science & Business Media.

Johnson, J. L., & Alderson, K. G. (2008). Therapeutic Filmmaking: An exploratory pilot study. *The Arts in Psychotherapy,* 35(1), 11–19. doi:10.1016/j.aip.2007.08.004.

Jung, C. G., Adler, G., & Hull, R. F. C. (Eds.) (1960). *Collected Works of C. G. Jung* (Vol. 3): *Psychogenesis of Mental Disease.* Princeton University Press.

Jung, C. G., & Hinkle, B. M. (1916). *Psychology of the unconscious: A study of the transformations and symbolisms of the libido; a contribution to the history of the evolution of thought.* Moffat, Yard.

Laing, R. D. (1972). *Knots.* Vintage Press.

LePage, P., & Courey, S. (2011). Filmmaking: A video-based intervention for developing social skills in children with autism spectrum disorder. *Interdisciplinary Journal of Teaching and Learning,* 1(2), 88–103.

MacLuhan, M. (1964). *Understanding Media: The Extensions of Man.* McGraw-Hill.

Mangin, D. (1999). *Cinema therapy: How some shrinks are using movies to help their clients cope with life and just feel better.* Health and Body.

Mann, D. (2010). *Gestalt therapy: 100 key points & techniques.* Routledge/Taylor & Francis Group.

McGee, D., Vento, A. D., & Bavelas, J. B. (2005). An interactional model of questions as therapeutic interventions. *Journal of Marital and Family Therapy,* 31(4), 371–384. doi:10.1111/j.1752-0606.2005.tb01577.x.

Minuchin, S., Nichols, M. P., & Lee, W. Y. (2006). *Assessing families and couples: From symptom to system.* Pearson Allyn and Bacon.

Mirzoeff, N. (2016). *How to see the world: An introduction to images, from self-portraits to selfies, maps to movies and more.* Basic Books.

Mitchell, W. T. (2005). *What do pictures want? The lives and loves of images.* University of Chicago Press.

Mozdzierz, G. J., Macchitelli, F. J., & Lisiecki, J. (1976). The paradox in psychotherapy: An Adlerian perspective. *Journal of Individual Psychology*, 32(2), 169.

Nardone, G., & Watzlawick, P. (2005). *Brief strategic therapy: Philosophy, techniques, and research.* Jason Aronson.

Perls, F. S. (1969). *Gestalt therapy verbatim.* Real People Press.

Perls, F. S., Hefferline, R. F., & Goodman, P. (1951). *Gestalt therapy: Excitement and growth in the human personality.* Dell.

Petruccelli, F., & Parziale, M. (1999). Tecniche di intervento in psicoterapia strategica. *Quale Psicologia*, 13, 13–37.

Petruccelli, F., & Verrastro, V. (2012). *La relazione d'aiuto nella psicoterapia strategica.* Franco Angeli.

Powell, M. L. (2008). *Cinematherapy as a clinical intervention: Theoretical rationale and empirical credibility.* [Graduate thesis, University of Arkansas]. https://schola rworks.uark.edu/etd/2984.

Rossi, O. (2003). La videoterapia nella relazione d'aiuto. *Informazione Psicoterapia Counselling Fenomenologia*, 2, 30–35.

Rossi, O. (2004). Le visioni della memoria – Un intervento di Gestalt a mediazione videoterapeutica. *Informazione Psicoterapia Counselling Fenomenologia*, 3, 12–23.

Rossi, O. (2009). *Lo sguardo e l'azione: Il video e la fotografia in psicoterapia e nel counseling.* Edizioni Universitarie Romane.

Rossi, O., & Rubechini, S. (2004). Le immagini autobiografiche: Una via narrativa alla percezione si sé. *Informazione Psicoterapia Counselling Fenomenologia*, 3, 14–23.

Ruini, C., & Fava, G. A. (2009). Well-being therapy for generalized anxiety disorder. *Journal of Clinical Psychology*, 65(5), 510–519. doi:10.1002/jclp.20592.

Sabatino, A. C., & Saladino, V. (2018). Dalla cinematerapia al Therapeutic Filmmaking: linguaggio audiovisivo e psicoterapia. *Quale Psicologia*, 11, 22–37.

Saladino, V. (2015). *Un caso di sexual offending: Aspetti psicologico-forensi.* [Postgraduate thesis, Accademia Internazionale di Scienze forensi].

Saladino, V., & Ricapito, G. (2020). *Introduzione ai processi decisionali e motivazionali.* Independently Published.

Schafer, R. (1992). *Retelling a life: Narration and dialogue in psychoanalysis.* Basic Books.

Schneider, I. (2002). Cinema and psychotherapy. In *Encyclopedia of Psychotherapy* (Vol. 1), 401–405.

Secci, E. M. (2005). *Manuale di psicoterapia strategica. Storia, modelli e strumenti delle psicoterapie brevi strategiche.* Edizioni Carlo Amore.

Secci, E. M. (2016). *Le tattiche del cambiamento. Manuale di psicoterapia strategica.* Youcanprint.

Sechehaye, M. A. (1951). *Symbolic realization: A new method of psychotherapy applied to a case of schizophrenia.* International Universities Press.

Shaw, J., & Robertson, C. (1997). *Participatory video: A practical approach to using video creatively in group development work.* Routledge.

Solomon, J. (2001). *The ancient world in the cinema.* Yale University Press.

Starobinski, J. (1989). *The living eye.* Harvard University Press.

Thénot, J. P. (1989). *Vidéothérapie: L'image qui fait renaître.* Greco.

Verrastro, V. (2004). *Psicologia della comunicazione: Un manuale introduttivo.* Franco Angeli.

Verrastro, V. (2008). *Psicologia dello sviluppo dei processi comunicativi: Un manuale introduttivo.* Franco Angeli.

Verrastro, V. (2015). *Le dipendenze comportamentali in età evolutiva*. Alpes.

Verrastro, V., Lilybeth, F., Pio, F. M., Albanese, C. A., Valeria, S., & Costa, S. (2018). *Me, myself and i (nstragram): Popolarità, self-concept e la percezione del corpo nei social network*. [Paper presentation]. XXXI Congresso Nazionale AIP, Torino, Italy, September 17–19.

Watkins, C. E. (1992). Developing and writing the life-style report. *Individual Psychology: Journal of Adlerian Theory, Research & Practice*, 48(4), 462–472.

Watson, J. C., Goldman, R. N., & Greenberg, L. S. (2011). Contrasting two clients in emotion-focused therapy for depression 1: The case of "Tom", trapped in the tunnel. *Pragmatic Case Studies in Psychotherapy*, 7(2), 268–304. doi:10.14713/pcsp.v7i2.109.

Watzlawick, P. (1977). *How real is real: Confusion, disinformation, communication* (Vol. 256). Vintage.

Watzlawick, P. (1978). *The language of change: Elements of therapeutic communication*. Basic Books.

Watzlawick, P. (1984). *The invented reality: How do we know what we believe we know? Contributions to constructivism*. Norton.

Watzlawick, P., Bavelas, J. B., & Jackson, D. D. (1967). *Pragmatics of human communication: A study of interactional patterns pathologies and paradoxes*. Norton.

Watzlawick, P., & Weakland, J. H. (1976). *The interactional view: Studies in the Mental Research Institute Palo Alto, 1965–1974*. Norton.

Watzlawick, P., Weakland, J. H., & Fisch, R. (1974). *Change: Principles of problem formation and problem resolution*. Norton.

Weiser, J. (2004). Phototherapy techniques in counselling and therapy: Using ordinary snapshots and photo-interactions to help clients heal their lives. *Canadian Art Therapy Association Journal*, 17(2), 23–53. doi:10.1080/08322473.2004.11432263.

Wheeler, G. (1991). *Gestalt reconsidered: A new approach to contact and resistance*. Gardner Press.

White, M., & Epston, D. (1989). *Literate means to therapeutic ends*. Dulwich Centre Publications.

White, M., & Epston, D. (1990). *Narrative means to therapeutic ends*. W.W. Norton & Co.

Wolman, B. B. (1965). *Handbook of clinical psychology*. McGraw-Hill.

Zeig, J. K. (1985). *Experiencing Erikson: An introduction to the man and his work*. Routledge.

Zeig, J. K., & Geary, B. B. (1990). Seeds of strategic and interactional psychotherapies: Seminal contributions of Milton H. Erickson. *American Journal of Clinical Hypnosis*, 33(2), 105–112. doi:10.1080/00029157.1990.10402912.

Chapter 6

Therapeutic Autism Narratives

An Integrated Approach

Anna Chiara Sabatino and Valeria Saladino

The Video-Pharmakon Therapeutic Model

Autism spectrum disorder (ASD) is a neurodevelopmental disease described by the *Diagnostic and Statistical Manual of Mental Disorders* (DSM-5) (American Psychiatric Association, 2013, 2014) based on the following criteria: persistent deficits in social interaction and communication, a restricted pattern of interests, and stereotyped behaviors. Individuals with ASD may exhibit peculiar cognitive profiles, characterized by aspects of executive dysfunction, and altered perception and information processing (Lai et al., 2014). These atypical developmental traits involve impairment in social, cognitive, and behavioral functioning, aspects that are often independent and heterogeneous in terms of complexity and severity. Indeed, the term "spectrum" identifies several clinical expressions of the disorder (Carter et al., 2005). Phenotypic forms include those with "high functioning" (HF) or level 1 and those with "low functioning" (LF) or levels 2 and 3. The disorder at level 1 presents with fluent language but deficits at the pragmatic level, normal cognitive development (IQ ≥ 70), deficits in social and relational functioning, and reduced empathic skills (Baron-Cohen et al., 1985); while levels 2 and 3 include individuals who need more support, with severe deficits in verbal and nonverbal functioning and social interaction. These levels of ASD also exhibit stereotyped and repetitive behaviors and below-average cognitive development (IQ < 70). The concept of "social functioning" is one of the key concepts that characterize autism spectrum disorder. Social functioning is a set of operations through which cognition, interaction, and social behaviors are integrated with each other enabling the individual to "negotiate" day-to-day with the environment (Kennedy & Adolphs, 2012). A deficit in social cognition can result in altered behavior (social behavior) and affect the functioning of the individual (social function). In individuals with ASD, social functioning differs from neurotypical individuals due to both qualitative and quantitative alterations, with deficits in verbal and nonverbal reciprocal social communication (Speirs et al., 2011). In addition, atypical individuals seem to have difficulties in emotional recognition through facial expressions (facial

DOI: 10.4324/9781003340508-7

recognition). These deficits are partially responsible for the alteration in empathic response to others' emotions, characteristically reported in the literature among children with ASD compared to children with neurotypical development (Lozier et al., 2014). It is also important to consider the presence of gaps in self-referential cognition, i.e., the ability to focus attention on oneself and one's own emotional states, as well as those of others (Lombardo et al., 2007). According to some studies, some of these alterations are attributable to the mirror neuron system (Perkins et al., 2010; Rizzolatti & Craighero, 2004) and to severe impairment of the areas devoted to play, reciprocity, and theory of mind (TOM). These neurons are activated both when an individual performs an action and when s/he sees the same action performed by others in person, but also in a video image, or in a still image (painting, sculpture, or photography), as Gallese and Goldman have shown (1998).

Socio-communicative deficits, as well as some dysfunctional behaviors presented by children and adolescents with ASD, can be a severely limiting factor for stable friendship relationships, especially among the peer group. The difficulty in understanding and being understood by others can result in severe stress in social situations, low self-esteem, feelings of inadequacy, mood disorders of the anxious/depressive type, and social withdrawal, especially in high-functioning individuals and adolescents (Lounds Taylor et al., 2017).

There are several intervention programs for autism spectrum disorder such as cognitive behavioral therapy (CBT) (Erskine, 1997), systemic-family therapy (Simon et al., 2020), music therapy (Geretsegger et al., 2014), psychomotricity (Jucan et al., 2021), speech therapy (Adams et al., 2012), and still others.

CBT is effective in promoting strategies of emotional and cognitive regulation, dysfunctions of which are often prodromes of future clinical psychopathologies (Ho et al., 2015). To educate patients in the use of functional behavioral strategies, therapeutic protocols have focused on programming training that would enable their development (Bruggink et al., 2016). An example is the CBT program designed by Tony Attwood (2004), which provides dedicated training for children and adolescents aged 9 to 12 years diagnosed with high- and low-functioning autism, divided into group sessions focused on recognizing and managing basic emotions. In addition to CBT, another form of therapy focusing on strengths and behavioral strategies applicable to children with ASD is strategic approach therapy (or strategic therapy, ST) (Ray, 2007), also used with childhood and adolescent disorders, such as behavioral and eating disorders, oppositional defiant disorder, attention-deficit/hyperactivity disorder, and psychosis. In therapy with children, ST provides a form of indirect intervention that acts on the parents, who become the main agents of change. The integration of psychotherapeutic approaches of creative-expressive forms, such as art therapies, can play a key role in the treatment of this specific target (Lusebrink, 2004). Art therapies, regardless of the clinical method, promote the recovery of residual capacities and the reactivation of psycho-affective development and cognitive structures, emphasizing the pragmatic and practical component of the therapy, which is neither merely observational and descriptive, nor oriented solely to the restructuring of normal interpretive performance of Self, others, and things, but rather aims at the involvement and awareness of the patient with ASD and her or his individual potential. For example, video ranks among the most effective art-therapy methods during childhood and adolescence and is educational, rehabilitative, and promotes well-being (Simpson & Slowey, 2011). In interventions dedicated to the autism spectrum, video is integrated into the form of video modeling (Macpherson et al., 2015), a vicarious learning technique and self-representation. This imitative strategy is particularly effective for individuals with ASD since, by focusing attention directly on targeted actions or cues, it engages them in an "as if" that relieves anxiety and neutralizes the emotional intensity and uncertainty of spontaneous social interactions. Through video modeling, children can see a person (or a character, played by an actor) on video, discuss its social aspects and its interactions with people and things, then evaluate their own relationship, and finally project themselves, through interpersonal interactions and imitation (Apple et al., 2005).

In recent years, several studies have focused on art-therapeutic intervention programs for enhancing social skills in ASD-HF, with positive results (Tanner et al., 2015). Mostly, studies focus on the potential for enhancing social cognition and social behaviors through specific training or treatments based on social skills (Olsson et al., 2017). Interventions focused on enhancing social cognition appear to result in an improvement in social functioning in adolescents with ASD-HF (Bishop-Fitzpatrick et al., 2017). However, the main difficulty remains maintaining learned behaviors over time and generalizing skills to daily life (Bellini & Peters, 2008). Some typical characteristics of individuals with ASD should be considered when planning interventions, such as the high level of anxiety experienced within social environments, especially if unfamiliar, the tendency to adhere to specific routines or repetitive/ritual behaviors, or extreme sensitivity to sensory stimulation; therefore, it would be preferable to support participants through individualized strategies and programs (Bellini & Peters, 2008). Moreover, neurotypical and ASD peers encourage the development of social interaction and self-acceptance (Stichter et al., 2012). In addition to video modeling, which has shown promising results in improving social and adaptive-behavioral functioning in children with ASD (Hong et al., 2016) – with respect to basic adaptive skills, imitation skills, and those related to pretend play – theater therapy is outlined as an additional and differently effective art-therapeutic option (Corbett et al., 2016). According to this therapy, acting is an interactive process that includes different aspects of socio-communication: observing the expressions and gestures, conversational turns, interpreting social situations, and expressing feelings or ideas appropriately through verbal and nonverbal communication. Theater therapy is a useful tool for intervening in the main deficits that characterize the disorder. Young participants train their skills in sharing, reciprocity, and awareness of self and others through theater/rehearsal exercises, role-playing, and improvisation. Role-playing for example requires imaginative and discursive skills and the maintenance of shared mental abstractions since the actor is required to put her/himself in someone else's shoes to speak and move as s/he would do and to collaborate with other participants to pretend a present, past, or future situation. The positive results of theater therapy were found in a study by Blythe A. Corbett and colleagues (2016) from which significant improvements were evinced in the group of children with ASD who had participated in therapy compared with the control group. For instance, ASD individuals who received the treatment maintained positive results on communication skills even after two months of follow-up, and a reduction of stress symptoms associated with social situations.

Therapeutic Filmmaking is an additional creative tool that directly involves participants in the production of their own movies from a perspective of self-confidence and awareness of their sense of identity. One of the strengths of this tool is the learning of social skills through the process of filmmaking. This is demonstrated clearly by one Therapeutic Filmmaking program, sponsored by the Autism Social Connection in San Francisco, which involved as protagonists 20–25 children with ASD and 15 neurotypical children. The results showed how the camera positively affected not only different aspects of socialization but also helped foster interactions between peers of the two groups (LePage & Courey, 2011). Through the techniques of filmmaking emerges the importance of the experiential modes of the creative process: the reactions of the child with ASD within the group are monitored and facilitated by the researchers, who show the participants how to deal with negative emotions and help the neurotypical children interact with their peers with ASD. Therapeutic Filmmaking includes a focus on building the relationship of trust among peers. This aspect also contributes to the exploration of one's identity and the acquisition of awareness. So, creativity, imagination, socialization, and awareness are implemented through the use of technology and storytelling, from interaction aimed at creation and group activities, in a context that allows children with ASD to perceive themselves, tell their stories, and see and recognize themselves in a circular and transformative videotherapeutic process (Sabatino & Saladino, 2018).

The Video-Pharmakon Intervention Protocol: Targets and Methodological Procedures

The Video-Pharmakon research-intervention project was derived from the agreement between the following associations and institutions:

- the Department of Human, Social and Health Sciences of the University of Studies of Cassino and Southern Lazio;
- the Department of Political, Social and Communication Sciences of the University of Salerno;

- the Department of Medicine, Surgery and Dentistry "Salerno Medical School";
- the Laboratory of Audiovisual Storytelling (LABSAV) of the University of Salerno;
- the Department of Medical and Surgical Sciences, University of the Studies "Magna Graecia" of Catanzaro;
- the Institute for the Study of Psychotherapies, Rome;
- the Cultural Association Gruppo Pensiero, Salerno;
- Sviluppo Psicosociale srl, Rome;
- Psicotypo – Association for Information and Updating in Psychology, Guidonia Montecelio.

The Video-Pharmakon project was approved as an observational and interventional study by the Campania Sud Ethics Committee and the Institutional Review Board of the University of Cassino and Southern Lazio. The protocol is aimed at children, adolescents, and young adults with autism spectrum disorder high-functioning (level 1 according to DSM-5), formerly Asperger's syndrome, aged between 8 and 25 years who are referred to the Complex Operative Unit of Child Neuropsychiatry of the AOU San Giovanni di Dio and Ruggi d'Aragona-University of Salerno, and their families.

The target group was selected based on the following inclusion criteria:

1   diagnosis of autism spectrum disorder – level 1 (DSM-5);
2   age 8–16 years, both genders;
3   good compliance of the parental couple in all phases of the project.

The only exclusion criterion was the co-existence of other behavioral and neuropsychiatric disorders that could interfere with the possibility of participating in the project. The novelty of this project is the application of parallel work in both the child and the family context. The circular and transformative process is mediated by audiovisual language, which allows the patient to be a spectator and producer of her/his film, and to recognize her/himself in new cognitive, emotional, and pragmatic performances.

This project is based on the strengths of ASD individuals and on the integration of neuropsychiatry, psychology, and audiovisual language theories and techniques.

The objectives of the project are based on the following points:

1   strengthening the personal autonomies, and emotional and socio-communicative skills of the child with ASD;
2   developing greater awareness and sense of identity;
3   providing a supportive space for families, especially the parental couple, as emotional containment;
4   providing the necessary tools for parents to manage dysfunctional aspects of the child in different family and social contexts.

The research-intervention team consists of a neuropsychiatrist who conducts the questionnaire assessment at time 0 and during follow-ups; a psychotherapist; and a filmmaker who conducts the assessment based on audiovisual techniques integrated with the therapeutic process.

The Video-Pharmakon protocol includes a scientific evaluation of the results at quantitative and qualitative levels ensured by the administration of the questionnaire assessment and by a series of pre- and post-intervention interviews. During the first interview, the project is presented to participants, children, and parents, who are aware of the protocol, techniques, and aims. Secondly, those who decide to participate sign an informed consent to the processing of personal data and audiovisual material. All phases of the protocol described below are videotaped to collect the useful material of the Video-Pharmakon to be administered.

Evaluation Measures

Participants involved in the study fulfilled a protocol of standardized tests to assess the quality and efficacy of the intervention. This protocol, administered and interpreted by the neuropsychiatrist, has a diagnostic purpose and is administered at the preliminary stage or time 0:

- Wechsler Intelligence Scale for Children – Fourth Edition (WISC-IV): A test aimed to assess the cognitive profile of children under the age of 16 (Lang et al., 2017; Wechsler, 2003);
- Wechsler Adult Intelligence Scale-Revised (WAIS-R): A test aimed to assess the cognitive profile of children over the age of 16 (Laicardi & Orsini, 1997; Wechsler, 1981);
- Autism Diagnostic Observation Schedule – Second Edition (ADOS-2): A test for the standardized, semi-structured assessment of communication, social interaction, and repetitive/stereotyped behaviors for individuals with autism spectrum disorder (Lord & Colombi, 2013; Lord et al., 2012).

Next, participants fulfilled a second standardized protocol aimed to evaluate adaptive and social skills. This protocol is administered at time 0 (preliminary assessment), time 1 (immediately upon the end of the project), and at subsequent follow-ups at 1 month, 3 months, 6 months, and 12 months:

- Neuropsychological Assessment (NEPSI-II): This test provides a neuropsychological assessment of the cognitive abilities of subjects aged from 3 to 16 years old (Korkman et al., 2007, 2011). Specifically, the following are evaluated: the sub-item recognition of emotions (RE), for testing the recognition of emotions through facial expressions; and the theory-of-mind sub-item (TOM), for the assessment of self and other's mental representation and process of thinking;

- Psychiatric Self-Administration Scales for Children and Adolescents (SAFA): This test evaluates the level of anxiety and mood disorders among children and adolescents from 8 to 18 years old (Cianchetti & Fancello, 2001);
- Child Behavior Checklist 6–18 (CBCL): This test is a self-report for parents and assesses the emotional-behavioral disorders in subjects aged 6–18 (Achenback & Rescorla, 2001; D'Orlando et al., 2010);
- Autism Diagnostic Interview – Revised (ADI-R): This is an interview for parents and caregivers and focuses on systematic and standardized observation of language, reciprocal social interaction, and stereotypical behaviors and narrow interests among children and adults (Rutter, Le Couteur et al., 2003, 2005);
- Social Communication Questionnaire (SCQ): This is a standardized questionnaire for parents/caregivers that assesses the communication, social, and interpersonal skills of children with autism spectrum disorder ages 4 and older (Rutter, Bailey et al., 2003, 2007);
- Social Responsiveness Scale (SRS): This is a self-report questionnaire for parents and investigates social-relational skills of children and adolescents aged from 4 to 18 years old (Constantino & Gruber, 2005, 2010);
- Vineland Adaptive Behavior Scales – II (VINELAND-II): This is a scale that assesses adaptive skills from birth to adulthood (Sparrow et al., 2005, 2016);
- Strengths and Difficulties Questionnaire (SDQ): A self-report questionnaire for parents, evaluating dysfunctional behavior in children and adolescents from 4 to 16 years old (Goodman et al., 1998; Tobia et al., 2011);
- Parenting Stress Index (PSI): A self-report questionnaire for parents aiming to assess parental stress (Abidin, 2012, 2016);
- Empathy Quotient (QE): A self-report questionnaire for parents, developed by the Autism Research Centre (Baron-Cohen et al., 2001) for testing the level of empathy in developmental age (childhood and adolescence).

Interviews

After the first evaluation, the team proceeds with the qualitative assessment through interviews conducted by the psychotherapist. The individual meetings last 60 minutes and have a double purpose: assess the participant's compliance with the intervention and collect data for diagnostic profiling. The interviews are videorecorded, and the filmmaker, in agreement with the psychologist, can ask additional questions, useful for the Video-Pharmakon administered in the other phases of the project.

The interview follows specific guidelines and investigates several areas, divided into thematic networks. This measure lasts 50–60 minutes for parents and 20–30 for children. The interview for children investigates self-perception and sense of identity; perceptions of parents; friendships; relationships with the school, classmates, and other family members. The interview for parents investigates self-perception and explores parental role; expectations toward children; family and couple dynamics; trust toward institutions; and extended family relationships.

Results Analysis

The RQDA analysis software (computer assisted qualitative data analysis software, CAQDAS) was used to perform statistical analyses of interviews, psychotherapy, and parent training sessions. This software allows semantic and conceptual analysis of the language and content of the transcripts. The observation of the team during the sessions is integrated and analyzed as qualitative data, and results.

IBM SPSS Statistics for Windows software (Version 25.0) was used to perform statistical analysis for quantitative data through parametric and nonparametric analysis of the standardized tests.

Protocol Phases

The intervention protocol has five phases, which are discussed in detail below.

Phase 1. Family System's Inspection

After the quantitative and qualitative assessment with tests and interviews conducted at time 0, the first phase of the protocol involves an on-site visit to the family's home. During this phase, the filmmaker and the psychotherapist interact with participants by inviting them to narrate their daily life and to show their fantasies, fears, desires, and needs, through role-play and ludic methods.

This phase creates a first alliance between the team and the family and facilitates compliance with the audiovisual tool, such as the camera. Indeed, the use of the video camera can stimulate reflections on daily dynamics, usually automatically acted. The inspection is useful in data collection on the family system and in the emerging of unconscious contents within the family member.

Phase 2. Documentary Videotherapy and Parent Training

The second phase is characterized by parental training, which involves parents/caregivers. During the sessions of parent training the filmmaker and the psychotherapist administers one or more Video-Pharmakon (footage of video material collected during the first phase). This therapeutic procedure of documenting and administering a video represents Documentary Videotherapy. According to the specific needs of the participants, the team can realize and administer more than one Video-Pharmakon, exploring them during the parent training sessions. Parent training, together with Documentary Videotherapy, involves 4–5 sessions in two months and guides parents in learning educational strategies useful in promoting the higher well-being of the family system. Indeed, Documentary Videotherapy shows the behavioral and contextual strengths and criticalities of the family, creating an audiovisual narrative that the participants can "re-watch" to be more aware of their dynamics.

In addition, the Video-Pharmakon reduces participants' resistance. Parents can interact with the filmmaker and the psychotherapist, commenting on and interpreting the video.

Phase 3. Therapeutic Filmmaking

In the third phase, the team involves children/adolescents to create a couple for Therapeutic Filmmaking, in which they are creators, scriptwriters, and directors of their own video. In this phase the filmmaker acquires the role of facilitator, who supports the creative process of video production, step by step, to achieve the narrative goals of the young participants.

During the first session, the filmmaker and the psychotherapist explain the phases of production, the main rules of communication, and the basic techniques of the construction of audiovisual narratives. A couple of participants proceed with the conception of the story, the composition of the storyboard, the filming, and the editing, following the planning developed together. Parents, meanwhile, are involved in parent training sessions and maintain a logistical support role, contributing to shifting the focus of the relationship from family to friendship relationship. The psychotherapist facilitates the interaction and interpersonal exchanges among peers and monitors the emotional and behavioral elements of the participants, promoting collaboration toward a shared goal. The main aim of this phase is to support and promote a process of subjectification, implementing intersubjectivity.

Phase 4. Cinematherapy and Documentary Videotherapy

In this phase, the young participants watch at the cinema, together with their families, the video realized during the Therapeutic Filmmaking phase. This moment is characterized by sharing the final product and assumes the role of therapeutic restitution of the project carried out.

The realized video represents, for both patients and families, a new perspective, emphasized by the transition from the home Therapeutic Set to the cinema, the actual final and elective setting of the autonomous and participatory Video-Pharmakon administration.

In this setting the psychotherapist facilitates feelings and emotions to emerge, reinforcing the patients with supportive feedback.

The viewing of the video at the cinema crowns the end of the process, of both the peer couple and their parents, who have acquired a mature and flexible view of the family system and parental and filial perception. After one week, both the parental couple and the children separately review the video together with the filmmaker and the psychotherapist, commenting on it and sharing thoughts and emotions about the content and experiences. At the end of this Videotherapy session the children/adolescents receive a DVD containing their film product with only the instruction to watch it whenever they want.

Phase 5. Outcomes Management

One month after the end of the Cinematherapy and Documentary Videotherapy phase, the team conducts a first follow-up with the same protocol of tests and interviews used in the preliminary phase of the study. The data collected from this follow-up aims to reinforce the strategies learned, positive outcomes, and family progress. The psychologist and the filmmaker edit a final Video-Pharmakon aiming to manage the positive outcome obtained. This video contains the audiovisual material collected throughout the project, the images from the preliminary conditions, the film made by the young participants, and the footage documenting the various stages of the intervention. This phase consists of two sessions in which parents and children participate separately. One week after the first follow-up, participants are administered the Video-Pharmakon related to outcome management: the psychotherapist provides the parental couple with specific prescriptions, to be carried out at home until the follow-up. After three weeks, participants again watch the Video-Pharmakon related to outcome management. The psychotherapist concludes the therapy with feedback on the behavioral strategies learned during the project, promoting future perspectives. This phase aims to provide reinforcement and to maintain the positive outcomes among young participants.

Follow-Up

The protocol includes four follow-up stages: (a) at one month after the end of the Cinematherapy and Documentary Videotherapy phase; (b) at three months; (c) at six months; (d) at 12 months from the end of the intervention.

Follow-up consists of the administration of the protocol and of the single interviews constructed based on time 0.

Intervention Tools

The protocol involves the use of specific tools in an intervention based on a strategic psychotherapy approach.

Video-Pharmakon. This tool consists of edited audiovisual materials produced during the project. The Video-Pharmakon has different characteristics and functions according to the phases in which it is administered. Within this protocol, in the phase devoted to Documentary Videotherapy, the videotherapeutic team realizes a first Video-Pharmakon to show to the patients their contingent situation, the starting point for change. This video documentary is packaged based on a careful selection of content by psychologists-psychotherapist and neuropsychiatrists, who identify one or more target behaviors (social or adaptive) on which to work through the Videotherapy intervention. This tool is structured considering materials from the interviews with parents and children and the on-site visit at home. Video-Pharmakon strongly connotes the visual language and function addressed in the methodological framework of self-video modeling, to encourage the reinforcement of positive behaviors previously assumed by the young participants through the playful reconfiguration of Self using the "as if" technique (see Chapter 5). Thus, this video led participants to review and reframe their behavior not on a structured and co-built script, shifting from the logic of "correct what is wrong". The self-image is represented by a narrative and prompts the person to reframe it. At the end of the Therapeutic Filmmaking phase, in contrast, there is the administration of the autonomic Video-Pharmakon, which coincides with the product made entirely by the young participants. The setting becomes essential in administrating the Video-Pharmakon. Indeed, cinema constitutes the culmination and crowning of the creative effort to produce a real film, which acquires the power to ratify the narrated reality and transform it from a narrative to actuality.

During the concluding phase of outcome management, the last Video-Pharmakon has a still different appearance and function: consisting of audiovisual materials of a hybrid nature and authorship, assembled according to the logic of intermedial editing. This video aims to restitute to the participants the realized process, from the first until the last session. Like the first Video-Pharmakon, the final one is tailor-made for the specific participant and should be watched individually.

This final Video-Pharmakon represents a synthesis between the recorded images of the participants by the team and the auto-produced images.

In the three types of Video-Pharmakon described, video modeling and theater therapy methodologies interact with those therapeutic approaches that are based on audiovisual storytelling (Cinematherapy and Videotherapy on its vision, Therapeutic Filmmaking on its production), to branch out into narrative documentary as representation and self-representation of a disorder and of treatment.

Parent Training. Parent training sessions, which involve the use of a strategic therapy frame, involve parents as a parental couple. Parents construct, with the psychotherapist guide, the main goals of the intervention. Through behavioral prescriptions, parents are educated and in turn, educate the children involved in the project according to shared and co-constructed needs. The family system commits to taking care of the disorder, thus dis-empowering the symptoms, enabling greater compliance, and facilitating the change. From the systemic and strategic therapy perspective, when an individual implements a change influences the entire system.

The parent training sessions contribute to the acquisition of functional tools in the management of distress experienced related to the disorder. The goal is not to change the child, but to help the family find its balance while respecting the identity of the individual. The first sessions involve a weekly meeting, then every two weeks until the training is completed. The tools acquired are maintained and used, through prescriptions given by the psychotherapist to maintain positive outcomes.

Spectauthors: Giacomo and Pietro

Considering the findings of the methodological premises, the application of the methodological protocol in the first selected pair of peers – Giacomo and Pietro – is described below.

Giacomo

Giacomo is a 13-year-old boy diagnosed with autism spectrum disorder level 1 (DSM-5). Specifically, due to his clinical features, compatible with Asperger's syndrome (DSM-IV). At the behavioral level, he presents difficulties in concentration and a tendency to continually search for stimulations and fix his attention on technological devices.

According to his cognitive profile (assessed through the WISC-IV Test) he shows specific competence. For instance, Giacomo has good skills in logical-sequential and inductive and deductive reasoning, excellent working memory skills, speed of processing information, visual-spatial perception, and organization skills. Regarding communication, Giacomo presents atypical communication modes, in terms of both verbal and nonverbal components, such as gestures and verbal expressions. Indeed, facial expressions appear limited and marked by elements of rigidity and reduced expressiveness.

The use of conventional, instrumental, or emotional gestures also appears limited and less frequent than in neurotypical development. Reciprocal social conversation is qualitatively inadequate due to the difficulty Giacomo has in respecting conversational turns and correctly interpreting the intonation, pauses, and other elements which characterize communication. Consequently, the adolescent presents difficulties in establishing spontaneous relationships with others, such as in reciprocity and mutuality of social interaction. Giacomo focuses his attention on specific content, e.g., computers and technology, and seems to not be aware of others' interests. He responds to questions but is not spontaneous, and does not ask referral questions, showing poor interest in others' thoughts, feelings, or experiences.

Regarding emotional skills, he shows low skill in processing, recognizing, and congruently responding to emotions. For example, when his parents have an argument, he does not correctly perceive the situation, reacting incongruously and showing limited understanding of his own and others' emotions.

These data are confirmed by the results that emerged during parent interviews (ADI-R; SCQ; SRS), which show the presence of a deficit in communication and mutual social interaction that significantly interfere in the child's daily activities. Parents report elusive eye contact, occasional social smile, limited mimicry, and gestures, poor interest in others as well as in developing peer relationships, with unfriendly social responses and difficulty in establishing friendships. In this regard, the SDQ questionnaire highlights significant problems in the relationship with peers, pro-sociality, and hyperactivity areas. In addition, the score obtained on the questionnaire for the assessment of the Baron-Cohen empathy quotient (QE) is extremely low and reflects a poor ability to understand and react to others' emotions. Also, the ability to decode emotions through facial expressions (NEPSY-II) and TOM is decreased, with difficulties in understanding the other's perspective and correctly interpreting social situations, thoughts, and intentions. In the emotional-behavioral profile (CBCL) assessment emerges an internalizing disorder, including symptoms such as social withdrawal and mood deflection, as well as issues related to lability attentional and physical hyperactivity. In fact, the adolescent's adaptive skills (VINELAND-II) appear deficient for his age, with an uneven profile regarding socialization and participation in group recreational activities.

Personal autonomies (e.g., choice of clothes, personal care), and domestic and community skills (e.g., respect for social norms, road signs, spatial and temporal orientation, organizational-decisional skills, planning, and money management) are less impaired. Parents have high levels of stress (PSI), associated with the parental role and behavioral characteristics of the child. The parental couple shows a willingness to interview, and in participation complain of acute anxiety related to the perception of not being able to interface with the issues of their child and a sense of strong social responsibility that leads them to experiment, with feelings of judgment by others as parents. These perceptions lead the couple to symptoms of hyperattention and control over their own behavior and Giacomo's routines. This control tends to schedule and schematize daily life, reducing the family's spontaneity.

In addition to school, Giacomo engages in several recreative activities, such as swimming class, horseback riding, and drumming lessons. Afterward, he spends his free time in computer games, programming systems, and software, and watches cooking programs. He describes the latter as his major passion. Sometimes these behaviors lead to arguments and conflicts with his parents, as Giacomo prefers to play with his iPhone, spend time on social media, and watch cooking programs instead of doing homework or hanging out with his peers. Despite this, Giacomo shows a good relationship with his parents, who educate him in respecting social rules to avoid problems at school. Indeed, teachers and educators are afraid that a lack of awareness of Giacomo about social behaviors may lead to acts of bullying. Giacomo often becomes aggressive when someone forbids him to use his iPhone or computer and does not always perceive the difference between what is a joke and what is serious. For example, his parents report some episodes in which, encouraged by classmates, he provoked other peers without fully understanding the situation. Giacomo has a very close relationship with his mother, who spends more time at home than his father and therefore also shows greater apprehension toward her son. Despite this, the mother leaves Giacomo free to go out with friends and have experiences without showing her anxiety. Giacomo's father works as a computer programmer, is very understanding about the attitudes of his son, and would like to be able to understand him more and adopt better strategies to support him in daily life. Giacomo is interested in his father's work and often helps him. The technology ensures a common and positive plane of interaction. Both parents are open-minded and cooperative, supporting and helping Giacomo with his daily challenges.

Pietro

Pietro is an 11-year-old child with autism spectrum disorder level 1 (DSM-5). According to his cognitive profile (WISC-IV), he is in the middle to low range. Pietro shows good skills in nonverbal logical reasoning, visuospatial organization, and abstract categorization; working memory skills also appear age appropriate. Pietro shows difficulties in processing visual information and maintaining attention, verbal skills and understanding of situations, behaviors, and rules. Pietro has some interests that often isolate him, such as the study of maps and Google Navigator. Some aspects of rigidity are also inferred in communication, in which Pietro presents a qualitative impairment of conversational skills, with a tendency to self-referentiality, failure in respecting turns, monopolization of conversation on topics of his own interest, and poor sense of reciprocity. Although his language skills appear age-appropriate, Pietro has difficulties in inferring from the context elements which are not explicit. He has a deficit also in the use of descriptive, conventional, instrumental, and informative gestures. Pietro shows difficulties in physical contact, not perceiving socially appropriate distances or the difference between formal and informal behavior. In fact, the adolescent is extroverted and invasive toward family members and strangers through kissing and hugging. In addition, his nonverbal behaviours are often incongruent with the context. The child communicates with a high tone of voice and uses inappropriate facial expressions and gestures, usually with the aim of drawing attention or showing his displeasure. For example, the mother recounts how Pietro often tries to attract attention when she is with other people, monopolizing the situation, crying, yelling, and getting nervous. Pietro has the same behavior as his peers. He has two best friends and is very possessive and jealous, due to the perception of exclusiveness of friendship. Consequently, when Pietro notes his friends playing with other children, he becomes aggressive and violent. So, Pietro has strong communicative intentionality, but he presents a deficit in the interactive process, which results in repetitive behavior and stereotypical/ idiosyncratic use of words or phrases. Indeed, the child has good skills in establishing spontaneous relationships with others but is not reciprocal in sharing emotions and feelings. Pietro does not show interest in others' opinions, offering information about himself with a specific focus on his interests, but without showing interest in his interlocutor's thoughts, emotions, or experiences. In addition, although Pietro shows facial expressions to express his own emotional states, these appear more rigid and less flexible than expected. However, he shows a high ability to process, recognize, and respond to others' emotions. For example, he understands when his parents are having an argument and tries to mediate conflict between them. Difficulties in socio-communication are confirmed by the scores obtained from the questionnaires self-reported by parents (SCQ; SRS), which show a severe impairment. Significant problems emerge from the SDQ questionnaire in the areas of emotionality, relationship with peers, prosociality, and hyperactivity. The empathy quotient questionnaire by Baron-Cohen is indicative of a low level of empathy, with a poor ability to identify others' emotional states. The test on facial recognition of emotions (NEPSY-II RE) reveals difficulties in decoding emotions through facial expressions and in understanding intentions, thoughts, and actions (NEPSY-II TOM). This aspect may relate to difficulties in understanding typical social situations and relationships (ADOS-2). Pietro also manifests poor tolerance for new situations and changes. For example, he feels passionate about cooking cakes following instructions. He often has an argument with his aunt, who cooks without following procedures or exact dosages: this is intolerable for Pietro. The interviews conducted with the parents (ADI-R) highlight the presence of clear difficulties in the verbal and nonverbal behaviors in social interaction: shifty gaze, rare social smile in response, reduced use of gestures, limited facial expressions, use of stereotyped expressions, presence of neologisms and idiosyncratic language, presence of inappropriate questions or statements. The relationship with the parents is conflictual, especially with the mother, who spends a lot of time at home and accompanies her son to school and in several activities. The level of parental stress (PSI) is high in both parents and related to the parental role and the child's characteristics. Parents show some concerns about the poor social-emotional skills of their son.

The mother also reports that she is afraid of leaving her son alone with peers, and this fear makes it difficult for Pietro to develop relationships outside the family context. On the one hand, Pietro tries to be autonomous from his mother, but at the same time, he seeks her protection from social situations. The child has never slept alone but has always been with his mother since he was five years old. This co-sleeping produces an intricate relationship that encourages an exclusive relationship with his mother and an exclusion of his father, whom Pietro perceives as distant and authoritarian. This exclusive relationship leads Pietro to interiorize the same fear of the mother, such as the fear of the dark, that causes nightmares in sleeping alone. Also, Pietro fears abandonment by his caregivers. Consequently, he avoids disappointing others to reduce the risk of losing them. For example, the mother chooses his clothes and activities, and his friends choose games. He never experiments with decision-making. From the emotional-behavioral profile (CBCL) emerges anxious-phobic-avoidant disorders (e.g., separation anxiety, specific phobias), externalizing behaviors such as dyscontrol impulse, acting out, hetero-aggressiveness toward caregivers in response to frustrations, attentional lability, and physical hyperactivity. The parental couple also shows difficulties in the education of the child, who often suffers from unclear and confusing communication. Finally, Pietro has poor adaptive skills (VINELAND-II). Extremely deficient are personal autonomies (e.g., Pietro does not dress, and does not independently provide for his own hygiene), domestic (e.g., poor/absent domestic cooperation), and community (e.g., difficulties in crossing the street, respecting signs, independently walking to a place, spatial and temporal orientation, planning and organizing one's activities).

Methodological Protocol

After the administration of the protocol, the therapist and the filmmaker conduct individually interviews with the participants (children and parents). The interviews are video recorded.

This setting is critical for introducing participants to the mental form of the patient-*spectauthor*.

Indeed, from the assessment, therapists and filmmakers create the basis for future interventions with audiovisual tools and techniques.

The interview is an intimate setting in which emerges content unaffected by the presence of other family members. Paradoxically, the presence of the camera and a peculiar setting closer to the film set than to the traditional therapist's office allows participants to feel like protagonists and not patients and to open up with less resistance.

During the first interview, Giacomo has a poor interest in sharing and communicating with the therapist and the filmmaker, not maintaining eye contact, responding in a dichotomous and incongruent manner, and progressively avoiding verbal and nonverbal communication. His attention is completely focused on the camera. The filmmaker proposes a role-play in which Giacomo should impersonate the role of the director of the interview, asking questions to the filmmaker. During the role-play, Giacomo's attitude changes. The child is attentive and keeps his gaze fixed on the camera and on the filmmaker, to whom he asks personal questions, showing interest. At the same time, Giacomo shares with the therapist and the filmmaker his attitude toward cooking.

Like Giacomo, Pietro at first does not show interest in the questions of the therapist but rather focuses on the place of the interview, analyzing and comparing it to other places he knows, showing elements of fixation on the route he followed to come and the aesthetical characteristics of the place. The same role-play was also proposed to Pietro, who, like Giacomo, reacted positively by showing himself capable of asking questions of the filmmaker, even in an incongruent manner (see Figure 6.1).

Regarding Giacomo's parents, they are open to dialogue and cooperative, disclosing about themselves and focused on what they would like to change in their family context and in their interactions with each other in their roles as husband and wife and in their roles as parents. As a parental couple they have the following goals for Giacomo: autonomy and concentration. Indeed, they report that Giacomo is easily distracted and avoids doing things alone. The couple set concrete goals for change to improve the quality of family life and their personal well-being as a couple. These elements lead to an alliance, which is essential for greater compliance during parent training. Pietro's parents, instead, show less awareness and more difficulty in expressing their own and the family's needs. Moreover, the proposed goals are unrealistic and based on the extinction of the symptoms of the pathology of their child, rather than on improving his quality of life. The interviews also reveal frictions in the couple that result in an incongruent and inconstant educative model toward Pietro. Indeed, Pietro's parents attribute to the disorder most of the behavioral issues of their son, reducing his liability.

The elements collected during the interviews are useful for the team to focus attention on strengths and critical elements during the first phase of the on-site inspection that takes place in the participants' homes. Indeed, during the filmed inspection in the family context emerge elements of daily life, critical issues, and problems on which to focus attention. The goal of the filmed inspection is to collect audiovisual material useful both as observational data to be integrated with the questionnaire scores and interviews, and as material for the construction of the Video-Pharmakon. For instance, at Giacomo's home, there was a great involvement of the mother in her son's activities.

Figure 6.1 Team and patient on the Therapeutic Set
Credit: Video-Pharmakon project

Giacomo has never been left alone, except at the request of the team, which needs to collect material in which the child can express his autonomy without being conditioned by the presence of the parents. When alone, the team observes the behavior of Giacomo while doing homework, playing computer games, and cooking. Specifically, he wanted to make chocolate on his own, a time when certain family dynamics emphasized the division of parental roles: the mother who tends to control her son while remaining at arm's length and allowing him to do it himself, and the father who does not participate in this dynamic. Both parents demonstrate cohesiveness in their educational model. In fact, the parental couple is united in the distribution of tasks and management of Giacomo, both expressing a desire to learn more about the son and to discern his needs and discomforts. Also on this occasion, as during the interview, a kind of performance anxiety emerges associated with the fear of social judgment: the worry of being labeled as "bad parents".

In light of what emerged from the interviews and the on-site visit, the first Video-Pharmakon of Giacomo and the parental couple was designed to show to the adolescent, and indirectly to the family, that Giacomo is already autonomous: statements about Giacomo's dream of being a cook and doubts about concentration are shown, complementing and contrasting with the very powerful images of the child cutting chocolate with a long knife with a razor-sharp blade, with appropriate attention to the culinary task and the potential danger of the action. Giacomo has been able to perceive himself as able to cook, without fear of hurting himself, showing that he does not always need to be guided by his mother's and father's rules, especially if what he does is rewarding for him. Parents realize the potential of their child and their ability to let him experiment without intervening. The therapist emphasizes the main positive characteristics illustrated in the Video-Pharmakon that acted as reinforcement and therapeutic restitution to both Giacomo and the family members.

Regarding Pietro and his family, from the interviews and the on-site visit emerged some dysfunctional dynamics and strong critical issues related to Pietro's fear of sleeping alone.

The team focused on an imagination exercise, in which Pietro was invited to be, for the camera and the videotherapeutic team, a "brave hero", able to defeat the ghosts and the darkness, by pretending that it was already night and time to go to sleep. In this representation, Pietro was the director and protagonist and decided how to realize the script, by giving the signal to stop after 58 seconds from turning off the light during the simulated "sleeping in the dark until morning". The mother also contributed to the scene, knocking on her son's door in the morning to bid him good morning. The team thus collected crucial material for the Videotherapy. In fact, the first Video-Pharmakon for Pietro focused on defusing a behavioral co-dependency, co-sleeping with his mother, and restoring to both the possibility of an alternative reality in which Pietro and his mother can sleep separately without having the fear of darkness or abandonment. This Video-Pharmakon returned a coherent and functional picture of dysfunctional behavior of Pietro. The application of self-video modeling substitutes the action of co-sleeping with the action of sleeping alone, modifying the same context, and re-enacting a different scene.

Such a re-enactment is, within the video, associated with Pietro's statements about his own fears and desires, and about his friends' and parents' perceptions. The Video-Pharmakon has a direct effect on the child's behavior due to the positive modeling and feedback derived from the action rather than from the self-imitative process of the behavior. Pietro does not imagine being "a hero" but becomes a hero during the action of sleeping alone and retains a representation of himself as a hero through video.

This is one of the main differences between the use of video within the therapeutic process as a means of change from the use of filmed behavior as a form of imitation and correction of actions. Observation of the Video-Pharmakon, accompanied by reflection on the identity process of the patient-protagonist, provides an opportunity to see beyond the images and the action, taking on even more powerful connotations than pure observation. Similarly, the Video-Pharmakon for the parental couple is based on some critical behaviors, such as not respecting turns in the conversation, or controversy in the educational model, in which the mother has the role of "despot" scolding the child, while the father divides himself from such responsibilities by avoiding punishment and arguments. The Video-Pharmakon shows these dynamics and stimulates a progressive involvement of the participants in a context of collaboration and inclusion in the psychotherapeutic process. This is followed by the first meeting of the peer couple, and the first Therapeutic Filmmaking session. The team (composed on this occasion of a psychotherapist and three filmmakers) proceeded to introduce the two participants who proved to be curious and involved. During this first meeting, the psychotherapist explained the main rules of communication: listen, work together, and use the camera only to tell a story. These rules are intended to demarcate any attitudes of prevarication and fixation. In fact, the common goal to realize a film together leads Giacomo and Pietro to set specific limits and rules and modify certain behaviors and attitudes that undermine cooperation and reciprocity.

In a second moment, the filmmaker explained how the cameras work and how to construct a story, i.e., the storyboard. Participants were asked to draw on A4 sheets of paper with colored markers the scenes of their story, divided into four categories: characters, actions, fears, and desires. Giacomo and Pietro discuss and propose content. Participants created their storyboards following the instructions of the filmmaker and decided together to be the protagonists of their film, describing their daily life. During the construction of the storyboard, Giacomo seems to feel more comfortable describing himself than during the interview. Indeed, this tool becomes a way for him to express himself without fear, a storyline in which it is possible to insert personal, creative, and biographical content in line with his own interests, sharing them with his partner Pietro. Giacomo describes his character as an aspiring professional chef who likes music and trekking. Music and cooking are in fact two constants in Giacomo's story. Pietro proves to be particularly conscious and creative in the construction of scenes, linking elements of his everyday life with those of his partner. Hooking on Giacomo's passions, Pietro, a lover of cooking, decides to impersonate a judge who tastes and grades the dishes prepared by Giacomo. Occasionally during Giacomo's turn, Pietro perceives himself as not the main character and the center of attention and shows irritation, aggression, and distraction, as well as little interest in technological tools, an aspect that leads him to ask Giacomo to explain the functions of the camera to him. However, Pietro consciously inserts himself as the main character in the story, expressing a desire to be considered.

At this stage, Pietro shows a strong tendency toward physical contact, use of gestures and vocalizations with both Giacomo and the team. Both participants incorporated elements of their everyday life into their story, including what they cannot do themselves or what they are afraid of and their greatest desires. For example, Giacomo does not like taking showers and Pietro is afraid of dogs. Participants use colorful drawings as a method to imagine, create, and represent fictional characters, and embody and impersonate their own fantasies, needs, desires, and fears. Protagonists act within an informal setting that is halfway between the didactic and the playful plan: the participants must fill in, respecting the turns, the three categories, entering the characters they wish to include in the film, their desires, and fears; if they want, they can involve one or more members of the team to collaborate in writing the storyboard (see Figure 6.2). This activity is aimed at refining, through a practical-ludic exercise, the communication and expressive skills of adolescents, minimizing and reducing the closure and self-centeredness that

Figure 6.2 Storyboarding all together
Credit: Video-Pharmakon project

usually characterizes the social relations of ASD individuals. It also fosters a didactic and emotional confrontation and exchange about important issues, such as their own desires and fears, allowed to emerge in a protected and non-judgmental setting. In this sense, Therapeutic Filmmaking promotes socialization and teamwork with peers and adults, acts through the reduction of defense mechanisms, and allows participants to share aspects of themselves that would otherwise be concealed. In addition, the storyboard is a basis for the therapist to identify the main goals, diversifying them by therapeutic levels: on the one hand, the aim is to increase the social-relational skills of the pair peers in the play-educational process, on the other hand, to intervene on the individual difficulties manifested by the participants. The construction of the film enables working on the therapeutic level. Therapeutic Filmmaking is based on the drafting of the storyboard and the realization of the scenes in a specific location. This activity requires flexibility in reacting to stressful agents, adapting to problematic and new situations, and in arrangements and the variability of schedules. During this phase, participants show cooperation and management of their divergent behavior from what emerged from the family interviews. For instance, Giacomo and Pietro cross the street according to the rules and without any suggestions by the family members, listen to and apply the crew's instructions in handling the camera, and, in general, train patience in organizationally complex situations, perceiving the tasks to be performed as a process leading toward a goal, but also a way to experience their independence without anxieties related to daily dynamics or parental expectations. In experiencing the role of both director and actor, the participants show remarkable psychological flexibility and excellent stress management. When one is the director, the other is the protagonist of the film, and vice versa (see Figure 6.3). In the role of director, the participant is

Figure 6.3 Ciak… action!
Credit: Video-Pharmakon project

responsible for giving directions to the partner and crew; in the role of actor, the participant, instead, listens and performs, respecting the set and the crew. Flexibly impersonating roles other than those known and maintained by the familiar context has leveled the rigidities and patterns of both participants and shifted the focus to empathic and listening skills.

Giacomo shows progressive spontaneity in mutual interaction, increasing eye contact, paying attention to his partner, and communicating his emotions. The exclusive focus on technology decreases and Giacomo helps Pietro when he perceived he needs it. For example, in shooting a scene Giacomo realizes that fellow actor Pietro cannot fasten his belt. Thus, he sets the camera aside, hands it to a crew member, and helps Pietro. Giacomo becomes increasingly aware of his choices and desires and can take care of himself in daily life. His passion for cooking, and his difficulties in showering alone, crossing the street, and telling his story, turn into a daily routine of a character who gets up, showers, and goes to a restaurant to work as a chef. The location in question, a real restaurant, hosted the young protagonist who was instructed and helped by the owners in setting a real actual meal, was judged by his partner Pietro, who, complementarily, in the plot acted as judge. At the same time, Pietro gradually learns to respect the physical boundaries of Giacomo, communicating through physical contact and facial expressions, showing a stronger need to share rather than to be the protagonist. Regarding co-sleeping with the mother figure and difficulty in making autonomous choices, for example in clothing, food tastes, and personal hygiene, these aspects are reversed in a narrative corresponding to Pietro's desire for autonomy, who as the protagonist of the film stages the day of a boy who gets up in the morning, chooses the clothes he wants to wear, washes, eats breakfast, and leaves the house only to return in the evening, say good night to his mother, and go to sleep alone. Another important element in Pietro's storyboard is the fear of dogs, a fear that was set aside on set and greatly reduced in real life. Indeed, the family decided to buy a dog. During filming in fact Pietro takes a small dog for a walk and very bravely faces his fear by learning to relate to the animal. Similarly, Giacomo's fantasy of cooking in a real kitchen and being a chef became a reality in the film and was then consolidated and embodied in a practical design dimension, in the teenager's future choice to attend hotel management school. In deciding, in the face of every narrative possibility, to recount their daily lives, habitual actions were obviously considered and included, such as getting up, getting dressed, brushing their teeth, taking a shower, cooking, and going out for a walk, but so too were critical events such as crossing the street alone and doing homework.

The process of Therapeutic Filmmaking acts on reality through a constant inside and outside of the script. During therapy, patients recite a script. This script becomes factual and concrete through the Therapeutic Filmmaking process. Once the filming phase was completed, the participants were involved in choosing the scenes to be included in the movie, becoming supervisors of the editing. Indeed, the couple of children/adolescents are directors and producers of their film: they are responsible for deciding which scenes to exclude and include, the soundtrack to use, and the title that best represents their story. For instance, since both protagonists love music, they decide to conclude their film with two musical self-produced sequences.

During the editing session, Giacomo demonstrates his ability in sharing his point of view and listening to Pietro, managing the decision-making process. Pietro also shows himself to be more mature and respectful of his partner, as well as proud of the film, representative of his friendship with Giacomo. After the editing meetings, the Cinematherapy phase saw the adolescents return as spectators, but this time together with their families, to watch their self-made movie at the movie theatre. This moment of sharing has the function of giving feedback to the young producers, and to transform the set into the setting and vice versa, promoting the change narrated in the film also in the lives of the two protagonists through their Self-Narrative Video-Pharmakon.[1] During the screening, Giacomo sits next to Pietro and comments on the scenes with him, sharing feelings of satisfaction and surprise at seeing himself on the screen and displaying congruent and spontaneous nonverbal communication. Pietro is attentive, embarrassed to see himself, but visibly satisfied. In watching their film, the children share their emotions, soliciting their partner's feedback several times, touching hands and whispering in each other's ear.

The cinema screening seals the therapeutic process of the pair and indirectly of the family members who witness the children's success.

During the Documentary Videotherapy Giacomo and Pietro watch the film again, this time individually in the office of the psychotherapist and in the presence of the filmmaker. Giacomo comments on the scenes most important to him, such as the scene where he cooks in a real restaurant and shares his impressions. At the end of the session, the team gives Giacomo the film on DVD.

Pietro also focuses his attention on the scenes that are most important to him, such as the scene where he sleeps alone in his room, showing himself participating and active in conversing with the team. He also receives the film on DVD and greets the team and Giacomo with much affection. Giacomo and Pietro supported each other, collaborating, highlighting each other's skills, and learning the meaning of effective communication, active listening, and the value of emotions and reciprocity. This is an example of how the storytelling intertwines with the life story to such an extent that it changes its course.

Together with Documentary Videotherapy and Therapeutic Filmmaking, the team works with the parental couples of both participants through parental training, which involves timed sessions (every week in the initial phase and every two weeks toward the final phase of the project) of therapy integrated with the use of Video-Pharmakon and therapeutic prescriptions. The parent training aims to support parental couples throughout the process to facilitate the integration of children's achievements and make family system changes based on congruent and verifiable goals. Parent training conducted by Giacomo's parents focuses on reducing anxiogenic and stressogenic symptoms related to perceived social judgment and the management of some of the boys' problematic behaviors and concerns about the future. To do this, the therapist structures, together with the parents, a set of verifiable and concrete goals to be implemented with prescriptions and tasks daily and evaluated weekly. Specifically, the parent training works on the modification of personal perception about the problematic nature of some of Giacomo's social behaviors and on the positive reinforcement of the parental resources. Parent training impacts different levels of individual and marital couple interaction and perceptions, encouraging parents to dedicate a space for themselves and their partner. This process of training leads to modifying oppressive and rigid routines and structuring new habits based on flexibility. The parental couple gradually learns to trust Giacomo (he goes out with friends), and they normalize behaviors previously pathologized and demonized as "symptoms of autism", de-emphasizing labels and shifting the focus to Giacomo's resources and needs. According to this perspective, parents interpret gestures enacted by Giacomo as forms of his personal expression and not as symptoms of his disorder. Based on the principles of the strategic approach, parent training disempowers pathology and changes the filters through which parents observe their reality, in this case, the couple and parental relationship.

Pietro's parents, instead, show problematic issues related more to the couple's cohesion and elements of conflict that emerge in their educational style of their son. Indeed, difficulties in communication and in following the rules, which are attributed to his disorder, can be related to this educational conflict between parents. Another problematic element concerns the affective "addiction" that characterizes the mother–child relationship and that hinders Pietro's development. Pietro perceives himself as "small" and behaves as such, reacting to frustration with aggression, demanding to always be the center of attention, and introjecting maternal fears, which is why he refuses to sleep alone. Progressively his parents establish a new parental pact in which they can see beyond their conflicts to only focus on Pietro and his needs. They unhinge the rigid mechanisms, such as the familiar role of the mother always present and apprehensive, and of the father, working and abstaining from educational decisions.

This process leads them to reflect on daily interactions and to question their educational methods and consequences. This intervention reduces stress levels related to poor functional strategies and, as with the Giacomo's parents, Pietro's parents regain their individualism as persons and couple, rediscovering the pleasure of being together as husband and wife and dealing with conflicts instead of avoiding them. As a result, the parents accept that Pietro is developing, and he cannot always be considered "a child". The parents become more confident in Pietro's resources, and he enriches his friendships and passions.

The final phase of the project includes two more sessions called "outcomes management" which aim to monitor and reinforce the positive results. During these sessions, the Maintenance Video-Pharmakon – conceived and edited by the therapeutic team – is administered to return the experience in its entirety to the participants. During the first session, both Giacomo and Pietro appear happy to meet the team again and to watch themselves on video, remembering the positive experience. Giacomo is attentive and focused on watching the video, introjecting the content that emerged throughout the therapeutic process; also, he reiterates that he wants to pursue the project of becoming a professional cook.[2] Pietro is very excited to see the team again and expresses these emotions by hugging the therapist and the filmmaker; he watches the Video-Pharmakon, focusing on the scene in which he was with the dog in the park.[3] The two participants are greeted with the prospect of seeing each other again after three weeks. During the sessions with the parental couples, instead, the main results obtained are discussed and useful strategies are provided for the maintenance and prevention of behavioral relapse of their children. Both parental couples are calm and aware, showing concerns about the future after the end of the project; but feeling protected by the presence of future follow-up meetings. The Video-Pharmakon is a reinforcement for couples, and the therapist provides specific prescriptions that provide continuity and reinforce autonomous parenting. An example of a prescription is to ask parents to write a letter for the therapist. The content of the letter is chosen by the parents. The therapist provides only one condition, that they write by hand and not by computer, and leaves it up to them to decide which topics to address – positive, negative, neutral, concerning their child, partner, or themselves. After three weeks, the participants were administered the Video-Pharmakon again, and the participants commented together on the progress of their routine in relation to the results and prescriptions carried out. From this session emerged greater awareness and autonomy from both children and parents. Specifically, parents realize that they had positive content to share, an aspect that was often devalued, reducing the value of anxiety and fear in their routine. The session on outcomes management aimed to monitor participants at a stage immediately following the intervention, gradually slating the concluding process without abruptly interrupting it, and strengthening the autonomy of the family system. During the follow-up phase at one month, three months, six months, and 12 months, the team verify the progress of the results through the protocol and the interviews conducted at time 0. The team met with Giacomo and Pietro and the parental couple, finding positive maintenance of the main behavioral outcomes of the therapeutic process. Giacomo is cooperative and spontaneous in his interaction by asking the filmmaker and therapist what they had done during the long period of absence, often touching the psychotherapist's face to get attention, and using gestures to show something important to him. Positive aspects and reduction of core spectrum symptoms were also noted during the follow-ups at three months and six months, in which no critical issues were revealed, except for some behavioral regression reported by the parents, who, however, report feeling able to manage them. During the last follow-up at 12 months, Giacomo recounts that he chose a school for professional cooking, remembering the scene in the film where he cooked in a real restaurant. During the session, Giacomo's parents express happiness for their son's choice, and it emerges during the interview how their apprehension has diminished, and their energies are focused on supporting their son rather than worrying by anticipating possible problems.

Pietro during the first follow-up is also visibly happy to see the team again and spontaneously tells in detail about his new friendships and experiences. Pietro is more reciprocal and attentive in answering questions from the psychotherapist and waits his turn when he wants to ask something to the team. His use of gestures is more congruent with the context. For example, when he tries to emphasize the emotional content, he uses nonverbal communication. During the second follow-up Pietro is more agitated and nervous due to a recent argument with his mother. When he calms down he shares the issue with the team, showing higher social and emotional skills and a congruent use of physical contact. In subsequent follow-ups Pietro shows calmness and positive interaction with the context, talking about the dog his mother gave him and about new friendships. Pietro's parents are more serene and able to handle stressful situations. They report being proud of the positive changes in their son.

Results

The effects produced by the intervention described are expressed in terms of the "change" it produced on certain socio-communicative, emotional, and behavioral aspects, which can be observed through a "before-after" comparison. The assessment of these aspects is based on clinical observations, interviews, and standardized tests, carried out at time 0 (i.e., baseline) and during the follow-up sessions. The observational assessments through interviews that occurred during the follow-up are complemented by the results of the test assessment. Indeed, positive results emerge regarding the pair of participants and their parents. Data become more stable over time. Specifically, regarding the children, from the interviews and semi-structured observations (ADOS-2), emerge some improving aspects involving the communicative-relational sphere.

Despite the persistence of the core symptoms of autism, both quantitative and qualitative improvements in social interaction are noted. In Giacomo, a higher interest in others (expressed through questions about thoughts, opinions, or plans) and a greater sense of social reciprocity (sustained gaze, more frequent attempts to initiate joint attention, respect for conversational turns, and less tendency to monopolize the conversation) were observed. Giacomo shows an improvement in physical contact and sharing of emotions. In addition, the relationship with a younger peer Pietro allowed Giacomo to face unexpected difficulties, solve unforeseen problems, and take care of another person, supporting him when necessary.

In Pietro, a qualitative improvement in social response was noted (more appropriate responses, keeping focus on-topic, respecting pauses of the conversation, gestures aimed at communication). The improvements in the social-communicative level are also confirmed by the results of the questionnaires administered to the parents (SCQ; SRS), which report higher scores for both participants. Another significant aspect is the recognition of emotions (NEPSY-II RE) by decoding facial expressions, a skill typically lacking in individuals with ASD. The two participants showed, at the beginning of the study, extreme difficulty in recognizing others' emotions, scoring the lowest on the standardized scale on the assessment test. Both children, at the end of the project, improve their abilities. Regarding the theory of mind scale (NEPSY-II TOM) there is a considerable improvement in both children. Empathic skills (QE), measured indirectly based on parental perception, are found to be increased in Giacomo and Pietro, with scores approaching or within the normal range. Parents report greater "attention" to the feelings of the other, a greater attitude of "caring", and a better ability to communicate emotional states. The assessment of the emotional-behavioral profile (CBCL) reveals some important differences, involving both emotionality management and externalizing behaviors, as reported by the parents. Specifically, Pietro had a reduction in worry and anxiety-phobic manifestations (specific phobias and separation anxiety toward the mother figure), but also in externalizing behaviors (reduced irritability, aggressiveness and disruptive behaviors, greater respect for rules and roles). Giacomo had lower scores related to social withdrawal and the inattentive component. Important differences also emerged on the adaptive skills profile (VINELAND-II). Pietro, at the end of therapy, acquired skills related to autonomy (e.g., dressing, washing, crossing the street, respecting shifts and rules in group activities, and cooperation in household activities) and reduced some dysfunctional behaviors that interfered massively with social and family life (e.g., maternal co-sleeping). In Giacomo, there is even greater improvement in personal autonomies (taking care of himself, choosing clothes to wear), organizational-decisional skills (planning activities in sequence), community skills (cooking, handling sharp objects, crossing the street), and social skills (cooperation in group activities involving adherence to shifts and regulations). Some dysfunctional behaviors are also reduced (less inflexibility and less tendency to repetitiveness). Finally, regarding the effects of Videotherapy on the parental couple, there is an overall decrease in parental stress (PSI) and in the stress arising from the "parental role". Giacomo's parents re-appropriate their personal space and increased confirmation of their positive parenting. The new "vision" of the family, returned through the video, leads to a greater awareness and acceptance of the peculiarities of their child and of the entire family system, which is functional in its uniqueness and no longer directed to the frustrating achievement of a forced "normalization" (e.g., acceptance of the child with no comparison with "typical" families). Pietro's parents show a positive view of themselves as a parental couple, valuing resources and not emphasizing critical points. In fact, positive educational modalities were discovered and built together with the team, through Video-Pharmakon and parenting training that allowed parents to perceive themselves differently, to explore their own abilities and potential. A fundamental point is that both parental couples have made gains from the understanding that "comebacks" and regressions can always happen and that the therapy and the course provided do not aim to magically eliminate them but to train the participants (adolescents and parents) to discover the resources needed to cope with such setbacks.

Spectauthors: Serena and Francesca

The protagonists of the second case are two ten-year-old children, Serena and Francesca, diagnosed with level 1 autism spectrum disorder according to the DSM-5.

Serena

Serena is a ten-year-old child, attends elementary school, and has a 14-year-old sister. Her global IQ is in the normal range (WISC-IV). The test assessment shows communication difficulties, as well as problematic issues in social interactions, as found by the analysis of questionnaires administered to parents (SCQ; SRS). Serena has high traits of self-referentiality and a tendency to continually fix her attention on numerical elements (calendar dates or multiplication tables). Serena has traits of affective immaturity related to poor tolerance of frustration manifested through strong fits of anger and crying in the face of defeat, especially in interaction with others and in sharing of emotions and thoughts; Serena seems to live in her own world. The child mainly expresses anger-related emotions, crying, yelling, stamping her feet on the ground, and physically and verbally attacking her interlocutor, tending to interact almost entirely aggressively and very rarely through affectivity, with caresses, kisses, and hugs. Even in terms of nonverbal communication, Serena avoids looking at and has a low ability to process emotions and respond congruently to the situation. For example, when she sees one of her family members crying or in a bad mood she tends to laugh, not recognizing their emotional state. Indeed, the results of the emotion recognition scale (NEPSY-II RE) are deficient in the attribution of emotional states. As for the theory of mind scale (NEPSY-II TOM), she has a poor ability to attribute and understand others, as also in empathic skills (EQ), measured indirectly from parental perception. Parents report poor attention to the other and a propensity for bullying and defiance. Aspects also emerged from the assessment of the emotional-behavioral profile (CBCL) from which aggressive attitudes are detected. Serena's daily routine is poor in terms of interactions; in fact, the teenager only goes to school and plays video games with her father and sister, doing no other activities or interacting outside the family context. Serena has a good relationship with her parents, who are often concerned about possible social interactions and are eager to protect her from outside judgments. Parents are afraid that Serena will be bullied by her peers, which is why they prefer to avoid contact with others. Despite this trait from which emerges a strong closure to the outside world, experienced as judgmental and frightening, family members welcome participation in the project as they believe it can help in reducing some of Serena's critical issues, as well as in decreasing parental stress (PSI).

Francesca

Francesca is a ten-year-old child, who attends elementary school and has a brother and sister aged 12 and 14, respectively. Cognitive level analysis (WISC-IV) shows a global IQ at the limits for her age. In Francesca mainly emerged aspects of immaturity and low tolerance to frustration, angry outbursts, a tendency to prevaricate, difficulty in cooperating and accepting compromise, and occasional hetero-aggressive acts. The assessment of the emotional-behavioral profile (CBCL) involves both emotionality management and externalizing behaviors. Francesca presents high difficulties in tolerating frustration and cooperating with others, showing bullying, not respecting turns in conversation, and not paying attention to interlocutors. Regarding nonverbal communication, Francesca shows chaotic and disorganized behavior, mostly trying to attract the attention of others, and monopolizing the interaction. For example, when in a social situation, Francesca seeks the attention of those around her, dancing, singing, and showing off to be the protagonist. This problematic nature of social interaction is confirmed through the analysis of questionnaires administered to parents (SCQ; SRS), from which emerge poor interest in others and in social reciprocity. On the emotion recognition scale (NEPSY-II RE) and the theory of mind scale (NEPSY-II TOM), Francesca shows low scores and a visible deficit in understanding and decoding the expressions and emotional states of others. Similarly, empathic skills (QE), measured indirectly based on parental perception, show low scores, confirming the results obtained through NEPSY-II. Francesca has a routine full of activities: in addition to school, she attends a dance class and a swimming class; she goes out with her classmates and her siblings, proving to be very dynamic. Despite her desire to stay with peers, she still shows strong self-referentiality and does not pay much attention to others' opinions, acting as if she were alone. Francesca has a good relationship with her parents. The mother is constantly present in her daily life and accompanies her daughter in various activities, while the father is less present and devotes himself to Francesca mainly in the evenings. The parents at first prove hostile and unwilling to get involved. However, after the assessment of the first test, both show great awareness of the importance of working together to ensure an improvement in the quality of life of the family system.

Methodological Protocol

Following the administration of the protocol of tests, the therapist prepared to conduct the interviews with the participants (children and parents). During the first interview, Serena is enthusiastic and curious about the team and the camera, showing cooperation and participation. Sometimes her answers are incongruent and vague, and she focuses on studying a calendar hanging on the wall. The filmmaker and the therapist engage Serena in the same role-play proposed to the first pair. At first, she is distracted and turns her attention to other stimuli, such as the camera or some objects in the room, but after a while she gets involved in the situation, asking the filmmaker questions, and actively participating. Serena tells a fantasy story in which she interweaves her inventions with elements of cartoons and stories she knows and has been fascinated by. She has a great imagination and fantasizes. This is an element that characterizes her isolation: she lives in her own world.

During the interview, Serena's mother recounts her everyday life and her tendency to isolate herself from others to avoid judgment and misunderstanding. She is very concrete and spends most of her time with her daughters at home, rather than outside. Her routine is based on Serena's needs, and the interview also revolves around her daughter's behavior and critical issues. Like the mother, the father also spends his time between work and home and sometimes goes for bike rides and follows online forums and projects on the topic. He is satisfied with his life and is focused on the present and on his family. Serena's sister presents aspects of closure and introversion during the interview, sharing only her passion for dance. She likes the idea of participating in the project because she has a passion for acting. She plays video games with Serena and sometimes they argue because Serena takes her things.

This is also in line with test evaluation. Indeed, Serena reacts negatively to frustration and all the family tends to perceive better staying alone; an attitude confirmed also during the on-site visit. This emphasizes elements of closure, as reported by the parents, who consider their isolation functional even for their daughter, who interacts mostly with them rather than with peers. This tendency accentuates Serena's unwillingness to establish relationships and her tendency to reject others and have intolerant reactions.

Francesca, like Serena, is comfortable being interviewed in front of the camera, especially given her propensity to be a protagonist, and she maintains the same position throughout the interview, posing for the video, narrating herself, and answering questions. During the role-play, Francesca is cooperative and consistent in asking questions of the filmmaker and affirms that during the project she wants to tell her story and describe her routine. Francesca is aware of what the team requires and is excited to collaborate with

Serena. The mother of Francesca is full-time engaged, driving her children to school and to several activities. However, she also spends time outside with friends. At home, her children identify her as "evil", due to her tendency to be always present. She spends a lot of time with Francesca, mostly concentrating on duty rather than on pleasure, and does not believe that her family presents specific issues, showing security but also closure toward what is new and toward the team.

The father works in a company, and in his free time, he takes his children to the countryside. Unlike his wife, he believes that Francesca should change some attitudes toward others because she has a problem relating to peers, showing higher confidence toward the project. Francesca's brother and sister are both talented, full of passion, and very sensitive to their sister's disorder, playing games and exercises with her to help with language and other issues. The brother spends his time between school commitments and afternoon activities and plays a lot with Francesca, occasionally fighting with her but still managing to get along with her. From the on-site inspection emerged an element that characterizes the organization of the household, the "chaos" characterizing the family's daily routine and consequently the attitudes of Francesca. Although described by the family as well integrated into the social context, Francesca shows a strong tendency not to respond to the stimuli proposed by the team and in no way respects the shifts in communication. The child tends to pose to emphasize her presence and to prevaricate in interaction and communication. These characteristics are reflected in the frenetic organization of the family system, which fills the days with activities and competition that consequently results in conflict among siblings. The family members have confused and disorganized interactions. The play between siblings is stereotypical, and Francesca does not realize rules and emotions because she is focused on competition. These are all characteristics that conflict with the symptoms that characterize the disorder.

In the first pair, characterized by two 11- and 13-year-old children, the first edited Video-Pharmakon was directly addressed. Serena and Francesca, instead, received a family Video-Pharmakon. Another aspect that distinguishes this second pair is the presence of siblings, an element that led to a re-evaluation of the interaction of the audiovisual tool with a larger family system and that included them as additional resources for the family system. The siblings of both peers played a key role in raising awareness and reshaping family dynamics, acting as a bridge between the parents and the young protagonists. The Video-Pharmakon for Serena and Francesca was administered to their families to show a first representation of their relationships and routine, as well as the essential elements on which to work. Both families have elements of dysfunctionality that affect their quality of life and adaptive skills. Both families perceive more than one level of problems: ASD of their children, emotional and behavioral consequences of the disorder, and the perceived social judgment about the parental role. In this regard, the first Video-

Pharmakon, aimed at the families, returned to them a very different portrait of themselves from their personal perceptions. The Video-Pharmakon aims to unhinge the participants' individual mental representations related to the idealization and devaluation of their role, encouraging them to see themselves differently and thus to change.

In Serena's case, the video focused on the sociability of the parents, the tendency toward closure and isolation, and the resulting difficulty in communication among family members. Moreover, the Video-Pharmakon shows the family's belief that it is necessary to protect themselves from the judgments of others to ensure greater serenity, especially for Serena.

The Video-Pharmakon quickly reduced the resistance of the family, enabling the parent training phase. This training aims to reorganize the dynamics based on greater openness and flexibility to promote positive behaviors in Serena.

In contrast, the Video-Pharmakon for Francesca's family emphasizes the difficulties in communication and in mutuality among members of the family, to lead to a greater understanding and reciprocity, and develop a common language that would facilitate especially in Francesca a greater understanding of social interaction. In fact, chaotic and disorganized communication did not help the child process external stimuli and led her to act through prevarication and anger. For instance, a video can show a series of images that captured several moments in which family members did not respect the rules of communication. Video can be a reminder of the importance of rhythms, environment, and interactions in influencing the style, conditions, and quality of life of children with ASD. This Video-Pharmakon was followed by the first Therapeutic Filmmaking session, in which Serena and Francesca met and the psychotherapist explained the main rules of communication.

Unlike the first pair, during the first Therapeutic Filmmaking session, the participants argued, showing aggression and a tendency to want to prevail in the relationship. However, their attitude changed when the psychotherapist and the filmmaker proposed a game, writing the rules explained by the therapist together on a poster board with a marker and comparing their opinions. During this exercise, Serena and Francesca showed positive interaction both with the team and with each other, shifting the focus from argument to task (see Figure 6.4). Afterwards, the filmmaker provided some useful instructions for building the storyboard and using the camera during the subsequent sessions of the filming. During the explanation, participants were invited in turn to film themselves with the camera and describe the main features of their partner, with the goal of creating their story, which should cover the following categories: characters, actions, desires, and fears. This exercise saw both participants involved and attentive in observing their partner, and in describing their characteristics. However, emotions were a missing element in this description. Therefore, the team proposed another game to stimulate their creativity through the processing of facial expressions. The game consisted of mimicking emotions and taking turns guessing them using

Figure 6.4 Describing and drawing feelings and emotions
Credit: Video-Pharmakon project

a "magic tool", namely a Polaroid, which takes and prints photos only when both participants mimic and guess the emotions correctly. This process allowed the participants to interact positively, test their ability to process and recognize facial expressions related to emotions, and enrich their storyboards. At first, both had some difficulty in recognizing the expressions mimicked by their partner, however, they show a positive reaction in being able to study and understand emotions and see the Polaroid take the photograph representing their face. Through this playful-creative exercise, the storyboard was constructed from mimicked emotions (see Figure 6.5). Both participants decided to represent their story by incorporating elements of everyday life.

Figure 6.5 The magic Polaroid
Credit: Video-Pharmakon project

Serena described the main activities that characterize her routine (getting up in the morning and playing with her sister); she also shared with Francesca her desire to have a best friend to rescue her from danger and to play with all the time. In Serena's story, Francesca represents "the best friend", a missing element in her life. The storyboard allowed the therapist to identify key points to work on throughout the Therapeutic Filmmaking process and to be reinforced in the next steps. For Serena, the objectives are improving flexibility in dealing with frustration and negative feelings; expressing and sharing emotions; promoting mutual interaction and social skills. Similarly, Francesca decided to describe her routine by involving her brother in one of the scenes. As in real life, the brother impersonates a very annoying character. Francesca adhered to the role suggested by Serena: the "best friend" and the "savior" who always helps her partner and spends free time with her. This role was for Francesca representative of her habitual attitude. In fact, the child often impersonates the role of a "teacher who explains how to do something" or corrects the behaviors of others. In the narrated story, this propensity is mediated by her friendship with Serena, who asks not to be corrected but to be supported and understood by her best friend. Again, the therapist identifies targets to work on: for Francesca, the tendency to be the center of attention and the propensity to attack and prevaricate in the relationship.

The storyboard is, as in the first pair, a meeting point for the participants to share their needs and desires. In fact, Francesca expressed her need to be important to someone and not just the protagonist of the scene, while Serena wishes to have a friend who understands and protects her. During the Therapeutic Filmmaking process, Francesca and Serena show a progressive ability to cooperate in organizing and filming scenes, handling stressful events, and adapting to the context according to the situation (Serena was shooting one of the scenes, falls and hurt herself, Francesca shows strong concern for her, taking care of her). Francesca demonstrates increasing mutual interaction with the team and with Serena and a decreased tendency to seek attention. Also, Serena shows more eye contact throughout the process, interacting with affection toward her partner (Serena takes Francesca by the hand and seeks her closeness, not physically or verbally attacking her). Both respect the rules and are flexible in switching roles as director and actor and in following the team's instructions (see Figure 6.6).

During the editing sessions, Francesca shares her opinions and selects with Serena the scenes shot, choosing the title of the film, respecting her turn to express her opinion, and listening to her partner. Serena, in turn, pays attention to Francesca's opinion, avoiding arguments and focusing on the editing process as a game to be played together, not a competition.

During the Cinematherapy phase, Serena and Francesca watch their Self-Narrative Video-Pharmakon[4] at the movie theatre in the presence of their family members (see Figure 6.7). Francesca is focused on the novelty elements of the situation, calm and quiet until the end of the film. Later, she

Figure 6.6 Serena and Francesca on the Therapeutic Set
Credit: Video-Pharmakon project

Figure 6.7 Serena and Francesca watching their Video-Pharmakon
Credit: Video-Pharmakon project

spontaneously takes Serena by the hand and expresses to her family and the team her feelings. Compared to the first assessment, Francesca shows a change in her perspective. Indeed, she decides to express her emotions to share and not to attract attention. Serena is also visibly happy, excited to see herself on-screen, and emotionally involved. Despite her strong emotion she remains silent throughout the film and responds positively to Francesca's initiative to come together on stage, to share her emotions with her parents and the team.

In the subsequent Documentary Videotherapy session, Francesca and Serena individually review the film in the psychotherapist's office. Francesca expresses her wish to see her favorite scene twice: Serena is sad because a child has blown up her balloon and Francesca helps her by giving her a new one. She tells the therapist and filmmaker that during this scene she felt very happy and close to her new friend Serena.

Serena shows interest in the scenes in which she acted with Francesca, expressing her desire to meet her friend again to play together and continue to be close, even after the end of the project. After the session, participants receive the film on DVD, thanking and greeting the team. During the process of Documentary Videotherapy and Therapeutic Filmmaking, the parents conduct parent training, in which, as in the previous pair, the video was used as a facilitating medium for a process of family awareness and collaboration in achieving the goals. The use of video, integrated with the various techniques of strategic therapy, has been highly effective in restructuring the dysfunctional mechanisms of the family.

In the specific case of Serena's family, the goal was to reduce isolation and encourage openness and socialization of all family members, showing how the dynamics of closure reinforce Serena's propensity for aggression and the progressive isolation of the other children, as well as a sense of loneliness and marginalization. Parent training improves parents' re-appropriation of their personal space and reduces stress levels derived from the perception of Serena as the "difficult child".

In Francesca's case, the Videotherapy aims to show the poor communication that influences Francesca, incrementing her prevaricating attitude. The new "vision" of the family resulted in parents' greater awareness and acceptance of the peculiarities of their daughter and a reorganization of family dynamics, based on the enhancement of listening and reciprocity, instead of competition. The parent training unveiled the family dynamic through the video and provided tools for families to support and intervene. This procedure shifts the attention from the frustrating achievement of a "normalization" to the recognition of one's own distinctiveness, a key aspect of the strategic psychotherapy approach.

After this phase, the Maintenance Video-Pharmakon, conceived and edited by the therapeutic team, was administered to both children and families, with the aim to return the experience in its entirety and to reinforce the behaviors and skills learned through the process. During the first administration of the Video-Pharmakon in the outcome management phase both Serena and Francesca were collaborative in talking with the team and happy to see each other again on video. The therapist's comments emphasize the positive results obtained. Serena reiterated her desire to make friends, as expressed during the construction of the storyboard and as emerged during the Therapeutic Filmmaking,[5] and Francesca was more willing to listen and focused on the needs of others.[6] Favorite scenes by both were those that capture their empathetic side, an aspect that was difficult to express during the sessions. Specifically, both recall with emphasis the storyboard construction phase and the use of the Polaroid that played a key role in the creative and expressive process of the couple. Serena's parents also were happy to see the team and share with them their well-being. For instance, Serena's mother presented herself with a well-groomed look and a big smile. Moreover, both parents expressed greater communicativeness and openness to dialogue. Parents investigate with the team any aspects related to Serena's behavioral relapses and both parents agree that their daughter is quiet and more sociable.

Francesca's parents are also cooperative and happy to see the team, although they do not express such contentment explicitly. They report no critical elements in their daughter. According to the couple, Francesca is calmer and more respectful of others.

The therapist provides behavioral prescriptions for the family, aimed at maintaining positive outcomes: specifically, for Serena's parents, the prescription is to focus more on the couple, as husband and wife; for Francesca's parents, the prescription is to do some activities together as a family.

After three weeks, the Video-Pharmakon were administered for the last time. During this session, the therapist highlights the effectiveness of the prescriptions and the therapeutic process. Both families reported having ups and downs but that they know how to deal with issues. Serena and Francesca occasionally present some behavioral regression due to high stress or a state of restlessness, but the parents feel more capable of coping with these situations, using strategies learned during the therapeutic process.

One month later, during the first follow-up, the team met with a couple of peers and their respective families. Participants fulfill the test protocol and do the interview. Francesca was very concerned about her parents and her sister, who was unwell. She seemed extremely focused on the family members and did not show any criticality during the session, sharing information and feelings about her family, showing that she was upset and interested in the sister's malaise and not just in herself. During the interview, the parents expressed strong concern about their elder daughter, not sharing apprehensions or critical regressions about Francesca. When Francesca does not follow the rules at home, her parents applied the communication criteria as outlined and explained during the project, to educate her.

Instead, Serena shares with the team her new friendships and activities. Serena's parents decided to be more open, letting their daughter out more, an aspect that led her to develop greater spontaneity. During the interview, Serena maintained eye contact and a composed posture, listening to the therapist's questions, and responding in a congruent manner.

After three months, during the second follow-up, Francesca shows some regressions in compliance with communication rules, as reported by her parents. Despite these regressions, during the session, Francesca is open to dialogue with the therapist and filmmaker and expresses the joy she experienced during Serena's birthday party.

During the second follow-up, Serena maintains her progress and recounts playing with Francesca during her birthday party. Serena remembers positively a scene she likes, in which she is in danger and Francesca helps her. In addition, Serena's parents decided to enroll her in a dance class to stimulate her social skills. Both parental couples show maintenance of achievements and an increased ability to look positively toward the future. The project is still ongoing for these two participant groups, who should conduct the last two follow-up sessions (at six months and at 12 months).

Results

According to the project described and based on the test evaluation and observational analysis of the data collected for this second pair of children, we can observe the improvement of Serena in her ability to process, recognize, and respond to emotions; a decrease in aggression and anger in defeat situations; and greater attention to the feelings of others and sharing of emotions. These aspects gradually emerged in the Therapeutic Filmmaking process, during which Serena expressed a desire to receive closeness and affection from a friend, namely Francesca. Like Serena, Francesca showed improvements in mutual interaction and in social and emotional skills. The child developed a progressive interest in the thoughts, opinions, and feelings of others, improving her ability to process, recognize, and respond to emotions. During the process of Therapeutic Filmmaking until the end of the project, Francesca modulated her aggressive and overbearing behavior toward Serena, cooperating with her and taking care of her, as a best friend. Regarding the test evaluation, participants produced improvements in some socio-communicative and behavioral levels, psychological well-being, and quality of life in their routine. Indeed, despite the persistence of the core symptoms of autism, some qualitative improvements in social interaction detectable in Serena are also detected through the analysis of questionnaires administered to parents (SCQ; SRS), which reported lower scores during the initial assessment. Regarding emotion recognition (NEPSY-II RE), visibly deficient at the beginning for Serena, at the end of the project she attests to an improvement that brings the score closer to the normal range. Along the same line, Serena reports improvement over the initial assessment in the theory of mind scale (NEPSY-II TOM). Also, the empathy level (EQ), measured indirectly based on parental perception, is found to be increased. Serena's parents report increased "caring" for their daughter and for each other's feelings, and an improved ability to communicate their own emotional states. These aspects also emerged during the different phases of the protocol, in which Serena showed a greater willingness to disclose with others, to provide help, and to share. Finally, from the initial assessment of the emotional-behavioral profile (CBCL), some important differences are noted involving mainly the externalizing behaviors, as reported by parents. In both children, greater tolerance to frustration and compliance with rules were found from the first session. Qualitative improvements in social interaction are expressed through more questions about the thoughts, opinions, or plans of others and a greater sense of social reciprocity, as also confirmed through the analysis of questionnaires administered to parents (SCQ; SRS). As for the emotion recognition scale (NEPSY-II RE) and that of the theory of mind (NEPSY-II TOM), Francesca shows that she has enhanced both skills. There is also evidence of increased awareness of social situations and empathic skills (EQ), measured indirectly based on parental perception. From the assessment of the emotional-behavioral profile (CBCL), are noted some important differences from the assessment stage, involving emotionality management and aggressive behavior. Another aspect is related to the remodeling of dysfunctional behaviors that initially made interaction with Serena difficult. Francesca over the course of the project has shown herself to be able to cooperate with others, accept different needs, and be able to compromise. Both parental couples reported lower levels of stress (PSI) and a greater propensity to find effective solutions and to think about the future in terms of change rather than fear.

Notes

1 Such a Self-Narrative Video-Pharmakon, totally created, shot, and edited by young participants, can be seen at the following link: https://youtu.be/Xc2le37m2n0.
2 Giacomo's maintenance Video-Pharmakon can be seen at the following link: www.youtube.com/watch?v=f6sXlda3SXU&list=PLU6miEzwFS61ZUVbZlEw_XLum3j06C8AT&index=2.
3 Pietro's Maintenance Video-Pharmakon can be seen at the following link: www.youtube.com/watch?v=fM2QzhqVpVs&list=PLU6miEzwFS61ZUVbZlEw_XLum3j06C8AT&index=1.
4 Such a Self-Narrative Video-Pharmakon, totally created, shot, and edited by young participants, can be seen at the following link: www.youtube.com/watch?v=izhOcbla0Us&list=PLU6miEzwFS61ZUVbZlEw_XLum3j06C8AT&index=6.
5 Serena's Maintenance Video-Pharmakon can be seen at the following link: www.youtube.com/watch?v=pD_huTuKFIs&list=PLU6miEzwFS61ZUVbZlEw_XLum3j06C8AT&index=5.
6 Francesca's Maintenance Video-Pharmakon can be seen at the following link: www.youtube.com/watch?v=73iIa8d0Q6g&list=PLU6miEzwFS61ZUVbZlEw_XLum3j06C8AT&index=4.

References

Abidin, R. R. (2012). *Parenting stress index, fourth edition (PSI-4)*. Psychological Assessment Resources.

Abidin, R. R. (2016). *Parenting Stress Index, fourth edition (PSI-4): Manuale* (A. Guarino, F. Laghi, G. Serantoni, P. Di Blasio, & E. Camisasca, Eds.). Giunti O.S.

Achenback, T. M., & Rescorla, L. A. (2001). *Manual for the ASEBA school-age forms & profiles*. University of Vermont Research Centre for Children, Youth and Families.

Adams, C., Lockton, E., Freed, J., Gaile, J., Earl, G., McBean, K., Nash, M., Green, J., Vail, A., & Law, J. (2012). The Social Communication Intervention Project: A randomized controlled trial of the effectiveness of speech and language therapy for school-age children who have pragmatic and social communication problems with or without autism spectrum disorder. *International Journal of Language & Communication Disorders*, 47(3), 233–244. doi:10.1111/j.1460-6984.2011.00146.x.

American Psychiatric Association. (2013). *Diagnostic and statistical manual of mental disorders* (5th ed.). APA.

American Psychiatric Association. (2014). *DSM-5: Manuale diagnostico e statistico dei disturbi mentali: Text revision* (M. Biondi, & M. Maj, Eds.). Raffaello Cortina.

Apple, A. L., Billingsley, F., Schwartz, I. S., & Carr, E. G. (2005). Effects of video modeling alone and with self-management on compliment-giving behaviors of children with high-functioning ASD. *Journal of Positive Behavior Interventions*, 7(1), 33–46. doi:10.1177/10983007050070010401.

Attwood, T. (2004). Cognitive behaviour therapy for children and adults with Asperger's syndrome. *Behaviour Change*, 21(3), 147–161. doi:10.1375/bech.21.3.147.55995.

Baron-Cohen, S., Leslie, A. M., & Frith, U. (1985). Does the autistic child have a "theory of mind"? *Cognition*, 21(1), 37–46. doi:10.1016/0010-0277(85)90022–90028.

Baron-Cohen, S., Wheelwright, S., Skinner, R., Martin, J., & Clubley, E. (2001). The autism-spectrum quotient (AQ): Evidence from Asperger syndrome/high-functioning autism, males and females, scientists and mathematicians. *Journal of Autism and Developmental Disorders*, 31, 5–17. doi:10.1023/A:1005653411471.

Bellini, S., & Peters, J. K. (2008). Social skills training for youth with autism spectrum disorders. *Child and Adolescent Psychiatric Clinics of North America*, 17(4), 857–873. doi:10.1016/j.chc.2008.06.008.

Bishop-Fitzpatrick, L., Mazefsky, C. A., Eack, S. M., & Minshew, N. J. (2017). Correlates of social functioning in autism spectrum disorder: The role of social cognition. *Research in Autism Spectrum Disorders*, 35, 25–34. doi:10.1016/j.rasd.2016.11.013.

Bruggink, A., Huisman, S., Vuijk, R., Kraaij, V., & Garnefski, N. (2016). Cognitive emotion regulation, anxiety and depression in adults with autism spectrum disorder. *Research in Autism Spectrum Disorders*, 22, 34–44. doi:10.1016/j.rasd.2015.11.003.

Carter, A. S., Davis, N. O., Klin, A., & Volkmar, F. R. (2005). Social development in autism. In F. R. Volkmar, R. Paul, A. Klin, & D. Cohen (Eds.), *Handbook of autism and pervasive developmental disorders: Diagnosis, development, neurobiology, and behavior* (pp. 312–334). John Wiley & Sons, Inc.

Cianchetti, C., & Fancello, G. S. (2001). *SAFA: Scale psichiatriche di autosomministrazione per fanciulli e adolescenti: Manuale*. Giunti O.S.

Constantino, J., & Gruber, J.(2005). *Social responsiveness scale (SRS): Manual*. Los Angeles Western Psychological Services.

Constantino, J., & Gruber, J. (2010). *Social responsiveness scale (SRS): Manuale* (A. Zuddas, A. Di Martino, L. Delitala, L. Anchisi, & G. Melis, Eds). Giunti O.S.

Corbett, B. A., Key, A. P., Qualls, L., Fecteau, S., Newsom, C., Coke, C., & Yoder, P. (2016). Improvement in social competence using a randomized trial of a theatre intervention for children with autism spectrum disorder. *Journal of Autism and Developmental Disorders*, 46, 658–672. doi:10.1007/s10803-015-2600-9.

D'Orlando, F., Grassi, M., & Di Blas, L. (2010). Uno studio di validazione del CBCL/6–18 e del TRF/6–18 nella tarda infanzia. *Giornale italiano di psicologia*, 37(4), 919–944. doi:10.1421/33434.

Erskine, R. G. (1997). *Theories and methods of an integrative transactional analysis: A volume of selected articles*. TA Press.

Gallese, V., & Goldman, A. (1998). Mirror neurons and the simulation theory of mind-reading. *Trends in Cognitive Sciences*, 2(12), 493–501. doi:10.1016/S1364-6613(98)01262-01265.

Geretsegger, M., Elefant, C., Mössler, K. A., & Gold, C. (2014). Music therapy for people with autism spectrum disorder. *Cochrane Database of Systematic Reviews*, 6. doi:10.1002/14651858.CD004381.pub3.

Goodman, R., Meltzer, H., & Bailey, V. (1998). The Strengths and Difficulties Questionnaire: A pilot study on the validity of the self-report version. *European Child & Adolescent Psychiatry*, 7(3), 125–130. doi:10.1007/s007870050057.

Ho, B. P., Stephenson, J., & Carter, M. (2015). Cognitive-behavioural approach for children with autism spectrum disorder: A literature review. *Journal of Intellectual and Developmental Disability*, 40(2), 213–229. doi:10.3109/13668250.2015.1023181.

Hong, E. R., Ganz, J. B., Mason, R., Morin, K., Davis, J. L., Ninci, J., Neely, L. C., Boles, M. B., & Gilliland, W. D. (2016). The effects of video modeling in teaching functional living skills to persons with ASD: A meta-analysis of single-case studies. *Research in Developmental Disabilities*, 57, 158–169. doi:10.1016/j.ridd.2016.07.001.

Jucan, S. A., Stan, C., & Stan, C. (2021). Use of multisensory room in the development of psychomotricity in students with autism spectrum disorder and intellectual disability. *Educatia*, 21(20), 48–55. doi:10.24193/ed21.2021.20.06.

Kennedy, D. P., & Adolphs, R. (2012). The social brain in psychiatric and neurological disorders. *Trends in Cognitive Sciences*, 16(11), 559–572. doi:10.1016/j.tics.2012.09.006.

Korkman, M., Kirk, U., & Kemp, S. (2007). *NEPSY-II: A developmental neuropsychology assessment*. The Psychological Corporation.

Korkman, M., Kirk, U., & Kemp, S. (2011). *NEPSY-II Second Edition: A developmental neuropsychology assessment* (C. Urgesi, F. Campanella, & F. Fabbro, Eds.). Giunti O.S.

Lai, M. C., Lombardo, M. V., & Baron-Cohen, S. (2014). Autism. *Lancet*, 383(9920), 896–910. doi:10.1016/S0140-6736(13)61539-61531.

Laicardi, C., & Orsini, A. (1997). *WAIS-R: Wechsler adult intelligence scale revised*. Giunti O.S.

Lang, M., Di Pierro, P., Michelotti, C., & Squarza, C. (2017). *WISC-IV: Wechsler intelligence scale for children: Lettura dei risultati e interpretazione clinica*. Raffaello Cortina.

LePage, P., & Courey, S. (2011). Filmmaking: A video-based intervention for developing social skills in children with autism spectrum disorder. *Interdisciplinary Journal of Teaching and Learning*, 1(2), 88–103.

Lombardo, M. V., Barnes, J. L., Wheelwright, S. J., & Baron-Cohen, S. (2007). Self-referential cognition and empathy in autism. *PloS One*, 2(9), e883. doi:10.1371/journal.pone.0000883.

Lord, C., & Colombi, C. (2013). *ADOS-2: Autism diagnostic observation schedule: Manuale*. Hogrefe.

Lord, C., Rutter, M., DiLavore, P., Risi, S., Gotham, K., & Bishop, S. (2012). *Autism diagnostic observation schedule, second edition (ADOS-2)*. Western Psychological Corporation.

Lounds Taylor, J., Adams, R. E., & Bishop, S. L. (2017). Social participation and its relation to internalizing symptoms among youth with autism spectrum disorder as they transition from high school. *Autism Research*, 10(4), 663–672. doi:10.1002/aur.1709.

Lozier, L. M., Vanmeter, J. W., & Marsh, A. A. (2014). Impairments in facial affect recognition associated with autism spectrum disorders: A meta-analysis. *Development and Psychopathology*, 26(4 pt1), 933–945. doi:10.1017/S0954579414000479.

Lusebrink, V. B. (2004). Art therapy and the brain: An attempt to understand the underlying processes of art expression in therapy. *Art Therapy*, 21(3), 125–135. doi:10.1080/07421656.2004.10129496.

Macpherson, K., Charlop, M. H., & Miltenberger, C. A. (2015). Using portable video modeling technology to increase the compliment behaviors of children with autism during athletic group play. *Journal of Autism and Developmental Disorders*, 45, 3836–3845. doi:10.1007/s10803-014-2072-3.

Olsson, N. C., Flygare, O., Coco, C., Görling, A., Råde, A., Chen, Q., Lindstedt, K., Berggren, S., Serlachius, E., Jonsson, U., Tammimies, K., Kjellin, L., & Bölte, S. (2017). Social skills training for children and adolescents with autism spectrum disorder: A randomized controlled trial. *Journal of the American Academy of Child & Adolescent Psychiatry*, 56(7), 585–592. doi:10.1016/j.jaac.2017.05.001.

Perkins, T., Stokes, M., McGillivray, J., & Bittar, R. (2010). Mirror neuron dysfunction in autism spectrum disorders. *Journal of Clinical Neuroscience*, 17(10), 1239–1243. doi:10.1016/j.jocn.2010.01.026.

Ray, W. A. (2007). In homage to Paul Watzlawick. *Family Process*, 46(3), 415. doi:10.1111/j.1545-5300.2007.00221.x.

Rizzolatti, G., & Craighero, L. (2004). The mirror-neuron system. *Annual Review of Neuroscience*, 27, 169–192. doi:10.1146/annurev.neuro.27.070203.144230.

Rutter, M., Bailey, A., & Lord, C. (2003). *The social communication questionnaire: Manual*. Western Psychological Services.

Rutter, M., Bailey, A., & Lord, C. (2007). *SCQ: Social communication questionnaire: Manuale* (C. Cianchetti, & G. S. Fancello, Eds.). Giunti O.S.

Rutter, M., Le Couteur, A., & Lord, C. (2003). *Autism diagnostic interview-revised*. Western Psychological Services.

Rutter, M., Le Couteur, A., & Lord, C. (2005). *Autism diagnostic interview-revised: Manuale* (R. Faggioli, Ed.). Giunti O.S.

Sabatino, A., & Saladino, V. (2018). Dalla cinematerapia al Therapeutic Filmmaking: Linguaggio audiovisivo e psicoterapia. *Quale Psicologia*, 11, 22–37.

Simon, G., Evans, M., Cano, F. U., Helps, S. L., & Vlam, I. (2020). Autism and systemic family therapy. *The Handbook of Systemic Family Therapy*, 4, 407–432. doi:10.1002/9781119438519.ch98.

Simpson, S. G., & Slowey, L. (2011). Video therapy for atypical eating disorder and obesity: A case study. *Clinical Practice and Epidemiology in Mental Health: CP & EMH*, 7, 38. doi:10.2174/1745017901107010038.

Sparrow, S. S., Cicchetti, D. V., & Balla, D. A. (2005). *Vineland adaptive behavior scales: Second edition (Vineland II), survey interview form/caregiver rating form*. Pearson Assessments.

Sparrow, S. S., Cicchetti, D. V., & Balla, D. A. (2016). *Vineland adaptive behavior scales: Second edition (Vineland II), survey forms: Manuale* (G. Balboni, C. Belacchi, S. Bonichini, & A. Coscarelli, Eds). Giunti O.S.

Speirs, S., Yelland, G., Rinehart, N., & Tonge, B. (2011). Lexical processing in individuals with high-functioning autism and Asperger's disorder. *Autism*, 15(3), 307–325. doi:10.1177/1362361310386501.

Stichter, J. P., O'Connor, K. V., Herzog, M. J., Lierheimer, K., & McGhee, S. D. (2012). Social competence intervention for elementary students with Aspergers syndrome and high functioning autism. *Journal of Autism and Developmental Disorders*, 42, 354–366. doi:10.1007/s10803-011-1249-2.

Tanner, K., Hand, B. N., O'Toole, G., & Lane, A. E. (2015). Effectiveness of interventions to improve social participation, play, leisure, and restricted and repetitive behaviors in people with autism spectrum disorder: A systematic review. *The American Journal of Occupational Therapy*, 69(5), 1–12. doi:10.5014/ajot.2015.017806.

Tobia, V., Gabriele, M. A., & Marzocchi, G. M. (2011). Norme italiane dello Strengths and Difficulties Questionnaire (SDQ): Il comportamento dei bambini italiani valutato dai loro insegnanti. *Disturbi di attenzione e iperattività*, 6(2), 15–22.

Wechsler, D. (1981). *Wechsler adult intelligence scale-revised (WAIS-R)*. Psychological Corporation.

Wechsler, D. (2003). *Wechsler intelligence scale for children, fourth edition (WISC-IV)*. Psychological Corporation.

Conclusions

Anna Chiara Sabatino and Valeria Saladino

Dominant narratives across medical humanities have been focused on the cultural construction of the notion of medicine as epistemic discourse and social practice, on the role of humanities in medical design of the disease as well as on the humanization of the clinical encounter in order to facilitate the anamnesis, the therapy, and the care. Among the main declinations, a more complex point of view arises, suggesting the critical integration and exploitation of a variety of methodologies, previously used by art and humanities research, into a peculiar human-centered dispositive, both narrative and therapeutic, in which audiovisual practices and languages acquire new healing potential for the particular target of suffering human beings. Based on the aforementioned premises, the book has investigated the Therapeutic Set as performative and methodological model, consistent with art therapy and narrative-based medical approaches, applicable in specific pathological conditions and health-care contexts. Within such a reflexive and operational framework including documentary studies and visual anthropology, self-representational and amateur theories, the Therapeutic Set becomes a media environment where the formative encounter, both technical and pragmatic, and finally ethical, between the self and the world takes place.

The Therapeutic Set is therefore described and contextualized as a transformative interplay between profaned cinematic dispositive and psychotherapy setting, dwelling on bodily involvement, audiovisual gestures and amateur self-representation to which active participants, storytellers of their own illness and treatment, are called in the making of therapy and narrative.

Video-Pharmakon research-intervention protocol consists of an integrated methodological and application approach based on strategic psychotherapy and audiovisual tools and techniques. Its consistent interdisciplinarity is aimed to promote effective integration and interaction between an audiovisual languages neuropsychiatry and psychotherapy, and to evaluate and analyze the relevance of this methodology in support and intervention of the core symptoms of autism spectrum disorder among children and young adults. According to the literature, the audiovisual language, integrated with the psychotherapeutic tool, could promote changes, interaction, and

DOI: 10.4324/9781003340508-8

collaboration, and enhance socio-communicative and relational skills in a specific target, such as individuals with ASD.

Moreover, the Therapeutic Set and Video-Pharmakon models, within a strategic psychotherapeutic approach, offer a dynamic perception of the setting as a tool tailored for the patient, the real protagonist and the author of her/his process of change. The therapeutic process that intervenes at the systemic level significantly contributes to the reduction of caregiver (parents and/ or guardian) stress and burnout by stimulating creative educational solutions. For instance, within families composed of parents and siblings, as in the case of Serena and Francesca, the caregiver is identified not only in the parental couple but also in the other children, who contribute to the family dynamics and problems associated with the ASD symptom. From a systemic perspective, which is part of the strategic approach, involving family promotes the identification of the elements of dysfunctionality among the members, endowing the symptom or behavior that maintains the problem. In the specific case of the two pairs of children, the symptoms and behaviors of the young protagonists held a key function in maintaining family balance. Strategic psychotherapy, unlike the approaches commonly used in the ASD setting, places only marginal attention on dysfunctional behavior and modeling, relying on the assumption that the patient has positive resources and potential to improve themselves. In this theoretical and methodological framework, the double dispositive narrative and therapeutic device allow an intervention not limited to the diagnosis of ASD and the treatments proposed by Evidence-Based Medicine. Indeed, our preliminary results, both quantitative and observational, lay the foundation for establishing new treatment approaches for individuals with ASD, especially for children and adolescents. Within the integrated methodology illustrated, one of the innovative aspects is the choice to involve pairs of peers with ASD, rather than designing the intervention with a mixed target (normative and ASD). The proposed creative activities allow them to experience autonomy and discover their own abilities, with the aim of promoting social and relational skills and avoiding social isolation.

Due to its observational-experimental structure, the Video-Pharmakon protocol has the following limitations: (a) difficulty in involving several numbers of participants; (b) impossibility of generalizing the data obtained, due to the small sample; (c) limited availability of professional filmmakers and strategic psychotherapists trained for an interdisciplinary and integrated methodological approach. Considering these limitations, therefore, our future goals will be focused on the implementation of the proposed methodology, through the further involvement of participants, with the aim of extending the considerations of the effectiveness and applicability of the method. In particular, the identification of a control group and the use of a waiting list and deferred treatment characterize one of the future strategies and a useful resource for subsequent applications. A further future prospect is an involvement in the protocol of a sample of young adults (age range 18–25 years) that would allow the exploration of the incidence and influence of expressive and participatory techniques in this specific target group. The involvement of this age range should consider the integration of methods more appropriate for young adults and could be an opportunity to explore new methods and applications of audiovisual languages with the strategic approach.

Finally, it is important to grow a network of professionals that will foster the dissemination of practices and strategies for training purposes, to increase the human resources employed in the project. In this sense, it is also desirable to export the therapeutic model to other contexts, both public and private, with the aim of offering additional and effective treatment proposals in response to the massive demand for support and intervention in the field of developmental autism spectrum disorder.

Index

psychic: apparatus 4–2; fragmentation 49; images processing 42; mechanisms 42; phenomena 42

For Product Safety Concerns and Information please contact our
EU representative GPSR@taylorandfrancis.com Taylor & Francis
Verlag GmbH, Kaufingerstraße 24, 80331 München, Germany